God and the Imagination

The Life of Poetry

POETS ON THEIR ART AND CRAFT

PAUL MARIANI

God and the Imagination

On Poets, Poetry, and the Ineffable

The University of Georgia Press
Athens and London

Published by the University of Georgia Press
Athens, Georgia 30602
© 2002 by Paul Mariani
Set in 10 on 13 Minion by Bookcomp, Inc.
Printed and bound by Maple-Vail
The paper in this book meets the guidelines for
permanence and durability of the Committee on
Production Guidelines for Book Longevity of the
Council on Library Resources.

Printed in the United States of America
06 05 04 03 02 C 5 4 3 2 1
06 05 04 03 02 P 5 4 3 2 1

Library of Congress Cataloging-in-Publication Data

Mariani, Paul L.
God and the imagination : on poets, poetry, and
the ineffable / Paul Mariani.
p. cm. — (Life of poetry)
Includes bibliographical references and index.
ISBN 0-8203-2407-8 (alk. paper)
— ISBN 0-8203-2408-6 (pbk. : alk. paper)
1. Religion and poetry. 2. Poetry, Modern—History
and criticism. 3. God in literature. I. Title. II. Series.
PN1077 .M29 2002
809.1'9382—dc21   2001008250

British Library Cataloging-in-Publication Data available

For Eileen

Here, now, we forget each other and ourselves.
We feel the obscurity of an order, a whole,
A knowledge, that which arranged the rendezvous,

Within its vital boundary, in the mind.
We say God and the imagination are one . . .
How high that highest candle lights the dark.

—Wallace Stevens, "Final Soliloquy of the Interior Paramour"

Contents

ℭ

Preface

❧

SHALL I SHOW my hand? Why not? I've been in the trenches long enough. So: to begin. Audience, artist, world, text. Four ways the critic/ teacher addresses his subject. They're all viable, important, all in their own way fascinating. But, as a teacher for the past forty years, the question, for me, has been one of audience. Students mostly, then the half-dozen stalwarts who have swarmed my lectures, and then some ideal reader (my wife, Eileen), and half a dozen dead and living writers, sometimes changing, sometimes fusing.

As for text: that too has always been paramount, more so than any theory. I read theory, but I suppose I'm too un-European and too much the Jamesian pragmatist ever to place theory before the poem. I distrust the usurpation of the writer by the critic, who uses a good piece of writing as a springboard to tell us about himself or herself, and I've seen too much of that sort of thing over the years. There are only a handful of contemporary scholar-critics I enjoy reading, and most—though not all—are working poets. Pound, Eliot, Williams, Hart Crane (in his letters, almost on a par with Keats), Berryman, Lowell. Harold Bloom and Terrence Des Pres among the straight critics (as in whiskey straight). Walter Jackson Bates and Richard Ellmann among the biographers. Others. In general I despise negative criticism, but especially by second-rate poet-critics who want to make a name for themselves (they don't, except as noisome two-week blackflies make their mark).

I came out of a certain historical moment. No surprise there. I'm old enough to remember American B-17s flying in clusters by the hundreds

over New York City in the summer of 1945, filling the fifth-floor tenement where I lived with a droning that lasted a long time and even
then—at five—gave me a sense of the realities of American power.
Working-class, Roman Catholic, Italian, Swedish, Russian/Polish ex-
traction. A year in a prep school leading to the seminary. Pius XII,
John XXIII (the good Pope), Paul VI, John Paul I, John Paul II. World
War II (with my father and other relatives stateside as well as fighting
in Europe and the Japanese-occupied islands). The black hole of the
Holocaust and its images, which have haunted me for over half a cen-
tury. The Bomb. The Cold War, the Berlin Wall, *Ich bin ein Berliner*,
Viet Nam, the deaths of the Kennedys, Jack and Bobby, Martin Luther
King Jr., Malcolm X. Twelve presidents: FDR, Truman, Eisenhower, JFK,
Johnson and The Great Society, Nixon hunkering down, Nixon de-
parting by helicopter from the White House lawn, stumbling Ford,
Carter, Reagan, Bush, Clinton and the scandals that paralyzed his sec-
ond administration, Bush redux. A life—white, American, male, married with three grown sons—in a particular context.

Artist and world. Two points triangulated by the poems themselves,
and the questions these points give rise to. How is it that we ever got
this text? What were the poet's concerns, obsessions, self-directives?
What sort of poet wrote this poem? What world did that poet come
out of? Who and what influenced the poet? Granted we can never get
back to ground zero—the moment that gave us the Ur text. Still, how
close *can* we come to recovering the psychogenesis of the poem? And
is it possible to reconstruct something of that electric moment and
so identify the complex linguistic strands that make up the self of the
poet, if indeed the poet can be said to have a self?

I see now that what I have spent thirty years doing is attempting on
another plane both what New Testament scholars have attempted to
do in reaching back into the Gospels to reconnect with the historical
Jesus, as well as what A. E. Housman and John Berryman (two very
fine poets) attempted with their reconstructions of the texts of the Roman poet Lucan and *King Lear*, respectively—except that for me it is
recovering the poet along with the poem.

So, then, narrative. The telling of a story. One man's way of getting prose down on the page, a man for whom the novel and short story are apparently not paramount concerns. Writing the self. Writing the other, by way of homage. And writing in a way that encompasses the ineffable. God and the imagination, as Stevens succinctly put it.

When I began writing, I came under the shadow of the New Criticism. The mode—at least as it was practiced then—seems quaint now, and unduly circumscribed, at least to many. But this was not the case forty years ago, when the academic world as far as poetry was concerned here in the United States was still under the aegis of Eliot, Ransom, and Tate. Pound, having only recently been released from St. Elizabeth's Hospital for the Criminally Insane, was surely under the double shadow of treason and anti-Semitism. Williams was still a special taste, the province of the Beats and the poets, but largely a figure outside the serious concerns of the academic world. Still, there were Richard Ellmann's biography of James Joyce, Jackson Bates's biographies of Keats and Dr. Johnson, and the complex, palpable worlds those biographies opened then for me. How much richer such lives were than the more specialized studies of text X or Y. And the writing of lives, the lives of the poets, I decided, was what I would pursue for myself.

Outside of a half dozen early *explications de texte* in the journals, I began by writing the kind of book that seems impossible to write these days (it was probably impossible then too, though that didn't stop me). And so: *A Commentary on the Complete Poems of Gerard Manley Hopkins*, which grew out of my dissertation under the guidance of Allen Mandelbaum and Wendell Stacy Johnson. A university press book—Cornell—published just short of my thirtieth birthday. A book that bridges—as best I could at the time—the world of the poem and the world of the poet, insofar as a life had shaped those poems. It satisfied at least three personal needs, as have all of my biographies since: the need to understand the poem, the poet, and the poetic/spiritual journey the poet traversed.

Stung by an early review—by a minor critic who has published virtually nothing in the intervening three decades—a review that pointed out that I had not paid sufficient attention to scholar Z, I undertook to write a critical text on everything written on the next poet I took up: William Carlos Williams. The book promised to review everything published on Williams from his beginnings in 1909 up to the moment I was writing, even as that moment became itself hopelessly historical. I look back on that time now mostly as a wasted two years when I could have been writing poetic epics. On the other hand, it proved a good homework book for my Ellmann-inspired biography of Williams: a work that all told took nearly ten years and earned me the princely sum of three thousand dollars and endless fame. Chalk it up to a labor of love that seems to have helped others interested in Williams, for which fact I am grateful. That book, *A New World Naked*, arrived in the fall of 1981. Since then there have been three other biographies: Berryman (*Dream Song*) in 1990, Lowell (*Lost Puritan*) in 1994, and Crane (*The Broken Tower*) in 1999, on the hundredth anniversary of the poet's birth.

In between there have been five books of poetry as well as a first book of essays, *A Usable Past*, published in 1984. Looking back at the seventeen years since the book was published, I find some of the same preoccupations I find in this collection. The same and different: five easy pieces on Williams, four on Hopkins, as well as six on post–World War II poets: Robert Penn Warren, Charles Tomlinson, Robert Creeley, John Montague, John Berryman, Robert Pack, and Thomas Merton.

And now what? Essays on the self, five of them, fragments of an agon, a partial bildungsroman, something between the River (of experience) and the Sound (of words on the page). Essays on the lives of poets and what goes into writing a life. The fiction of biography. Occasional pieces, too, as in my first book of essays, which allowed me to write about poets I admired or loved, but whom I would otherwise not have written about: Hardy, Frost, Rilke, Kinnell. Essays written for special occasions, as talks: at Middlebury College and the Bread Loaf Writers' Conference, Colorado Springs, Smith College, New Harmony, Harbourfront in Toronto, the Writers' Collaborative in New York, and the University of Massachusetts, where I taught for thirty-two years before going on to Boston College. Many of these essays grew out of my biographies, either as steps toward the writing, or in the wake of publication. Of the twin essays on the connections between Lowell and Berryman and Crane and Williams, the first provided the transition into *Lost Puritan*, while the second was written after *The Broken Tower* and *A New World Naked* were published. Editors and friends asked for specific essays—on Kinnell, on Hardy, on Frost—the cries of their occasions being anthologies, symposia, festschriften.

The shadow of New York, from which I exiled myself a third of a century ago for the pastoral Eden of western Massachusetts, looms large over many of these pieces, as well it should. And now, just days after the destruction of lower Manhattan by a surprise attack on the World Trade Center, while bodies are still being recovered, I am finalizing the typescript. The ironies are almost too unbearable to contemplate. Meanwhile, my preoccupation with the ineffable, the Mystery, looms ever larger in my work. The subject, I begin to see, really does seem to call to the writer rather than the other way around. So be it. You write about what you can in the best way you can and hope in that way to gather your listeners about you.

Paul Mariani
SEPTEMBER 2001

Acknowledgments

⚭

FOR ALL who gave me the chance to work out the ideas developed or suggested in these pages, especially Greg Wolffe at *Image*, Rev. Jim Martin and Rev. Tom Reese at *America*, Bob Pack and Jay Parini at the University of New England Press, my heartfelt and lasting thanks. A special word too to Ron Hansen, Philip Levine, Edward Hirsch, and Bill Heyen for their splendid support over the years. And to Barbara Ras and Daniel Simon, for believing in this project and for seeing it through.

A number of these essays were originally talks, some of which were subsequently reshaped for publication in magazines and anthologies. The following five are published for the first time:

"Writing Lowell," Harbourfront Reading Series, Toronto, October 15, 1994.
"The Hole in the Middle of the Book: Absence and Presence in Biography," Middlebury College, 1994.
"Hardy's Heartbreak," Middlebury College, 1995.
"Reconfiguring Flame: The Art of Biography," Smith College, Northampton, spring 1998.
"Frost among the Poets," keynote address at Bread Loaf on the occasion of the 125th anniversary of Frost's birth, fall 1999.

The following were originally delivered as talks and subsequently recast for publication:

"Lowell on Berryman on Lowell" was originally delivered as a talk at a Berryman symposium held at the University of Minnesota at Minneapolis St. Paul.

"Summoning the Dead: Politics and the Sublime in Contemporary
English Poetry," the earliest essay in this collection, was originally
delivered as a lecture on the awarding to the author of the Chancellor's
Medal at the University of Massachusetts in 1984.
"The Ineffability of What Counts" was delivered as a keynote address at
the Image conference at New Harmony, Indiana, in the fall of 1992.
"Toward a Sacramental Language" and "God and the Imagination" were
keynote addresses delivered at the Glen Eyrie conferences in Colorado
Springs in the summers of 1995 and 1996, respectively.
" 'The Unshapeable Shock Night': Pain, Suffering, and the Redemptive
Imagination" was originally presented at Loyola Marymount
University in the fall of 1998.

The other essays here were written expressly for publication. But
every essay has been revised for publication here, some of them sub-
stantially. For their interest and support I want to thank the following
publications:

"Beginnings," *The Gettysburg Review* 4, no. 3 (summer 1991). Reprinted
in *The Bread Loaf Writers' Anthology of Writers on Writing* (Hanover:
University Press of New England, 1991). Selected by Robert Atwan as a
notable essay for 1991 in *The Best American Essays 1992*, ed. Susan
Sontag and Robert Atwan (London: Ticknor & Fields 1992).
"Class," *New England Review* 15, no. 2 (spring 1993).
"Hopkins As Lifeline," *The Hopkins Quarterly* 25, nos. 1–2 (winter–spring
1998).
"*Quid Pro Quo*," in *Introspections: American Poets on One of Their Own
Poems,* ed. Robert Pack and Jay Parini (Hanover: University Press of
New England, 1997).
"Eight or Nine Ways of Looking at a River," *Preservation Magazine*, nos.
52–53 (May–June 2000).
"The Brain That Hears the Music," in *The Bread Loaf Anthology of
Contemporary American Essays,* ed. Robert Pack and Jay Parini
(Hanover: University Press of New England, 1989).
"Kinnell's Legacy: On 'The Avenue Bearing the Initial of Christ into the
New World,' " in *Under Discussion: On the Poetry of Galway Kinnell,* ed.
Howard Nelson (Ann Arbor: University of Michigan Press, 1987).

"Lowell on Berryman on Lowell," *The Gettysburg Review* 4, no. 4 (autumn 1991). Rev. and rpt. in *Recovering Berryman: Essays on a Poet*, ed. Richard J. Kelly and Alan K. Lathrop (Ann Arbor: University of Michigan Press, 1993).

"Staring into the Abyss: Robert Pack's Later Poems," in *At an Elevation: On the Poetry of Robert Pack*, ed. David Haward Bain and Sydney Landon Plum (Middlebury, Vt.: Middlebury College Press, 1994).

"Hart Crane's 'O Carib Isle!': 'Clenched Beaks Coughing for the Surge Again,'" in *Touchstones: American Poets on a Favorite Poem*, ed. Robert Pack and Jay Parini (Hanover: University Press of New England, 1995).

"Summoning the Dead: Politics and the Sublime in Contemporary English Poetry," *NER/BLQ* 7, no. 3 (spring 1985).

"The Intensest Rendezvous: On the Poems of John of the Cross," *Spiritual Life: A Quarterly of Contemporary Spirituality* 37, no. 3 (fall 1991).

"The Ineffability of What Counts," *Image*, no. 5 (spring 1994).

"Towards a Sacramental Language," *Image*, no. 12 (winter 1995–96).

"God and the Imagination," *Image*, no. 18 (winter 1997).

"'The Unshapeable Shock Night': Pain, Suffering, and the Redemptive Imagination," *America* 180, no. 5 (February 20, 1999).

I. WRITING THE SELF

Beginnings

❧

I CONFESS I MUST RELY for the truth of what follows by calling only on memory now. First of all, there's the matter of the lost letters, letters I wrote home to my mother in 1956 and '57, during the year I spent at the Marianist Preparatory School in Beacon, New York, as a postulant seeking entrance into the priesthood. Those letters, sent home at the rate of one or two a week, I long ago saw cut to shreds and thrown away by my poor mother during one of her low points. In the work of a single afternoon, she made a sacrifice of whatever symbols of her past she could lay her hands on, which, on this occasion, unfortunately included not only many old family photographs but those letters I wrote her from Beacon. Years ago I came to the realization that that loss was one of the chief reasons I have spent the past twenty years as a biographer poring over the letters of other writers and why, as a poet, I find myself preoccupied with trying to retrieve segments of my past from the cold ash of history.

Images, then, of the old Marianist Preparatory in Beacon, New York, a third of a century ago. The large recreation room off the study hall, with its two ping-pong tables, its stacks of metal foldaway chairs, its comfortable, seedy old lounger. I still see in my mind's eye the four-square, four-storied Victorian structure with its oversized drafty rooms, its high ceilings, its tall dusty windows overlooking Mount Beacon and a rising Easter moon. Upstairs: the cream-colored classrooms where we learned Latin and English and history and—on the top floor—the large dorm with its ancient, public porcelain washing troughs and its tiny infirmary off to one side. Thirty to forty boys, aged thirteen to eighteen, all testing the wings of their fledgling vocations.

The building is gone now, along with the chapel, the rectory, the toolsheds, the dining hall down the road that housed the handful of German nuns who fed us. Even the chlorine-leaking pool, surrounded by its green wooden dressing stalls, is gone. I spent a year here, from one September until the following July, in the Society of Mary: the Marianists. And since my name was so cleverly embedded in the order's, I took it as a youthful, onomastic sign that I was destined, not only for the religious life and the priesthood, but to spend my allotted span in this particular order.

The last time I visited Beacon, seventeen or eighteen years ago, I was already married and the father of three sons. I had stopped there on my way home to western Massachusetts after lecturing on literature to the assembled freshmen cadets at West Point. By then there was a new bridge across the Hudson, so that Beacon was almost on the way home. In truth, even if the bridge had not been there, I needed to go back then and see the place again. By then, however, except for the macadam road and the expanse of elms and maples that had dotted the old estate, everything had changed. The buildings had been razed and a new public school stood now in its place. My only consolation that midmorning was seeing Mount Beacon shimmering in the distance like the shadow of God, and even that had been denuded of the old funicular railway I had once ridden to the top of the world.

Images from those ten precious months at Beacon still flood my memory, rising with a frequency and vividness out of all proportion to the relatively short time I spent there. Most of the memories are peaceful beyond belief—low clouds hanging beneath Mount Beacon, bob-sledding through a rush of pure white powder, robins jack-hopping across an acorn-studded patch of field. Perhaps it is merely the nostalgia of youth, but I seemed to live closer then to the changing seasons, and can still summon the smells of late summer, the awesome cracking of boughs all through the long night following a powerful winter ice storm. But I also know from the few surviving letters I wrote others at the time that there were moments of intense loneliness, moments when I would have given anything to be back home with my family and friends.

I do not know what exactly happened to my religious calling, whether it died or whether it underwent a transformation into something else. But I do know that when I returned home in late July I still believed I was going on to the novitiate at Mount Marcy, New York, in two months' time. And yet something in the smell of roses and the translucent honey of those golden oldies, Presley's "Love Me Tender" foremost among them, taken together with the promise of dating girls from the local high school, became forces against which I no longer cared to struggle. So, when the time came to get on with my vocation, after a short, intense struggle with myself, I decided not to return.

Still, I count that year as the real beginning of my abiding love of writing. The Marianists were—are—a teaching order, and with hindsight I can see that I was fated to be a teacher. I can actually date that knowledge to an overcast November afternoon in the fall of 1956, while I stood on the frozen playing field guarding a soccer goalpost. I remember that time so vividly because it is linked in my memory with those black-and-white images tacked up on the study-hall bulletin board from *Life* magazine. The images show the bodies of the dreaded NKVD spattered with lime to help them decompose, and other images of Hungarian freedom fighters, some no older than myself, holding machine guns as they fought to realize a new order.

For a moment that afternoon, the soccer ball and both teams had collected at the other end of the field and I was suddenly left alone to daydream. Then, out of nowhere, I saw an image so powerful and seductive I can still call it up with the weird uncircumscribed passions of my youth. It is the vision of a pretty cheerleader in ponytail. She keeps her eye on me as she goes through her cheering exercises, and I find myself following her every move, at the same time promising *le bon Dieu* that, when I finally leave the order, I will bring the same dedication to teaching that I would have given to the priesthood.

I can see now that what I was doing then was making a bargain in the crassest manner possible. But, as an old brother explained, when his false teeth suddenly fell out of his mouth in the middle of his lecture and he had to force them back in without further ceremony, *Necessity knows no law.* So too with the bargain I made that November afternoon, when there was no one to witness what had just transpired but God. I still find myself checking to see if I've kept that youthful covenant. Since that fall when John Kennedy was shot, seven years after my boyish daydream and covenant, I have been teaching university students. And, though the world has undergone its own massive metamorphoses politically, culturally, and economically in the long intervening years, I have kept my promise.

But Beacon was also the place where I learned things that now seem idealistic to the point of the delusional and the banal, as if a young Don Quixote had set off to conquer the world and its recalcitrant words for the greater glory of the Word, armed only with a leaky pen. To begin with, mine was not what you would call a literary family. Work, hard work, was what was wanted and demanded at home, at least by my father. There were six kids when I was at Beacon, and the seventh and last arrived two weeks after I returned home. My mother named my new sister Regina Maria, since, splendid dear romantic that she was, she believed she had just sacrificed her oldest child to the Marianists and saw my sister as a gift from God to replace the loss of her firstborn.

During the war—the Big One, as he called it—my father rose to the rank of Tech Sergeant. He spent most of his tour of duty at the Aberdeen Proving Grounds in Maryland, instructing others in the repair of heavy equipment and testing the new Sherman tanks that were about to be shipped overseas. Whatever else he may have learned, he certainly learned order and discipline, a discipline he early passed on to his children, so that to this day I find myself "policing the area" (i.e., the yard) of my Victorian house for stray litter and cigarette butts before walking through the door.

In our family, outside of the ubiquitous comic books and the daily newspapers, to read was to read textbooks as a way of educating oneself for landing a good job, preferably—as my father hoped, Depression child that he was—a safe civil-service job with a pension. The novel, short story, or the rare poem I read were all assigned in class, pored over not for themselves but as a way of getting on. I laughed to myself when I read somewhere that Robert Frost thought the real descendants of the New World Puritans were the Catholics, with their strong sense of duty and responsibility. How, I wondered, had Frost found out our secret? For even into my thirties, I had difficulty with Wallace Stevens's dictum that good writing must give pleasure. Did that mean that pleasure was an end in itself? And wasn't that suspiciously like engaging in sex without having children, something, as the old schoolmen had taught, *contra naturam*?

And yet my father was an avid reader of history, especially biographies of church figures like Cardinal Spellman and Pius XII, or political figures like Churchill and Eisenhower and Senator McCarthy; the last my father firmly believed had saved our country from the Red Peril. My mother's reading habits were both simpler and more complex, and since she held a full-time position at the Doubleday Book Company's offices in Hempstead, she sometimes brought home books for me to read. Rudyard Kipling's *Jungle Book* was one, Thomas Merton's *Seven Storey Mountain* another. Besides her monthly perusal of *Reader's Digest*, she read every one of James Michener's novels, as well as romantic novels by the carton, and sometimes she read even riskier things. Once, around the time I came back from Beacon, I found on her dresser in a brown-wrapped plain cover a paperback copy of Henry Miller's *Tropic of Cancer*.

Once I lectured my brother, Walter, eighteen months my junior, for wasting his time reading Jack Kerouac's *On the Road* instead of something more uplifting, like the moral writings of Epictetus, as I was then doing. That was back in 1959, at the end of my freshman year at Manhattan College, and I shudder when I think what a pompous ass I was. Still, for the most part, my family hardly ever discussed the books they read. The most I ventured, being first in my family to go to college, was to rehash some of the ideas my philosophy teacher had lectured us on in class. I'd spin out some idea, such as Plato on the ideal of Justice, and, when the talk threatened to become esoteric, my father, at the other end of the long table, would fix me with a stare and pontificate that there was nothing right or wrong but thinking made it so, a signal that the college bullshit session was about to come to an end.

So much for reading. To write meant writing letters, preferably business letters, or a curriculum vitae for a job. In our family there was no precedent for writing to "express oneself." That was something I did not even begin to take in until I started teaching at UMass-Amherst in the late 1960s, by which time I had a Ph.D. and three kids. By then, having already taught Hunter and Lehmann undergraduates, as well as rookie cops and homicide detectives from among New York's finest and—in my spare evenings—tired stenographers and bank clerks who took Continuing Ed. classes, I felt I could at least write *about* literature. And did, including baroque essays on Carlyle and Conrad and Austen, *explications de texte* of Chaucer, Donne, and T. S. Eliot, and—eventually—a dissertation on Hopkins.

But except for a one-semester course in creative writing in my senior year at Manhattan College with John Fandel, a gentle and patient poet, I did not dare to spend time writing anything more creative than literary essays until I was in my early thirties. Writing about literature, and—better—teaching it, was acceptable because it had a social purpose. Moreover, from my father's perspective, it put bread and butter on the table. One did what one had to to survive. In the meantime, the dialogue with poetry, like my earlier dialogue with God, continued to bide its time, patiently, waiting in the wings.

In 1973, after the Italian poet Giovanni Giudici read my handful of unpublished poems, he told me in his inimitable way that it was time I stopped playing the altar boy before the altar of art and became a priest of the imagination. That, of course, links up with my experience at Beacon, and the only thing in favor of this anecdote is that it is true. But Beacon was the real beginning, though there is not much in the way to mark the beginning. Perhaps there is something of the maternal about all such modest beginnings: a harboring, a nurturing, the sense of a disembodied smile hovering over an author's infant word. It is not unlike the Christmas story, perhaps, which in retrospect forms the first act in the later retelling of the story of our lives. Our preconscious life as it is retold by our mothers seems to be the only time when history takes second place to our mewling, princely egos.

I wish I could remember the name of the outdated navy-blue-covered literary anthology that the brothers gave us high-school seniors to read that year. Or find the notebook I so meticulously kept, outlining the introductions to the various historical periods of English literature with such meticulousness that I wound up virtually transcribing the entire text to my notebook, page by page exact, believing the physical act of copying would help embed those literary "facts" on my brain. Or that is how I remember those hours in the darkening study hall, panning the ore of that old text in the hopes of discovering gold.

There was something very special as well about the books I pored over that year, including not only books I and II of the *Aeneid* but also a scholarly life of my namesake, St. Paul, which I studied for months, mysteriously delighted with the figure of Christ's disciple seated at the feet of that wise Jewish scholar, Gamaliel. For my seventeenth birthday, my mother—at no small sacrifice—bought and sent me, along with a pair of imitation leather shoes, a copy of Mackinlay Kantor's just-published Civil War novel, *Andersonville*. This I read greedily, a piece each day during my few free moments, until Brother Clyde, skimming it for objectionable material, discovered a passage about pigfucking and suggested I turn my attention to other books for the time being.

As an antidote to Kantor, he suggested I read the Catholic apologist G. K. Chesterton with excursions into Hilaire Belloc. Belloc I found vicious and half mad and quickly abandoned, but I did manage to read more than a dozen of Chesterton's Father Brown detective stories, his life of St. Francis, and *The Everlasting Man*. I even read Chesterton's biography and expressed such an interest in this Catholic writer that I eventually managed to get a pass into Beacon, a mile away, to do research at the public library. The freedom of that was so novel as to feel like freedom itself, and I spent part of that afternoon just walking the streets of the town. Thinking of that afternoon still rouses in me the half-formed image of a girl rising phoenixlike above the smoke of autumn leaves burning in small, tended piles on those impossibly innocent streets.

The history of the American Revolution is also tied in with these memories, for General Washington and the Continental Army had been sequestered across the river two hundred years earlier. Beacon is a river town, located on the eastern shore of the oil-stained, still-majestic Hudson, with Newburgh—Washington's headquarters—directly across from us (in those days it was still reached by ferry) and West Point twenty miles to the south. On a brilliantly cold mid-February day around Washington's birthday, we all rode the ferry as its huge, antiquated engines churned the boat through large ice floes, taking us to visit Washington's headquarters. I remember standing engrossed near the prow, shaken by the anti-Catholic pamphlets I'd found in the ferry station, published by some fundamentalist sect out of Tampa, which asked in a heady, terrifying, illiterate style how any right-thinking American could actually believe in some wafer God or pay allegiance to the scarlet whore of Babylon.

It is the iambic chuff Chuff chuff Chuff of the straining ferryboat's pistons vibrating through the floorboards and up through the soles of my shoes I feel now even as I write, and that brings to mind my first effort to write a serious poem. It was the beginning of Lent, and a call from a local convent had gone out for poems on a Lenten theme. The prize for the best poem was ten dollars, and I was intent on winning the prize so that I could buy something for my mother's thirty-fourth birthday. But how *did* one go about writing a poem, anyway, I wondered?

At a loss, I went up to Brother Clyde at his desk at the front of the study hall and asked him. In the appendix to my literature textbook, he explained, was a glossary of literary terms with a definition of the various meters and a discussion of line lengths and rhymes. No matter that someone named Allen Ginsberg was making history in San Francisco with his long, unrhymed Blakean verse lines and had already caused a wild stir with something called *Howl*. I do not believe anyone at the Prep had even heard of Ginsberg or his *Howl*, and in any event I would no more have been allowed to read that poem than I'd been allowed to read *Andersonville.* Poems, as my tattered textbook informed me, should rhyme. Everybody knew that.

Poems, I learned, were marked by lines of metrically recurring feet, usually in units of four or five, but could have as few as one or as many as seven or eight. If my textbook spoke of metrical shading and variation, I paid no attention, and wouldn't have understood these nuances anyway. Besides, I'd just been pressed into service as an auxiliary drummer for the Marianist Prep's ragtag marching band and at the moment had percussion on the brain. Like the atom in my physics textbook, the foot was the essential building block of the world of the poem, and was made up of a stressed syllable linked at either end to one or two (relatively) unstressed syllables. Leaving aside the problematic issue of the double-stressed spondee, no doubt invented by some troublemaker who couldn't leave well enough alone, there were four possible kinds of feet, and out of these the poet strung together his poems the way a jeweler strung pearls on a string. There was the rising iambic foot, which went dah-DUM, and the mirror image of this called the trochee, a falling rhythm that went DUM-dah. Then there was the galloping anapest—dah-dah-DUM dah-dah-DUM—and, finally, the lugubrious chant of Longfellow's dactyls that had informed his *Hiawatha.* This one went DUM-dah-dah DUM-dah-dah and was somehow faintly epic and heroic.

For my Lenten poem I chose the iambic foot, strung along the line seven times. This combination, I could not help feeling, would give my effort a certain nobility and epic expansion and, since seven was a sacred number, it would gain by that as well. I would also employ rhyming couplets, seven of them, which would add up to fourteen, in imitation of the fourteen Stations of the Cross, which the poem meant to commemorate. What I did not know at the time was that I was using the old fourteener or poulter's measure, whose long lines naturally break into breath units of four feet and three. In other words, the ballad or hymnal form.

The lines themselves would march smartly across the page, exactly as we did whenever we postulants went off to mass or to the refectory for meals. In spite of my best intentions, however, the poem spent itself after only twelve lines, and these I soon regrouped into three squads of four, each of which displayed about as much subtlety as a Roman phalanx. At the top of the page I wrote the obligatory dedication, "J. M. J.," followed by the title, "Forgive Me," in turn followed by the mini-phalanx of the poem. In spite of its curtailed length, I was anxious to have it follow the course of the Via Dolorosa, and filled out the long lines with as many baroque and redundant modifiers as my piety and zeal could muster, meanwhile trying to remember to look into my heart and write. Here was what I wrote:

> I help to beat and scourge Your back a bloody crimson red
> And place a crown of prickly thorns upon your regal head.
> Your sacred name and character I mock and ridicule.
> O Lord each time I flee your love I prove myself a fool.
> I hurt and help to make You fall along the Dolor's way,
> And scorn Your mother and the others as they watch and pray.
> I strip Your garment from Your limbs and from your whip-lashed skin.
> Yes, all of this I do to you when I commit a sin.
> I help to drive the ugly nails into Your feet and wrists,
> And mock Your kingly deity with sland'rous waving fists.
> Each time I sin against Thee, Lord, I help to break Your heart.
> Lord, help me hate my sins and evermore from them depart!

In the course of writing those lines, the beat of which I kept tapping out on my desk to make sure it conformed, I managed to evoke most of the traditional images of the Passion, on which the entire community had been daily meditating for weeks, plus a touch of Poe's "The Raven," all wrapped neatly into the rhythms gleaned from my careful reading over the years of various store-bought birthday cards. I can see too that the poem's logic is not unlike an Ignatian meditation made specifically for someone with the attention span of a Peter Quince: the composition of a particular place—a grand guignol version of the Via Dolorosa, trombone crescendos and all—followed by a meditation on the significance of place, and ending with a petition.

What else? The verb "help" is there five times, turning with a jack-knife spring at the end as the help shifts from the youthful torturer to a plea to the Victim, no doubt an encoded cry for help from that Victim in getting through the poem. Is it any wonder that, five years later, as a college senior, I fell instantly and irrevocably in love with the alternating stress and feather-light modulations of Father Hopkins's sprung rhythms, whether in the hammering opening of "Thou mastering me God" or the heartbreaking rhythms of his elegy to a dead blacksmith, cut down in his prime, when Hopkins had prayed the man might be forgiven "all road ever he offended."

The poem completed, I submitted it (that is the word one wants) to my superiors, who in turn sent it on to the local convent, and about a month afterward I learned that I had been awarded the ten dollars. From our little religious store I bought a very modest gift for everyone in my family, and a very good (plastic) rosary for my sometime Lutheran, sometime Baptist mother. I had looked in a book, much as my father had taught me to look in his automotive books to learn how to change spark plugs or an oil filter on anything from a '55 Chevy to a Nash Rambler, and now I'd learned to write a poem. Better still, it had paid off in cash. Everyone, except perhaps the poor nuns and my readers, were winners.

That it would take a lifetime of listening to the play of the wind through the shagged pines, the sound of one's self breathing, and the phrasal modulations that constitute one's unique voiceprint, as well as attending to the shifts and jagged counter-movements present in all sorts of music, from country to Buddy Holly to Bessie Smith to Mozart and Debussy and back to Charlie "Bird" Parker, as well as what one hears in Catullus and Virgil, Dante and Chaucer, Keats and Whitman, Williams and Berryman and Lowell, could not then have occurred to me. In the beginning, I could only hear and register the percussive strokes of the snare and marching drum, or the tic-tic-tic of an engine's valves and pistons, both as sharp and as defined as all ethical and moral issues then seemed to me, as they repeated their iambic and anapestic imperatives of "thou shalt, thou shalt *not*."

That May I entered my second and last contest, this one held by the Marianists themselves for the best poem and the best short story about the Order's founder, Father Chaminade. With the hubris of the as-yet-unbested, I entered both contests, writing nothing less than a poetic epic, again in fourteeners—the poem has mercifully disappeared forever—that focused on Father Chaminade's rooftop escape while the Girondist forces of revolutionary Paris sought to guillotine him. I then wrote an eleven-page biographical novella centering on the life of the founder. As it turned out, I was co-winner in both contests, which for me had the antiseptic feel of kissing one's grandmother. Worse still, I had to swallow the bitter aspic that competition even among the forty of us could be more formidable than I had been led to expect.

Reading over one's juvenilia, Stevens has written, can give one the creeps. Still, we have to begin somewhere, impelled forward with nothing but a hope that turns out to be ninety-nine percent illusion. It is like trying to outline the aurora borealis as it flashes across the deep heavens on a late summer's night. Angels cheer us from those vast heights, and at first we dream they are performing fiery cartwheels for every fresh copulative we add to noun. Or, if not angels, then perhaps a cheerleader going through her paces on a field, rampant on dun gold. As we feel the loss of our bodies press upon us, we are sometimes compensated by old daydreams that seem to become fresher and more vivid even as they—and we—recede into the past. Perhaps it is only a light, an *ignis fatuus*, after all, that we end up following, a light riding fitfully across the chalkboard of the mind, on which are scrawled huge symbols in a language we cannot read. We look again, and now the light is bouncing gaily across a silvered screen on which the words of some old song have been written, as with those old sing-alongs we watched on holidays in the study hall that long ago disappeared. It was a light by which we learned to stitch words together once—dah-dee-DUM dah-dee-DUM—until such time as we could teach ourselves to sing.

1991

Class

A SATURDAY MORNING in the early spring of 1962. It's not even seven. I've been up late, working the A&P night shift till midnight, then reading for classes till three. I'm tired. I want to sleep. But he's standing at the base of my bed, my father, twisting my big toe. In that half world between oblivion and nightmare I want to lash out and kick him hard for making me go through this fucking Steppin Fetchit routine again, but of course I don't. *Walter,* is all he says. As usual he's in his heavy black workpants and olive-drab shirt and boots, the gray hair of his crew cut bristling, his face lined and ruddy, a half-moon of oily dirt beneath each of his fingernails. He wants me up and in the truck in fifteen minutes. We're going to pick up Uncle Louie, his older brother, then head down to some bar in Garden City I've never even heard of. I look over at Walter's bed, which hasn't been slept in.

Now we're inside the bar. Outside it's a bright spring morning, but in here everything's the color of fish mud. There's broken glass everywhere: plate glass, broken beer bottles, amber and green. Chairs, some of them smashed, lie on their sides and backs. The glass panels on the front door have been kicked in, the glass in the bay window facing the parking lot smashed. My father's talking to the owners, the brothers DeNofrio. Walter, up from Georgia on furlough, two of his friends, Wilbur—whom I know—and a blond kid named Hurley—a linebacker from Post, whom I don't—stand off to the side. They're tired, bruised, and sheepish. Hurley's jaw is gashed; the back of Walter's head is bandaged. A Nassau County cop is trying to talk the brothers DeNofrio out of jailing the three of them.

Here's what's happened. It's one in the morning. Walter and Wilbur have already left the bar and are getting the car. But Hurley, who's had too much to drink, has decided to smash somebody's face as he exits, and suddenly there's a brawl with four guys swarming him. There's a shout, and Wilbur and Walter run back to help. But the door's already locked. Through the glass they can see Hurley flailing as he starts to go under. Wilbur goes right through the glass door, and then two guys are on him. Walter goes in to pull one of them off and someone brings a bottle down hard on his head. Stunned and pissed, he turns like a puma to see a shadow moving backward across the bar. In the underwater melee someone shouts that the cops are coming and then suddenly everyone is heading for the exits. Walter and Wilbur and Hurley start up the block toward the car. They're almost there when a cruiser comes up from behind, the spotlight raking their bodies. *How'd you know it was us?* Walter hears himself saying, blood matting the back of his head and soaking his jacket. . . .

I can tell just how pissed my father is by how fast his jaw is working. He's come to assess the damage for himself. He knows what a door and a couple of mirrors cost, and wants to talk turkey with the brothers DeNofrio. He knows that half of what they're saying is a bullshit act to cash in on the fight. It's the way they keep pushing the cops to have his son and the other two thrown into jail. But he also knows the DeNofrios have the law on their side and he hates tangling with smart-ass lawyers and the unfathomable legal system, and now he just wants the thing settled. After all, anyone can see the bar's just a hole in the wall. And what of the others who created mayhem and then took off? What about them?

Fifteen minutes, twenty. He pleads, cajoles, waves his hands. And soon it's "goombah" and "kids will be kids," and one of the DeNofrios finally cracks a smile and he's got him, he knows, and then he's taking some bills from his wallet, and collecting what he can from Walter and me and the others. He makes them apologize to the owners and, though it takes some doing, because they know they've been set up, they do. Each will come up with another one and a quarter. The officer also plays his part. Better, he tells the DeNofrios, in the low voice of authority, to drop the charges and take the cash. Having played the grand guignol act out as far as they can, the brothers relent.

But my father's not quite finished. Outside he goes up to Hurley and grabs his face in his strong right hand. I can see Hurley's huge right fist going into a clench. It's clear he's not used to being handled like this. But then he thinks better of it, for it seems my father is only inspecting the fishgape gash on his jaw. It ain't too bad, my father tells him, but he should get it looked at. For a moment longer than he needs to he holds Hurley's face rigid in that right hand of his, and what looks like a gesture of concern turns out to be his way of letting the kid know this bullshit will not be repeated. At least not with his son.

I'm standing over against the car with my brother, who is hurting and pissed. Fuck if he's going to shell out a month's Army wages, he tells me. "Look," I say, "you don't pay up, you'll have the DeNofrios and their lawyers on your ass for months, maybe longer. And what if the Army finds out? Or down the line some employer? Is it worth a hundred and a quarter to let so many bastards have that kind of power over you?"

"I'll think about it," he says. And for once he does.

THE POWER OF money. The power of those with the power. Then as now. No escape. No escape even now from this question of class in this so-called classless society of ours. To stare—at fifty-two—once more into the smoky mirror and count the palimpsest of crosshatched scars. No escape. I think neither my wife nor my sons can understand what this issue of class has cost my parents and siblings and so has cost *them*, except as they've registered the shock waves of insane anger break through the surface of an otherwise comfortable, middle-class existence over the past quarter century. Class. *America's dirty little secret.*

You know the best things in life is for free, I can hear my brother singing. *But you can give them to the birds and the bees. I want money.* After all, it's about money, isn't it? Money: that fucking soul-numbing drug. For some there's the early attempt to escape the worst aspects of the "situation" into which one was born. That's where the myth comes from, isn't it? The one about the prince waking up to find himself with two peasant stepparents, one twisting his toe, living in some shit-eating, humble cottage, struggling to make enough to eat.

But where does one escape *to*? Into the philosophers' circle where poets stroll about in puce leggings discussing poetry like something out of *Il Cortegiano*? And yet what world is *not* barbed-wired with its own demands? Were Lord Byron and Percy Shelley finally any better off than Keats? Were Lowell and Bishop for all of their personal capital any better off than Berryman or Phil Levine? All your life, in spite of whatever you do to alter things, and even if someday according to the "norms" you "make it" as a professional, or as a writer, you will always feel a cut below those with the pedigrees. Those with the ivy league pedigrees. Those with the gargantuan salaries and vast pampered country estates. Those who serve you *bons mots* that go off in the depths of the mind for years after like detonating depth charges, so that some hunchbacked cretin living in the fens there will always want to smash those who make you taste the old bitterness of your first world.

Bill Cosby addressing the assembled faculty at the University of Massachusetts two years ago, reminding us—with our hands out as our patrician governor began dismantling our flagship state university—that he—Cosby—made and would continue to make more than any of us, and (what was also true) probably as much as most of us put together. No doubt he had the bitter truth on his side. But what, one wonders, could have prompted him to take that particular occasion to remind us of that truth? Race issues at UMass? Or the underlying class issue of a black kid from Philly who had made it to the top, and made it in part by capitalizing on his working-class background?

Bill Clinton: Arkansas boy with his Lincolnesque beginnings, in the photo as a boy shaking hands with the mythic Jack Kennedy, the hope of having the mantle passed on to him shining in the young man's eyes. Bill the Rhodes Scholar, Bill the Yale and Oxford graduate, spending two hours with the editors of the highbrow *Atlantic Monthly*, even as he avoids the editors of the proletarian *USA Today* and *Reader's Digest*. Bill, connecting with the college crowd, even while his advisors remind him that he shines best working the crowds in shopping malls, interstate truck stops, bowling alleys, in short the people he thought to leave behind with his stepfather long years ago. You know that Cosby's and Clinton's ways out of the morass have been your exit too, their embarrassments and preoccupations your own. The advanced degree your meal ticket, as you watch yourself half in disbelief becoming one of them, one of the new breed of college professors from the working class who could find breathing space in the magic kingdom of language, surreptitiously pocketing the food others are freely offered at the banquet table.

And yet, against that, the flickering example of not counting the costs, of sharing what you have with others. Learned how? Learned where? From one's mother, who took what she could to give to her kids, as on the marble capital in the Upper Room in Jerusalem glimpsed earlier this year, three years after her death, the only image in that whole room spared by the iconoclastic Muslims: a mother pelican feeding its young from her lacerated breast. Like my mother, bled dry, until her only solace came from drinking. Or did this irritating altruism come from that year in the seminary in Beacon, New York, when there was actually time to think and to meditate, to listen to the little German priest reciting Virgil and the amniotic rhythms of the Latin?

> Dum Argolici reges vastabant bello debita Pergama
> que arces casuras inimicis ignibus, non rogavi
> illum auxilium miseris, non arma tuae artis que opis,
> nec volui exercere te, carissime conjux. . . .

> [While the Greek kings razed those walls, Troy's walls,
> with those wasting fires, I did not ask you to help
> my wretched friends, did not ask your aid, did not
> press you, my dearest husband. . . .]

Or did the example come from my wife, Eileen, who came from a modest white-collar family but who, like many such families, I see better now, avoided tearing itself to pieces with money worries and the clay-logged succor of sexual fantasies and alcohol, keeping away from unbridled anger, anger hot enough for a father, desperate for the failing words, to break his wife's fingers with his fist, because she stood there trying to stop him from smashing his son's—this son's—face with that same right hand?

Ah, here's the rub. No one lives in the magic kingdom of language for long without harking back to the very past that may no longer want either you or your language. And yet, as soon castrate yourself as cut yourself off from that past. To deny those roots, one learns, leads to neurosis, sterility, madness, spiritual death. Better to pay homage to the household gods than to try and seal them off in the basement.

A cousin telling me, with implacable iciness, that he has divorced himself from his brother, that it's bullshit this thing that blood is thicker than water. Then watching him over the next few years as his blood freezes in his relations with everyone.

A friend, refusing to acknowledge the effects of a past that held alcoholic parents and messy, working-class beginnings, becoming, as her economic situation climbed skyward beyond her wildest expectations, a chilling, suicidal elitist.

Another friend, so damaged by childhood trauma that for thirty years she managed to block out her past, only to find, as she tried to recover the childhood she'd lost, that her body had locked on her, paralyzed by the frozen river of repression even as she began to recover.

Recover. It's an interesting word that cuts two ways. We recover something by getting it back. But we recover too by covering something up again. So one retrieves something, only to hide it from view. Isn't that what happens when we write? Don't we re-cover something we thought was gone even as we bury something else?

IN SPITE OF our outward show of gregariousness, the men in our family have turned out to be largely reclusive. It is they who have found a hundred ways to be alone and will go to any lengths—legitimate or otherwise—to achieve the drug of solitude. Even at family gatherings, it's not unusual to be joined in the corner of the basement, where one thought to escape with one's ham and potatoes, by one's brother.

Part of the difficulty no doubt is the inevitable claustrophobia that comes with crowding a family of nine (eleven with live-in relatives) into a small cape cod, the sense of airless constriction remaining even after thirty years, even when there's no one else about in the three-story Victorian you call home. Which says nothing of the women, who have had to find other, even less satisfactory, ways to cope with the Sisyphean weight of the past. It troubles me that this should be so, that the voices of the women should have been silenced, for their stories are just as important to understanding the wreck of our past. It's as if their tongues had been ripped from them long ago.

Itys. Tereu. The distant trembling notes of the nightingale recalling the violence. The lonely cry of the train slogging through the hills to the east of here at three in the morning. My dead mother.

For my brothers the early out was through the military. For me—with my hearing disability—it had to be something else. Words. Even the seminary was preoccupied with words. Writing them, reading them, teaching them. I remember how happy—and guilt-ridden—I felt the day Walter told me he was being shipped out to Korea, because it meant our second-story shared bedroom would be mine alone: four slant green and brown walls and a cubbyhole with a lamp and desk at which to read Epictetus and Aeschylus and the medieval philosophers of light while Presley and Billy Holly and the unfamiliar, heady music of Bach and Mozart played in the background. My own Skinner box, and it was good. At least for the month it lasted, until my father invited Frankie to move in with me.

Poor Frankie. His father and my father had been cousins, had grown up together in an Italian ghetto in Manhattan in the shadow of the 59th Street bridge. The cousin had been drafted and sent to fight with the army in France and then Belgium, and there, at the Battle of the Bulge, retreating, the chain he was hanging to on the back of the truck had snapped and he'd fallen under the wheels of the oncoming truck in the convoy, its lights out, and then another and another. . . .

That left Frankie for my father to watch over. Now, at eighteen, Frankie was through with the New York public-school system and try-ing to find work. I remember giving him something funny to read in the newspapers and Frankie eyeing me before he put the paper down. He looked trapped. What was the matter, I asked him. No sense of humor?

He looked at me, and I could tell he was near tears. *I can't read*, he said simply. Like that. *I can't fucking read.* I could feel an inaudible sucking in of air, as if he'd just told me he had cancer or was going to have to do time.

A. The past. The thing we keep trying to make sense of.
B. The present, the moment of relative tranquility. As now, as here. The thing we have been given to make sense of the past.
C. The place the imagination creates when it tries to connect A and B. Call it the kingdom of language, the place where the past and the present fuse to form the remembered past.

It's hard to sit at a desk like this and write. Hard because all sorts of wild things begin stirring again: the demons barely, just barely, appeased by the honey of language. In truth, as I've told my wife, the memories of the past have become more—not less—unbearable with the passage of time, so that it would seem better to leave them alone. Except that the old adage sticks like a thistle: that those who refuse to examine the past, and the class issues snaking through that past, are doomed to repeat it every waking day of their lives.

Besides, for a writer, out of the tortured descent into the past a difficult beauty can sometimes be forged. If I were still living in that first world, working in a gas station, a factory, or a diner—as I sometimes feared I might be stuck—my poems, my preoccupation with words, would have been left to drift off into thin air, as so much of one's past, thanks to silence and death, seems to have done. On the other hand, if one did not have roots in a particular world, say the world of Astoria, Manhattan, Beacon, Levittown, Mineola, Richmond Hill, Flushing, what could one say?

Money. The fear of never having enough. It has pushed me—like so many others—to a succession of stopgap jobs, murderously necessary at the time, in retrospect grist for the writing mill. Working the nightshift at the old Atlantic & Pacific. Pumping gas and cleaning toilets at Scotty's Esso and the Sinclair station across from the Nassau County courthouse in Mineola. Washing dishes in a Garden City diner. Shredding classified government documents with byzantine numerical formulas into the early hours of the morning in a small office room behind the local movie house for an alcoholic boss who paid up weeks late if he paid up at all. Cutting the transparent, sickly sweet knobs from the plastic turtle bowls that the troglodytic machine clanked out at the rate of one every fifty-three seconds. Loading the droppings of two Appaloosas and four palominos into the dump truck come rain come sunshine each summer morning at seven. Painting the bottom of Camp Baumann's Day Camp pool a robin's-egg blue, the merciless sun turning one's back a blistering red, while my foreman-father, inured by hard work himself, inured to it by *his* tar-roofing immigrant father, watched over his motley crew.

Seventeen years ago I sent my first manuscript book of poems to a university press for review. They were family poems, mostly, the book itself a pale version of Joyce's *Portrait of the Artist As a Young Man.* Months later the word came back in effect dismissing not only the poems, but—what to me was unforgivable—dismissing the very existence of the world I'd written about. Who, the reviewer had written, could possibly be interested in the world of a working-class American family at midcentury and beyond? Or at least *this* family? My suspicion is that the reviewer was an academic socialist. That would work, wouldn't it?

It's one thing for a writer to paint a realistic portrait of the family in which he has invested nothing less than his life. It's quite another for some insensitive outsider to dismiss it. It's good that such university reviews are anonymous, for I still find myself wanting to smash that blank and stupid face. Of the changes that have come over the past few decades, few have been more welcome for me as a writer than the increasing recognition of a plurality of voices, including those from working-class backgrounds, sound *and* dysfunctional.

But then I remember that I left my blue-collar world long ago. Sure,

I still mow my lawn, weed the garden, paint the house. But I have my cars fixed, my house cleaned, my kitchen rebuilt by carpenters, my washing machine repaired, my antenna removed, all by members of the working class, all jobs my father and two of my three brothers still do for themselves. Sometimes, on my way to teach classes in Bartlett Hall, wearing a blazer and tie, I note the janitor sweeping the hallways or mopping the men's room, jobs I did for twenty-five cents an hour in my father's gas station back in the 1950s, and in truth I feel closer to him than I do to my most of my colleagues and students.

Many of my poems still take as their subject my first world. The cape cod we lived in at 70 Colonial Avenue, across from the high-school football stadium, was long ago sold, the children—married and with kids of their own—scattered over the country, from Vermont to Hawaii, our father remarried, at last retired from all his makeshift jobs, including the last one he had fixing trucks and snowplows for the town of Hempstead. It was a job he took, proud as he was, to earn a small pension, his other pension having been taken from him by the simple twist of a pen. You'll find him on the Maryland seashore now, riding his bicycle by the edge of the Atlantic, up and down the town's streets, still checking the construction on each new building as it goes up. As for my mother, having put up a winning struggle with alcoholism and a losing one with lung cancer, she died just before she was to retire, her last job a nurse in the V.A. drug counseling center in Syracuse. Instead of working behind the counter of a diner somewhere on Route 17 near the Delaware Water Gap—my father's persistent dream for holding the family together and giving them all jobs—I teach poetry, lecture, give readings. Most of my days—I still can't believe this—are spent writing, for which I actually get paid. Writing the lives of poets, writing criticism, writing poems.

And still class seeps into everything. It enters into the subjects one writes of, it enters the lungs and is expelled in one's language and syntax, in the rhythms one uses. It stains everything. It's behind almost any subject I talk of. Like any vantage point, it has its limits even as it helps one keep to what is important. Sure, a writer struggles to expand his subjects and lexical range, to—as they say—broaden his view. But isn't it home one always starts from? So one reads of the worlds of Ashbery and Merrill, who belong like Hecht and Nemerov and Hollander to quite other worlds, though one's deepest instincts are with those who share backgrounds closer to one's own: Wright's Martin's Ferry, Kinnell's New York, Levine's Detroit.

How difficult to speak of what presses one most closely, without overly investing in the I. But "why even speak of *I*, which interests me not at all," Williams reminds himself in that great, teeming epic of working-class America he called *Paterson*. Yet there it is: Williams's diagnostician's eye trained on the living, fallible, embarrassed autobiographical I.

Consider the peasant staring up at the stained-glass windows in the church and reading there the life of Christ, or the lives of the patriarchs and saints in resplendent, hagiographic, soothing blues and greens: exempla for the pilgrim's journey. So too with the poet who follows the narrative thread of other poets' lives, including the roaring boys: Rimbaud and Berryman, Hart Crane and Dylan Thomas, lives of incredible concentration and love amidst a too-rapid dissolution.

Williams, working the life of the suburban doctor against his great need to be a writer. Berryman, working the life of a gifted teacher, scholar, and poet against the siren call of the bottle. Lowell, revising himself and his poems over and over in a lifelong attempt—like some great Dutch realist of the seventeenth century—to understand the dark drama of the self against the oceanic drag of history. Or Bishop, like Wordsworth, working the *absence* of both mother and father into nearly every poem she ever wrote.

The writer makes himself out of what he translates, in the act transforming the life of another writer into something personal, something of one's own. Pound—citizen of Idaho and Philadelphia—translating the late-Republic love poet Propertius as a way of coming to terms with the mind-numbing insanity of World War I. Lowell of Boston transforming Baudelaire's luminous darkness into poems of his own, or reworking *Benito Cereno* into a personal dialogue on the issue of race. Bishop's preoccupation with a young Brazilian girl's life in the interior as a mirror of her Nova Scotian years. Levine's returning again and again to the impossible dream of the Spanish Republic, Barcelona his holy city. Berryman's dream of the Zen gardens of Ryoanshi, Kyoto becoming for him a consoling and multidimensional touchstone by which to measure the hectic fever of his splendid *Dream Songs*. And again the omnipresent issue of class in all the choices a writer makes, as well as in the desire to retreat into the magic kingdom of self-made language. To move, for whole moments at a time, beyond the clamant issue of one's origin and stamp.

Biography. Writing the lives of the poets by way of homage. Another act of translation by which to continue one's dialogues with the dead. A way of entering a world of riches that would otherwise remain off limits. In this the poem differs, for it allows one to celebrate one's own world, to re-cover what would otherwise be lost to time and silence. What does it mean, for example, for someone like myself to follow the uneasy Brahmin existence of a Lowell? What does it mean to take the lessons learned, say, from a perusal of *Life Studies* in order to create my own life study: Boston and New York and London shifting perceptibly to Mineola and Amherst, the voice changed, the preoccupations, the expectations, the mode of address: all, all changed in large part by this issue of class.

Berryman in natty tweeds and Oxford tie rubbing Philip Levine's jacket sleeve between the thumb and forefinger of his right hand, eyebrow slightly raised, the slight grin, as if to say, "Where *do* you get your clothes, Mr. Levine?"

And yet one knows past worlds can only be re-covered by a language equal to the occasion. In this, it seems, we are all equal in our trials: Villon as much as Sir Philip Sidney, Dickinson as much as Mrs. Browning. Part of the difficulty is in deciding on which words to use, the problem here being having at one's disposal too much language, or language inappropriate to the occasion, revealing a truth other than what one thought one was revealing. As Mailer does in his portrait of Robert Lowell in *Armies of the Night*, in the act of describing Lowell's patrician slouch showing us his own uneasy preoccupation with pedigree and class.

So too—to compare small with great—with my own poems, in trying to deal with one's past in mock-epic strains, or in a skittery, polysyllabic discourse replete with mythic overtones that quickly— one sees now—crossed over into the Cambodia of the mannerist and the baroque. As when fifteen years ago one tried to deal for the first time with the reality of a mother's attempted suicide. How difficult— then *and* now—to keep the mind on what happened that night. How easy to slide off into the unreal, consolatory dream world of language itself. And yet it was a traumatic enough event that I can still see my sixteen-year-old sister's eyes going blank as a wall of self-protective amnesia descended over her, mercifully covering over the episode in oblivion, so that she wonders now if the event ever actually happened.

But you do not get far with silence. Better to learn to trust language, the common language, though to do this, we learn by slow degrees—is anything *but* common. It's a learned response, and difficult, this primary attention to truth and clarity. One might even call it, paradoxically, the final, earned, aristocratic use of language. We think this common language belongs to our first world, but it doesn't, for that first world lives now only in the fictive re-creation of a wordless past that nevertheless keeps reminding us *it* is at the heart of our experience. To re-form the past, it seems, we are destined to deform it.

It's the fall of 1960. It's late, after eleven. I'm at the kitchen table and again I'm reading. In their bedroom I can hear my parents arguing over the fact of too little money and too many bills. I'm pretty sure my mother's been drinking. I mean, I *think* she had to be drinking to do what she did. But at this particular moment in 1960 I don't know, and don't want to know. I look up from whatever I've been reading to see her slide by me in silence, open the back door, and go out. A minute passes, a year, then thirty-five years. Once more I hear the Pontiac start up in the one-car attached garage, and of course I go on reading, afraid to stop. More time passes, fifteen, twenty, thirty minutes. There's not a sound from anywhere inside except the intake and expulsion of breathing. The smell of gas exhaust begins filtering from the bedroom to the kitchen. My sister, four years younger than I, comes down from her bedroom, asks frantically what that smell is, then goes past and outside. Then she's back, saying now she's had it. As she brushes past me, I can see her mouth set, her beautiful brown eyes go blank.

In the cage of kitchen light, in his long johns, my father stands in the hallway, his voice low and cracking. Go out and get her, he tells me, and I go. Outside, it's Mineola. There's fog everywhere, and fumes, and in the shadow of the kitchen light I can see drizzle swirling. There's the eerie Bessemer-like glow from the plastics factories a block away, just beyond the empty stands of the football field.

It's crazy, the whole goddamn thing is crazy, and in truth I am afraid to look through the back door of the garage at what I will find. The door's shut tight, but the old Pontiac's in there and it's humming. Through the dizzying fumes I can just make out my mother's head. She's upright in there, behind the steering wheel, but she isn't moving. The shock of it all is, I see now, that she's only thirty-seven. Thirty-seven: fifteen years younger than I am now, as I sit here trying to reconstruct this scene. But a hard life with an army sergeant and seven kids have made her look older and haggard. I think: she's my mother, for Christ's sake, not a goddamn kid sister or daughter. What's worse is, that in all of this, I cannot make out her face.

I put a handkerchief over my nose and mouth, push in with my shoulder as the metal hook bounces off the cement floor, and force open the door. Then I'm pushing up the overhead garage door and staring down at the cipher of my mother. I try opening the driver's side but she's locked it. I bang on the window next to her ear, but she's not moving. *Come on, Mom, get out of there*, I am yelling. And still no movement. I can see the glow of the radio lights on the dashboard, but I can't hear the music. Again I bang on the door, the window, ready to smash it. And now I'm pleading at the same time that I'm trying to seem as if I'm in control. *Please, Mom, for Christ's sake, come out.*

And then my dead mother stirs once again, turns off the engine and unlocks the door and rises, her bathrobe visible beneath her raincoat, and goes past me and inside the house, past my father, past my sister, who is standing, I think, in the shadow of my father, and goes into the bedroom, and no one says anything, and I turn out the light in the kitchen, and go upstairs to greet the unquestioning oblivion of sleep.

I KNOW THEY mean well, the people with causes. But I think now that most of them really don't get it. I'm sick of the rhetoric of the liberals as well as the rhetoric of conservatives, of the Marxists, the feminists, of my university colleagues, of the shallow irony of the deconstructionists, of most minority spokespersons, of the background noise of the *New York Times*, of those radio and TV talk shows that have eaten up so much of my life with what passes for news.

By the thousands people, especially the little ones, the weak, the powerless, are starving to death in Somalia. You see their skeletal heads and swollen bellies and the look of despair on their faces. In the streets of Sarajevo people are blown up or shot dead as they stand in line for bread or dodge through the streets to get to their jobs. And in households in this so-called classless society of ours, where the question of a wobbly recovery (that word again) remains paramount in the media, hundreds of thousands of people from hurting families—many on welfare or barely eking out blue-collar livings—each day are dying, though it often takes years to finish the job.

You do what you can to ease your pain. Rhetoric, the breezy quip, the language of "I know how you feel," when you don't. All of it less than nothing. Money matters, power matters. Sometimes, you think, they could make all the difference. And yet, part of you knows that, as important as it is, it's not by bread alone that we live. After all, there's also the word, the right word, the felt word, the sacred word, the words of felt stories, felt poems, words with blood on them. Sometimes they even manage to cut clean through the issues of class and race and gender, through whatever traps us into our Balkan states. And sometimes, you learn, they say something that actually matters.

1992

Hopkins As Lifeline

❦

I greet him the days I meet him, and bless when I understand.

IF I HAD NOT DISCOVERED Hopkins, I would have had to invent him. It was the spring of 1962, my last semester at Manhattan College, that cluster of buildings that rises on the hill above the Seventh Avenue IRT at its Bronx terminal. On the other side of the elevated, beyond the four bars and two bookstores, Van Cortland Park slumbered. There were trees. I lived thirty miles away—an hour and fifteen as they say in New York—out in suburban Long Island, and was given a ride each weekday morning and evening in a hearse-gray '57 Ford driven cautiously by my friend, John Monahan. Back home, I gulped down dinner, then drove my father's truck to my job each weekday night, working from 6:00 until 10:00, stacking shelves in one or another of the local A&Ps. Back home, I studied until 2:00 in the morning, then rose at 6:30 to begin another day. Weary of watching rats run about in mazes and writing up statistics that most of us jerryrigged anyway, I transferred over to English from psychology at the last possible moment. Even I had to admit to myself that I loved literature—especially English literature—and needed it the way one needs air or water.

Even without the prospect of a job after college, I was not to be deterred, any more than I'd been deterred at sixteen from attending Marianist Prep with the idea of someday becoming a priest. All I knew was that nothing else touched me the way a book did. Not only Shakespeare, Dickens, and Melville, but Homer, Aeschylus, Aristophanes, Dante. My father, who had seen his dream of running a gas station go under several years earlier, and who wanted his seven kids to become self-sufficient as soon as possible, scratched his head. What business did I as the oldest have taking English, he grumbled, though—thanks to my mother—he did not stop me.

Manhattan College is run by the LaSalle Christian Brothers, whose mission is to teach, and they taught splendidly. We had a core curriculum in those days, perhaps too exclusively based on the western classics, but a wonderful education for all that. A small group of us—perhaps one hundred humanities students surrounded by a sea of more practical engineering and business majors—lined up the civilizations one after the other and let them wash over us: the Egyptians, Babylonians, Persians and Jews, the Greeks and the Romans (freshman year); the Early and Later Middle Ages, with a heavy dose of Thomist philosophy (sophomore); the Renaissance, Reformation, and the Enlightenment (junior); Romanticism and the Age of Revolution, followed in our last semester by the later nineteenth and first half of the twentieth centuries.

These we pursued with a four- and five-pronged assault: history, literature, philosophy, the arts—visual and aural. What was lacking were great swatches of Africa, South America, most of the Asian rim. Still, it was a foundation, though one soon to be dismantled because most students found it too demanding. Then too there were the social upheavals of the 1960s: the Civil Rights movement, Viet Nam, the feminist movement. Indeed, the demographics at Manhattan, like New York itself, were changing. Soon women would be admitted to the all-male domain of the school, and the Irish would give way in part to a new generation of Spanish-speaking students.

But there was another thing as well. As a young Catholic I missed the presence in much of English literature of modern Catholic writers. What had happened to the tradition I'd studied that had included the New Testament, the early Church Fathers, Augustine, Francis of Assisi, the medieval philosophers of light, Dante, Chaucer, Villon, Shakespeare, Cervantes, the English metaphysicals, Pascal? Yes, there were Waugh and Morris West, and of course James Joyce, that spoiled priest

whose portrait of Irish Catholicism seemed so cold, so aloof, so analyt-
ical. And there were the heady English and American moderns—Yeats,
Eliot (at least an Anglo-Catholic), Pound, Dylan Thomas, Auden (another Anglo-Catholic).

But who—this is the way I framed it then—who spoke for what
was dearest to me? Yes, I knew the Protestant Reformation in England had won the day—there was Spenser and Donne and Milton
to remind me of that—but were there no Catholic representatives?
Had the great Catholic literary tradition in English—the world's lin-
gua franca—simply disappeared? And yet I was surrounded by Catholics. Italian, Polish, German, and especially Irish Catholics, young
men from Manhattan and Brooklyn and the Bronx whose fathers and
mothers lived in modest attached houses or tenements, labored in tall
offices or on the subways or as police officers and teachers and postal
workers, and proudly displayed portraits of Padraig Pearse and the
post office on O'Connell Street framed in their foyers. Sundays year
in and year out I was surrounded by Catholics at mass—the age-old
Latin responses about to give way to the transformations undertaken
by an interim pope who had called for a council to get some fresh air
into the churches and had in the process changed the world.

Then, in my final semester at Manhattan, Dr. Paul Cortissoz assigned me—randomly—the poetry of W. B. Yeats to fathom and then
present to my classmates. Jim Blake, my Beta Sigma fraternity brother,
who affected a kind of Irish agnostic world-weariness, had been assigned some damnable Jesuit named Hopkins. Did I want to swap with
him, he dared me, over a styrofoam cup of tepid coffee in Plato's Cave?
American astronauts—John Glenn among them—were preparing to
take heaven by storm. Without knowing it, so was I. I looked at a poem
called "The Wreck of the Deutschland." It was long, and I cannot say
I understood it. But the language. The language! "Thou hast bound
bones and veins in me," the words sang,

> fastened me flesh,
> And after it almost unmade, what with dread,
> Thy doing: and dost thou touch me afresh?
> Over again I feel thy finger and find thee.

I felt like someone who has just picked up four aces in a hand of poker. I clutched the words to my chest. Yes, I told him, I'd swap him my Yeats for this. In truth, I had just fallen in love. Done, Blake slammed his hand down on the formica table top, glinting that crooked smile of his. Done.

And so it began. The more I read the more I fell in love with the language, the explosive syntax, the passion. But it was not just how Hopkins sang. After all, Dylan Thomas had exploited that same Welsh richness in *Under Milkwood*, which I'd seen performed in the Village the year before. More important was the sense of the man that flashed from the page, his way of making the spirit speak.

Everywhere I felt a kind of subtext—what Hopkins calls a poem's underthought—sustaining and deepening the poem's meaning. Poem after poem seemed irradiated with a kind of sacramentality. More, there was an intelligence about the lines, a formal intelligence that refused to dissolve no matter how closely I scrutinized the words or the silences between the words. Atoms whirred in those spaces, creating a kind of intense inner light.

This and other immensities I tried sharing with my classmates when it came my turn to address them. Of the actual presentation I remember nothing beyond a sense of delight. I found it difficult to transmit to a group of young men whose preoccupations were anywhere but in this gray classroom on a gray day in March. I remember too a sort of pounding in my ears, which the professor put down charitably to enthusiasm but which Blake read as a sort of Italo-American lunacy. "Felix Randal the farrier, O is he dead then? my duty all ended." That was one line that played inside my head day after day. And here was another: "So some great stormfowl, whenever he has walked his while / The thunder-purple seabeach pluméd purple-of-thunder." Rich, variegated, a poetry striving to be heard among the angelic choirs. But so too the sparer, starker pitch of "No worst, there is none. Pitched past pitch of grief," or the final lines of that other sonnet written in blood:

> I see
> The lost are like this, and their scourge to be
> As I am mine, their sweating selves; but worse.

In the years to come I would discover that Wallace Stevens too had picked out the line from the Purcell sonnet to breathe in like some exquisite nosegay. And once, many years later, teaching at Bread Loaf, I remember Donald Justice quoting the lines above from "I wake and feel the fell of dark," pausing before the final two words, as if to stress that, yes, this was what hell must feel like. Then Hopkins adding almost as an afterthought that whatever he was going through, hell itself was worse. But all that was later. For now Hopkins was mine and mine alone. No one else among my classmates, for most of whom poetry was at best a chore to be endured on the road to getting the B.A., seemed much to care about my discovery. Well, all right, I thought. It was like finding a wallet on the sidewalk flush with bills that no one else seemed interested in claiming.

Then graduation, then an M.A. at Colgate, and marriage, and the pursuit of a Ph.D. at the City University of New York, with classes on the tenth floor of Hunter at 68th Street and Third Avenue. More studies—Latin, Greek, German, French, Old English, Middle English, Linguistics, Dante with Allen Mandelbaum, Chaucer with Helaine Newstead, the Victorian novel with Irving Howe, Victorian poetry with Wendell Stacy Johnson, Modern poetry with Norman Friedman. I taught radical students at Lehmann College in the Bronx amid demonstrations and protests, then took the subway downtown to 23rd Street to teach police officers—Frank Serpico among them—the two groups like the *Titanic* and its iceberg colliding finally at Columbia, one side, taunted, at last pummeling the other with their nightsticks. And then my own sons coming—Paul in 1965, Mark in 1966, and John in 1968, Eileen giving birth to John just a week before I donned my exquisite medieval garb to receive my diploma.

What would I do my dissertation on, Helaine Newstead, the no-nonsense director of the graduate program in English demanded to know. My mind buzzed. I had affected the style of *Sartor Resartus* much to the puzzlement of everyone. Carlyle, I said. Carlyle and the French Revolution. But Newstead sensed a hesitancy in me. She had read my prose. Carlyle and I a good match did not make. I retreated, re-grouped, returned a month later with another brilliant idea. Cardinal

Newman, I said. *The Idea of a University*. Again she discerned an inner conflict. No, she said, addressing me like some Zen master. I had yet to find my double. Again I retreated. What did I really wish to do, I kept asking myself. Finally, it dawned on me. Hopkins. I would undertake to write a commentary on the spiritual and aesthetic development of Hopkins's sonnets, which in his case came to the bulk of his work. The project seemed manageable. Newstead listened. Yes, she said, do it. She would help me get food on the table while I toiled daily in the library stacks unraveling Hopkins's poems. I was twenty-six, ready to take on the world, to bulldoze my way in where angels . . .

Steadily, from nine to five, in a small carrel at Queens College, for a year, I wrote. After dinner and putting the kids to bed, I wrote some more. Regularly, I sent off the accumulating chapters to my readers. Word came back from on high. Continue. Finally, in November 1967, I turned in a four hundred-page typescript and managed to defend my thesis successfully. To celebrate, Allen Mandelbaum took Eileen and me out to see *Bonnie and Clyde*. I smiled, feeling I had been through worse. Months later I met with Bernie Kendler, an editor at Cornell University Press. In the cafeteria at Hunter, between classes, we spoke. Revise the book, he offered, include all of Hopkins's poetry, and they would consider publishing my manuscript.

Later that year, in a farmhouse in Hadley, Massachusetts, I worked assiduously on my commentary while two of my sons ran about the room knocking each other over, and the other, placidly, looked on from his crib, smiling his Buddha smile. "The Wreck," "The Loss of the Eurydice," "The Blessed Virgin," "The Leaden Echo and the Golden Echo," "Brothers," "The Bugler's First Communion." Each of these in due time was scrutinized, analyzed, entered. Meanwhile I taught Modern poetry, the classics, and composition to undergrads at UMass-Amherst. The Viet Nam war dragged on. Johnson refused to run for re-election, Martin Luther King and Bobby Kennedy were gunned down, riots erupted in Chicago, Nixon assumed office. In February 1970, just short of my thirtieth birthday, *A Commentary on the Complete Poems of Gerard Manley Hopkins* was published to almost total silence. I waited for the *New York Times* to announce the presence of a bright young luminary and waited in vain.

I turned to other things. Raising a family. Writing biographies of Williams, Berryman, Lowell, and Crane. Criticism, essays, reviews, five volumes of poetry. But in all these years—thirty-six of them since I first opened and read him—I have never been very far from Hopkins. I think of him daily, and he's everywhere in my own poems. There are also the essays and reviews, and there are mentions of him as a touchstone in each of my biographies, for he figures strongly in all but the Williams biography, Williams somehow not hearing or being unwilling to hear Hopkins's richness as against his own plainer New Jersey speech.

But there's more. There's the fact that Hopkins has entered into my blood in even deeper ways, at the level of spirit. I've learned as much from him in terms of the Real Presence in the Eucharist, the midnight watches, the dark night, the small steady joys, the essential innocence underlying life to which we are called to witness. My oldest son is himself a Jesuit in the California Province, teaching Mandarin Chinese at Bellarmine Prep in San Jose, getting ready as I write this to move on to theology. It took me two and a half years to make the Long Retreat with my parish priest directing me—a man who had trained with the Jesuits—and I've made my share of modified eight-day retreats. Each morning now I rise and drive up the country roads to make the 7:00 A.M. mass. Sometimes I lector, sometimes I distribute communion. In short, I am blessed. And there is another thing I have been wanting to do. Go back now, toward evening, to write the life of Father Hopkins, and get what the lives I've read—informative as they are—all seem to miss: the Real Presence that sustained him through his years as a Jesuit and did what he said fidelity did for another saint, Alphonsus Rodriguez:

> crowd career with conquest while there went
> Those years and years by of world without event
> That in Majorca Alfonso watched the door.

Those lines, written in the last year of Hopkins's life, speak as much to my sense of Hopkins as they do of the humble Jesuit saint he in turn celebrated at the end.

1997

Quid Pro Quo

❧

Just after my wife's miscarriage (her second
in four months), I was sitting in an empty
classroom exchanging notes with my friend,
a budding Joyce scholar with steelrimmed
glasses, when, lapsed Irish Catholic that he was,
he surprised me by asking what I thought now
of God's ways towards man. It was spring,

such spring as came to the flintbacked Chenango
Valley thirty years ago, the full force of Siberia
behind each blast of wind. Once more my poor wife
was in the local four-room hospital, recovering.
The sun was going down, the room's pinewood panels
all but swallowing the gelid light, when, suddenly,
I surprised not only myself but my colleague

by raising my middle finger up to heaven, *quid
pro quo*, the hardly grand defiant gesture a variant
on Vanni Fucci's figs, shocking not only my friend
but in truth the gesture's perpetrator too. I was 24,
and, in spite of having pored over the *Confessions*
& that Catholic tractate called the *Summa*, was sure
I'd seen enough of God's erstwhile ways towards man.

That summer, under a pulsing midnight sky
shimmering with Van Gogh stars, in a ructive,

cedarscented cabin off Lake George, having lied
to the gentrified owner of the boys' camp
that indeed I knew wilderness & lakes and could,
if need be, lead a whole fleet of canoes down
the turbulent whitewater passages of the Fulton Chain

(I who had last been in a rowboat with my parents
at the age of six), my wife and I made love, trying
not to disturb whoever's headboard & waterglass
lay just beyond the paperthin partition at our feet.
In the broad black Adirondack stillness, as we lay
there on our sagging mattress, my wife & I gazed out
through the broken roof into a sky that seemed

somehow to look back down on us, and in that place,
that holy place, she must have conceived again,
for nine months later in a New York hospital
she brought forth a son, a little buddha-bellied
rumpelstiltskin runt of a man who burned
to face the sun, the fact of his being there
both terrifying & lifting me at once, this son,

this gift, whom I still look upon with joy & awe.
Worst, best, just last year, this same son, grown
to manhood now, knelt before a marble altar to vow
everything he had to the same God I'd had my own
erstwhile dealings with. How does one bargain
with a God like this, who, *quid pro quo,* ups
the ante each time He answers one sign with another?

RANDALL JARRELL ONCE SAID something to the effect that a poet, prepared to stand in an open field over a lifetime of waiting, would be lucky to be struck by lightning half a dozen times. He was talking about the vast disparity between preparedness—keeping one's pencils sharpened and erasers ready as one went through the daily exercise of writing—and the times when the poet senses inspiration has arrived. By inspiration I suppose Jarrell meant something like the welding of music to the precise curves of a complex, shimmering emotion. I feel that way about "Quid Pro Quo."

Like you and you, I too have spent weeks and months sweating over a particular lyric, trying to get the thing right. One poem I wrote two years ago, called "Then," is just such an example. Originally it had a complex Rilkean scaffolding and three days of intense talks with Robert Bly—at UMass for a conference on Rilke—holding it up. In its early stages it was hung with Rilkean angels and attitudes before I finally eased all of them out the door in the name of a New World pragmatic simplicity. "Quid Pro Quo," on the other hand, came to me largely in a single sitting for reasons I can only guess at. And it's because the poem still haunts me (and apparently others) that I want to talk about it in the hope of better understanding it.

Here's how I remember the poem's psychogenesis. In the spring of 1995 my wife and I were reading through the Gospel of St. John, a short passage each morning. We'd been at this for nearly two months when, one Sunday morning toward the end of Lent, sitting at the kitchen table, we came to the passage in John 13 where Jesus tells his disciples that he is about to be betrayed by someone close to him. Suddenly a shiver went through me as I remembered an incident that had occurred thirty years before at Colgate. It was something I don't believe I'd ever told anyone about.

I was twenty-four then and had been married just seven months. I was teaching four sections of freshman English for a small-enough salary. My wife was in the local hospital in Hamilton recovering from her second miscarriage, and I was sitting in an empty classroom late one afternoon with my friend, Mike Begnal, a freshman instructor and Joyce scholar. There was a glacial feel of Siberian winter over everything. I remember Mike looking at me with that characteristically bemused, inquisitorial glint of his through steelrimmed glasses like the spoiled Irish priest I imagined him to be, and his asking me what I thought *now* of God's ways toward men.

I was broke, terrified of being unable to go on with my education—the one way I saw out of my working-class background—and completely unprepared emotionally or economically to become a father. My wife and I were Catholics and here, for the second time in little more than half a year, the rhythm method of birth control had inexplicably failed. No one at a liberal Protestant bastion like Colgate, I believed, could really understand how a young graduate student would allow himself to get into such a predicament as I now found myself. In truth, as sad as I was at this second miscarriage, something in me felt relieved *and* guilty, though thirty years later I still find myself mourning for the babies that might have been and must remain forever now mere possibility.

And so, when Mike quoted Milton's tag about my justifying God's ways now to men, without thinking about it I raised my middle finger up to the heavens. Lapsed Irish Catholic though he was, his face registered a sort of bemused shock at what I'd done, followed by nervous laughter on both our parts. My own reaction was more complex. Had I really just done such a thing? And if I had, had I meant it? Could I now erase the gesture? Those feelings would quickly sink underground, to surface again over the years. As on the particular Sunday morning I mentioned earlier, when I read the words *One of you will betray me*.

In the fall of 1964 I began graduate studies at Hunter College in midtown Manhattan. One of the first courses I took was with the noted translator and poet Allen Mandelbaum. He was thirty-seven, and dressed impeccably after the Italian fashion. He had just joined the Hunter faculty after a thirteen-year sojourn in Florence and Rome, and was already preparing his brilliant translation of the *Commedia*. It was in his class that I came across the passage in canto XXV of the *Inferno* where the tormented thief makes "figs / of both his fists, and raising them, cried, / 'Take that, God, these are both for you!' " Reading those words, the classroom at Colgate reemerged from the glacial depths for a moment, before sinking back again.

The question one has to consider—and it is the same question Job's God responds to—is just who is this poor forked yammerer, this pisspoor inquisitor who insists on knowing God's deepest designs. Is this metaphysical questioner the same who had lied to the owner of that camp for boys up in the Adirondacks that he was in fact an expert canoeist, so that he and his wife might have a rent-free place for the summer and meals and rent money at summer's end for a small apartment in Flushing? Was he the same individual who allowed the owner to talk him into taking a too-huge group of boys down the splendid lakes that make up the Fulton Chain, including some too small to portage their own canoes? It turned out to be a miscalculation that led to my trying to shoot the lower rapids with my charges in tow rather than try yet another time-consuming portage, and this with darkness coming on.

There's a moment that still sticks out vividly in my mind. We are between sections of punishing whitewater, and have turned a bend in the river. It is about eight in the evening and a doe has come down to the water's edge to drink. As I approach in the lead canoe, having signaled to the boy in front not to stir, and with the others straggling behind and out of sight, the doe looks up at me with its large round feminine eyes and will not scare. And then, as I come within feet of it, the ten canoes straggling behind me, each with its two or three boys paddling and laughing as they follow this twenty-four-year-old who has put their lives in jeopardy, the doe slowly turns and disappears into the darkening shadows.

And then the reality of where we really are is back with me again. Bats circle and dive above us, the swirling silver-flecked waters grow darker and darker. We are soaked through now, there are still the final rapids to negotiate, and I am praying to the same God whom I had earlier signed to please—*please*—get us through this and out onto the stillness of the lake without anyone capsizing or getting hurt. Or worse.

Somehow we make it through without mishap—a miracle in itself—to find ourselves out on the still black waters of Long Lake under a beautiful rising moon. As soon as we can make a ridge, we camp for the night, build small fires, eat the packaged stew we've brought, and sleep the sleep of the dead. In the morning a storm looms on the horizon, and when I ask my young charges if they want to continue on like troopers or admit defeat and go back to camp, they opt for camp. Who can blame them?

Sed quaeritur: Is the speaker in this poem any more prepared—than the reader, say—to receive a sign from God that he will read aright? Does he—this young husband and soon-to-be-father—understand even the human relationships he's in, much less his relation to the divine? This drama I have tried to capture in the poem itself: the headstrong syntax, the nervous asides, the comic appeal to the speaker's Catholic intellectual credentials. Underlying all of this shuttling back and forth of language, however, there remains the underlying seriousness of one man's relationship to his God.

There is also the question of the speaker looking back now through the lens of Hopkins and Van Gogh on the sheer beauty of that particular moment in the Adirondacks. There is too that hole in the cabin roof through which all that starry beauty looks back down on the young speaker and his wife. Not of course that I understood this at the time, for the reality of that night and the morning of my first son's birth (Passion Sunday, April 4, 1965) still has the power to awe me. So this is the grace that was granted in spite of the speaker's impatience and rebellion and gracelessness.

More time elapses. In the wink of an eye a quarter century falls away, and the embryonic drama continues to unfold. The speaker, older now, but essentially one with that younger self, watches as his son and namesake kneels before a small altar in a Jesuit chapel in Los Angeles with a group of other young men—Irish, Italian, Vietnamese, Filipino, Latin American—and prepares to turn over his life to the same God the speaker had once had his own awkward dealings with.

The poem consists of nine sentences, some of them short declarative statements, some of them baroque in their twisted convolutions the way Stevens's are in "The Comedian as the Letter C." Eight sentences followed by a question, for which the reader—like the speaker—will have to provide his or her own answer. Seven stanzas, each seven lines long: a sense of completion and of rest, like the Lord who created the world in six days and rested on the seventh, his work completed.

For all the poem's speed and rush of syntax, there's a grand stillness about it, as if it were an ikon of some sort: the speaker's restlessness countered by God's hand supporting him and his young wife. Four relationships: the man and the woman who open the poem, the young father and his infant son, the speaker young and the speaker older, looking back on his brash younger self, though not exactly in Wordsworthian tranquility.

And finally the relationship of the speaker to his God, the same one he has underestimated more than once, trying to make the Lord of subatomic particles AND the Lord of exploding new galaxies over into *his* own sorry image. There's a lesson here, not much different from the one Dante and Milton and Herbert and Berryman—to compare great things with small—have also given us, but a lesson worth repeating.

1996

Eight or Nine Ways
of Looking at a River

❧

A STEAMY JULY AFTERNOON in lower Manhattan three or four years ago, the temperature near the one hundred mark. All morning I've walked about Greenwich Village and the Lower East Side, looking for signs of Hart Crane's having passed this way. I want to get inside the poet's mind by glimpsing the buildings and landscapes—however altered—he would have known here eighty years ago. And given that this is New York, a city that eats its past the way a sow eats her young, I know it is not going to be easy recovering that world. Here and there traces of cobblestone pavement, the streets and alleys following the haphazard planning of the city's colonial forebears, the mid-nineteenth-century brownstones and Georgian structures Poe, Melville, and Whitman walked among. One imagines Crane in this or that structure: some two-story brick-fronted building with central hall, already converted into apartments back in 1920, the poet playing his striated records on his wind-up Victrola, typing on his portable late into the night, as moths circle the electric bulb above his head and ghostly words offer solace:

> Through the bound cable strands, the arching path
> Upward, veering with light, the flight of strings,—
> Taut miles of shuttling moonlight syncopate
> The whispered rush, telepathy of wires. . . .

But it is the Brooklyn Bridge, one sees, that Crane kept coming back to, finally locating an apartment at 110 Columbia Heights, on the Brooklyn side of the river that flows east. The building itself is gone now, torn down after World War II, the space now part of the Watchtower complex. I know portions of this river, have known them since anything I can remember, though my part of this flowing, this curriculum in a purple twilight, lies further uptown: at Astoria, or just above the Queensboro Bridge, or—a bit later—down at 51st. Now, on this sweltering July day, walking across the Brooklyn Bridge, as millions of others have done, and with Hart Crane's *The Bridge* haunting my mind, I am seeing the river again, this time from a great height. And not, at least this once, from a car. No, this time I take in the view almost like a tourist, or—better—a recording angel. There below lies the vast sweep of the river, the rotting piers, the eternal seagulls whirling and dipping, the low-rise tenements and the trees, maples and sycamores, as in Crane's day, and—above me—the massive cathedral-like gothic piles supporting the untold miles of bound steel cables.

There's so much history here. For this is Roebling's dream, first the father's and then the mother's and son's. Boss Tweed and Tammany Hall, Walt Whitman's vista in "Crossing Brooklyn Ferry," Gov. Al Smith's boyhood haunts, City Hall, the South Side piers, the Woolworth Building—that "nickel-and-dime tower" paid for and built by the department store mogul, the city's tallest skyscraper for over two decades, until the Empire State Building went up in 1931, rising incredibly in spite of the worst depression the country has ever seen. Hart Crane's "white buildings," the title of his first collection of poems—1926—gleaming in the light of a summer day. An impossible dream so beautiful, so charged with erotic vitality, it hurts, as it hurt García Lorca when he was here in the 1920s, and hurt Scott Fitzgerald's Jake Gatsby, and William Carlos Williams, looking at this same city from the vantage of that other great river, the Hudson, and dreaming of its tall buildings and women from the cemetery rise in Rutherford, New Jersey.

Hart Crane wrote once that he wanted to be remembered, always, as looking at the great Manhattan skyline from the window overlooking the East River from his rented rooms at 110 Columbia Heights. In all seasons he stared out on the impossible city gleaming before him, Odysseus bewitched by his Circe. "Every time one looks at the harbor and the NY skyline across the river it is quite different," he told his mother in May 1924,

> and the range of atmospheric effects is endless. But at twilight on a foggy evening . . . it is beyond description. Gradually the lights in the enormously tall buildings begin to flicker through the mist. There was a great cloud enveloping the top of the Woolworth tower, while below, in the river, were streaming reflections of myriad lights, continually being crossed by the twinkling mast and deck lights of little tugs scudding along, freight rafts, and occasional liners starting outward. Look far to your left toward Staten Island and there is the Statue of Liberty, with that remarkable lamp of hers that makes her seen for miles. And up at the right Brooklyn Bridge, the most superb piece of construction in the modern world, I'm sure, with strings of light crossing it like glowing worms as the L's and surface cars pass each other going and coming.

How extraordinary, he summed up, "to feel the greatest city in the world from enough distance," from some vantage where one could see it in something like its full splendor and vitality. Too often, walking its streets, lost among its canyons, with the blare of taxis and trolleys behind him, or the clack of the elevated cars overhead, one was simply "too distracted to realize its better and more imposing aspects."

Standing there, along the escarpment overlooking the East River on this July afternoon, I suddenly understand Hart Crane's New York, his lost Atlantis, his benzene-rinsed white buildings rising majestically across the wide waters of the river. I have studied with wonder the grainy black-and-white images of this river preserved on damaged celluloid from the 1920s: ghost tugboats wheezing up the river past steamships bound for Buenos Aires, Liverpool, and Calais; sailing ships moored in the harbor along the wharves on South Street; the gothic pilings of the Brooklyn Bridge slowly rising. Or, downriver, Lady Liberty with her colossal torch welcoming immigrants to the new world, my own grandparents from Italy, Poland, and Sweden somewhere among them.

But this river and this city seen from this vantage, even with Hart Crane's windows at 110 Columbia Heights long vanished along with Hart Crane: this struck with the force of a revelation. People walked past me, deep in thought or conversation, or just walking their dogs, while I stared and stared. In the mind's eye I see it still, and will probably go on seeing it for the rest of my life: a river, a force, the Woolworth Building and Wall Street directly ahead or slightly to the left, the World Trade Center for the moment erased with a flick of an eye. And up to the right, the cathedral of the Brooklyn Bridge sleeping in the afternoon sun, its enormous force for the moment placated.

CONSIDER FOR A moment the lenses of Picasso, Juan Gris, Braque. The river as Cubist mélange, from eight or nine vantage points.

Christmas night, 1995. Returning with my family from Greenwich Village, the station wagon loaded with gifts, up around 70th Street on the FDR, heading north and stuck in a glue of traffic. Movement by inches, if at all, and tempers flaring. On the other side of the steel divider, headlights zooming south. Ahead of us a river of taillights flashing dully, then brighter, as cars inched to a full stop. Twenty minutes, half an hour, four or five city streets traversed, swearing. Everyone growing tense. Then the phosphor-red flares, and police officers directing us to the left. Then the sight of the ambulances lined up on the extreme right, and three cars badly smashed, their passengers being rushed to the huge hospital on our left. Here, in the anonymity of the great city, a life or several lives have just ended. I catch myself looking out beyond the ambulances at a massive tug churning through the darkness of the river. A vision of le néant, the Abyss.

Summer 1947. I am seven years old and have come down to the river. There is a park here at the eastern end of 51st Street, where my mother has often brought my brother and me to play. But today I have wandered down here alone, crossing the FDR to walk out on some of the ancient rocks facing the river. Somewhere near here Nathan Hale, a Connecticut schoolteacher and spy for General Washington, rowed ashore on a reconnaissance mission, was intercepted by British troops, tried, and hung. History. That world, like colonial New York, long gone. Like nature, this city abhors a vacuum. If it can be built upon, New York will build on it. Only here, and out in the river, as Williams noted, is there any sign of the original Manhattan island: three small rock outcroppings, too small for building on, and left now only for the gulls to crap on. I stand at the edge of the water here and look out, desiring to embrace this river. Only a man in a topcoat, alone and off to the left at the highest point of the outcrop, intrudes on the scene. Weirdly—if anything that happens in New York can truly be said to be weird—I find the man addressing me. I watch him as he pulls something from inside his coat. A derringer, he says, as he points it at a low-flying seagull.

Driving down from Massachusetts, I often take the FDR down to the Village or midtown. And there is the river, off to my left, the railroad bridge, the islands with their buildings, a few trees, the 59th Street Bridge that for years was my landmark. Cobblestoned 61st, between First and Second Avenues, where my father was born in an Italian enclave, mostly people from Milano, Turino, and the hill towns east of Genoa. Here too in the late 1930s my young mother came, fresh from Paterson, New Jersey, with her widowed mother, a good-natured, hard-drinking Swedish flapper whose husband—my grandfather— had joined Black Jack Pershing's army in Texas. His name was Harry Szymborski, and once, a private in the U.S. Army's Sixth Cavalry, he rode a horse named Red across the Mexican border in pursuit of the elusive Pancho Villa. Nineteen sixteen: the same year a boy named Hart Crane decided to make his name in lower Manhattan, two miles downriver from this spot. Forces melding in the imagination, married yet isolated, like those islands gleaming in the river.

Nineteen forty-eight. My step-grandfather, Hank Cosgrove, married to my Swedish grandmother, walks his daughter, my brother, and me along the walkway edging the river around 70th. A bracing breeze comes in off the water. The sun beats bright as a bell off the wave caps in chiaroscuro fifths. Hank has a package of animal crackers in his pocket, from which he has been carefully doling out treats. He points to an island out in the river, to some derelict buildings there. His father, he says, died on that island, fighting a fire. They went into the building and the flames trapped them, he says, and the men died there. His father, a big New York Irishman, was one of them. He was a hero, Hank says into the air, at no one in particular. Can I have a cookie, I say.

Great flakes of wet snow falling on the river, the whitecaps roiling, coursing southward to merge with the great Atlantic, far from the Christmas lights of Macy's and Bloomingdale's. The gray gulls sullen, withdrawn and unblinking, perched on the tops of the rotting piers, themselves slowly going under, to merge, as everything will, with the river.

The Williamstown Theater, midsummer, three years ago. My wife and I have driven up to this college town in the northwest corner of Massachusetts to see a play called *Dead End*. The setting is New York City in the 1930s, a drama rife with the issues of social justice during the American Depression. The set is a piece of New York in remarkable detail: brick and marble-fronted buildings along the river at 53rd, tenements and a posh hotel side by side, representing the stark economic contrasts endemic to New York. The actors are dressed in the film styles of the 1930s. Like them, too young to have known this world firsthand, I let my memory roam, checking the accuracy of the set against the black-and-white films of the period, against photographs of the period. The acting is good, the accents believable, but the scene is wholly imagined, for these buildings never existed in this place, right up against the river. Still, it's all somehow right. My mother swam this river as a girl. A strong swimmer, she dared the whirlpools up near the Hellsgate Bridge, aptly named. I recall boys swimming in the polluted waters in a film I saw as a boy back in the 1940s. It was called *Naked City*. Real boys swimming in black trunks or in their underwear. But a fictive murder and fictive cops, fictive lines recited above a celluloid river. The river remembered, the river imagined. And the real river, like God, flowing outward forever. Yesterday, today, and tomorrow. *Per omnia saecula saeculorum.*

In the spring of 1932 Hart Crane was returning from Mexico City with Peggy Cowley, the ex-wife of an old friend, a woman he imagined might become his wife. It was the nadir of the Depression, Crane's millionaire father had died the year before, broken by that same Depression, leaving his son virtually nothing. Crane was returning to New York and the East River by ship and was 275 miles north of Havana when he did what he had been daring to do for years and killed himself, leaping from the ship's stern and disappearing beneath the waves. The body itself was never recovered. Fifteen years later his mother's ashes would be scattered from the midsection of the Brooklyn Bridge, that metaphysical span in a physical world, a bridge reimagined by the poet himself. From here his mother's ashes might descend, like black snow, to merge with the river below. Perhaps in time in this way she would be reunited with her only child, from whom she had been estranged in his last years. A belle in New York once, dancing the latest steps, the Charleston among them. Now she too, like her Hart, has made the great leap.

The traffic this winter day along the FDR, heading in either direction, as well as along all the approaches to the river, has been backed up for nearly an hour. Once again everything has come to a standstill. The bright morning sun reflects off a thousand car windows and seems to be laughing. The eighteen-wheel rigs and the buses too are sitting idly, diesel fumes misting the air. It's New York on any given day, really. Only the river, with its ghostly clippers and steamers, its spent history renewing itself as the eye moves along its whitecaps, seems to be moving, inexorably, onward.

2000

II. WRITING LIVES

The Brain That Hears the Music

CONSIDER FOR A MOMENT the figure of the failed artist, Salieri, in Peter Shaffer's *Amadeus*, confronting for the first time a sheaf of Mozart's musical compositions. Salieri, in health, with some modicum of power, the court composer who has had to struggle like most mortals for whatever recognition he has achieved, staring now in wonder and despair at the manuscripts of this interloper with the deranged laugh, this Mozart, this genius touched with the gift for a musical composition of the first magnitude. Salieri in middle age and Salieri old, knowing that his own work at best exists to be corrected and parodied by this lout, this boisterous roustabout, this, this divine artist. "Astounding," he sighs, and the notes of the compositions he has been reading take wing now and begin ascending, seeming to touch the very sills of something beyond his ability even to articulate:

> It was actually . . . It was beyond belief.
> These were first and *only* drafts of music.
> But they showed no correction of any kind. Not one. . . .
> He had simply written down music
> already finished in his *head*.
> Page after page of it, as if
> he were just taking dictation.
> And music. Finished as no music is *ever* finished.
> Replace one note and there would be diminishment.
> Displace one phrase and the structure would fall.
> It was clear to me that sound

55

I had heard in the Archbishop's palace . . .
that was no accident.
Here again was the very voice of God.
I was staring through the cage of those meticulous
ink strokes at an absolute beauty.

I think all poets must at one time or another have known this Salieri well, having seen his quizzical, sharp, terrified face in the plate-glass window or the bathroom mirror. It is a feeling shared by many writers when they see good work—excellent work—done by others. Admiration, yes, a stammer of assent to say lightning had flashed off the page, but—as William Carlos Williams says—fear too that others can write so well.

The music that haunts our ears and—once heard—will not let us rest. "Atem der Statuen. Vielleicht," Rilke has struggled to say it. "Stille der Bilder. Du Sprache wo Sprachen im enden" [The breathing of statues. Or, maybe, the stillness of paintings. You, speech where speech ends]. Many kinds of music will do to demonstrate a point. Mozart of course, but why not, at least for Americans, the complex registry of responses we feel toward the gospel singer belting out "Amazing Grace" or "What a Friend We Have in Jesus," or—again—the chords resonating in us when we hear Bessie Smith do "Yellow Dog" or "Empty Bed." Or Williams, sick of what he calls the syrupy red-and-green candy music of Latin love songs, no longer of any use to him in his sickness, attending rather to the music accompanying an old burlesque dancer jiggling her buttocks in mockery before a dozen bald heads in some cheap nightspot in Juárez.

Certainly that music in that place was enough for Williams, crippled by his first stroke, become a joke to himself, enough to move Williams to poetry once again. Watching the woman mock the music she dances to, he hears a music that fits this "artist" perfectly. Enough to help him make his way back from his disabling stroke by giving him the courage to find a limping, broken music to fit his broken brain and broken world. Walking back across the border to El Paso, one world separated from another, his scattered brain begins to find its music:

> What in the form of an old whore in
> a cheap Mexican joint in Juárez, her bare
> can waggling crazily can be
> so refreshing to me, raise to my ear
> so sweet a tune, built of such slime?

Now he hears the nightclub music begin to detach itself from its occasion and hover over him, signaling for him the music of his desire, "as when Casals struck / and held a deep cello tone / and I am speechless." Speechless: breathless. But also an acknowledgment of his inability to capture in words what it was he felt hearing Casals, a feeling that forever after changed him. Now, again, here in Juárez, he has heard it, a music consonant with his own complex human condition, and he is grateful. Grateful for having found even in hell a music to console him: "I *am* a poet! I / am. I am. I am a poet, I reaffirmed, ashamed."

"But who could call back now the web of sound," Donald Justice writes in "The Sunset Maker." He too has felt something of this same poignancy in the loss of one of the old lovers of music. No, not Mozart, but one Eugene Bestor, remembered now for six notes "Flying above the staff like flags of mourning." A "ghost-music materializing," hovering over the book itself, so that I am moved almost to tears for a man I do not know (if he ever existed) and by a music I cannot even read:

> A brief rush upward, then
> A brief subsiding. Can it be abstract?—
> As Stravinsky said it must be to be music.
> But what if a phrase *could* represent a thought—
> Or feeling, should we say?—without existence
> Apart from the score where someone catches it?
> Inhale, exhale: a drawn-out gasp or sigh.

A lifetime's practice at the piano or at one's desk, playing the keys, trying to get down on the page something of what moves one. And doesn't it come down to ghost music in the mind of the poet who remembers and who, if we are lucky, records it for us:

> The perfect ear, the technique, the great gift.
> All have come down to this one ghostly phrase.

> And soon nobody will recall the sound
> These six notes made once or that there were six.

In *Foreseeable Futures*, Bill Matthews too notes that hunger for a music touched aslant in the jazz-riff interstices between two notes. What is the real burden—in its musical sense as well—of our attempts to get back through the music to touch the dead composer himself? As if we could. Touched to the heart by Purcell's music, Hopkins speaks of the composer's "abrupt self" flashing off the score when we least expect it, always in the side glance and never by staring directly at the face of the artist. That would seem to be the most of it.

Matthews hints at the same sort of thing when he writes of the unearthing of Bach's tomb at the end of the last century in "Leipzig, 1894." And what was there to see, he asks, in this return to the original ground of the poem? What was there to hear from the now-decomposing artist, in the bones of a medium-built man over which the music of our breathing hovered? And when we were finished staring at the place from which the music had originated, what would we have learned? After that, the dark phosphorescence of the mystery would still have kept its distance. How end such a search but as Matthews has ended, with the lanterns tossing

> their heads this way and that.
> The harder I listened, the deeper I heard us breathe.
> What music, after all, had we disturbed?

A plangency, *sunt lacrimae rerum*, such as Virgil and Horace heard for the passing of all things. The cry too of our desire to hold them, if only for a moment. As in "Blue Notes," waking to hear somewhere in the recesses of the mind a song, the

> few splatters from an evaporated eloquence
> we can't reconstruct for all the cocaine
> in Bogota or winter wheat in Montana.

An evaporated eloquence, the unheard melody that tortured Keats so exquisitely, as if he too had heard Charlie Parker or Bessie Smith belting out the blues. "All the cocaine / in Bogota." In that shrug a world glimpsed, a world lost.

A world lost. Here is Berryman's *Dream Song* 68, composed in the nation's capital the day after Christmas, December 1962. White, middle-class Henry, listening to Bessie Smith belting out the blues, does a two-step across stage-center in "two—three seconds," as he hears

> the house is givin hell
> to *Yellow Dog*, I blowin like it too
> and Bessie always do
> when she make a very big sound.

Then, having touched that chord, the sense of loss complicated by the sense of guilt. "Strange horns" he hears now, Pinetop Smith hitting him some chords, then Charlie Green playing trombone. Strange horns: the horns of an automobile clashing with trombone and sax, an accident, an ambulance taking Bessie to a whites-only hospital, not admitted, Bessie dead. And now, thirty years later, Berryman celebrating White Christmas in the shadow of the White House, all of it taking on a new definition through Bessie's dying eyes:

> they all come hangin Christmas on some tree
> after trees thrown out—sick house's white birds',
> black to the birds instead.

Schubert too could move Berryman to tears, and did, capturing in the flagstaff score the cry of a heart broken by something gone forever like a lost first wife, a pain beyond what one would have thought possible:

> like a man
> dragged by his balls, singing "Oh yes"
> while to his anguisht glance
> the architecture differs: he's getting on,
> the tops of buildings change, like a mad dance,
> the Piazza Navona

recovers its calm after he went through,
the fountain went on splashing, all was the same
after his agony.

You find your music where you can. "Just as my fingers on these keys /
Make music," Peter Quince a.k.a. the younger Wallace Stevens wrote,
"so the selfsame sounds / On my spirit make a music, too." Music *is* desire, a giving over of oneself completely to a condition of being, rather
than meaning. "Music is feeling, then, not sound," this Mount Rush-
more of huge unsatisfied hungers wrote:

And thus it is that what I feel,
Here in this room, desiring you,

Thinking of your blue-shadowed silk,
Is music. It is like the strain
Waked in the elders by Susanna.

Of a green evening, clear and warm,
She bathed in her still garden, while
The red-eyed elders watching, felt

The basses of their beings throb
In witching chords, and their thin blood
Pulse pizzicati of Hosanna.

Consider too the cadences of Linda Pastan's "Overture," with its in-
structions on how we bring that sure music, half heard, "almost remembered," over into the poem. Here Pastan has transformed the idea
of musical overture by way of metaphor into the way we "almost" remember the music which startled the poet into song:

soon we will find ourselves
thinking of weather—
a cold front rumbling in—
or of applause, not for the self

(not for the self, then, which has by now disappeared into the music,
where we are one with the music while it lasts)

but for someone we watch
bowing at the edge
of a pond whose waters,
like the cello's darkest waters, part
letting the melody
slip through.

As if for the first time. That signature of the fictive Mover. Not to copy the music, but to imitate, Williams insisted. Which means the verb, the word as action, detaching itself to create a new song, albeit a diminishment of whatever it was that first startled us. It is always a music played—foot by foot and breath by breath—against a music half heard and half remembered, and, even though the poem wins in bringing into being some new song, it must always lose against the music it weeps to recall.

"And the things of this world," Jorie Graham has it in her "Eschatological Prayer," the things of this world

were everywhere happy
to be so grazed . . .

sifting the minutes from the dust from those three
almost repeatable
notes
on which the whole unbearable song

depends. . . .

You could reach almost in
to where the notes and the minutes

would touch.

A gesture toward the intangible, that most exquisite of moments before the composing music gives way to "the airplane factory now closed and converted / into a temporary / slaughterhouse." For such are the "conversions" of the human condition: the ecstasy of music giving way at the turn in the road that returns us to the prose quotidian and the dust, the boredom, the loss.

Still, the poem gains its strength from bowing to that ghostly music, the muse, the mother. This is because the music—the *arpeggio* of the flute or the thrum of the shawm, the *pizzicato* of the clavichord or the banjo twang—is inextricably bound up with a world lost. For that first (lost) world always evokes a world of other images: Bonnard's colors and a concert hall, or a friend, as with Justice, or the moon glimpsed over a mountain seen from the back seat of a car late, a rowboat drifting on a lost summer's day, three Appaloosas in a field playing, a mother singing on a winter's night before an upright.

D. H. Lawrence too understood this, and gave us, in his superb lyric "Piano," an understanding of desire and loss in terms Freud himself might have dictated. And Lawrence did this in some of the most extended couplets in the language, as if the swelling tide of the music itself might break through the lines themselves:

Softly, in the dusk, a woman is singing to me;
Taking me back down the vista of years, till I see
A child sitting under the piano, in the boom of the tingling strings
And pressing the small, poised feet of a mother who smiles as she sings.

In spite of myself, the insidious mastery of song
Betrays me back, till the heart of me weeps to belong
To the old Sunday evenings at home, with winter outside
And hymns in the cosy parlour, the tinkling piano our guide.

So now it is vain for the singer to burst into clamour
With the great black piano appassionato. The glamour
Of childish days is upon me, my manhood is cast
Down in the flood of remembrance, I weep like a child for the past.

Even Eros can have its great horns clipped in the peaceable kingdom of the imagination, a creature become all quarter, half, and whole notes, flats and sharps. Even Priapus, as Williams knew, might become the impossible Unicorn finding the woman among the millefleurs and lilies, who calls for his death and transformation. It must give pleasure, Mozart and Stevens remind us, the pain of loss transformed into the music of our nostalgias.

"How terrible must life become before / music no longer can transform disgust?" a grieving Robert Pack has asked, as he catalogs the detritus of a world at least his blessed Mozart was spared. In "Within Measure" the music of Pack's lines snarl with the despair of having to bear witness to "clogged birds oozed up on oil-clotted shores," the "sulfur-infiltrated trees," "ghostly radiation in the air," the "noise of motors everywhere / gnawing like locusts in a plague." Against that, what? The burden of the poet's music in a darkening time, the attempt to render the healing notes glimpsed in Mozart and now given back in Titian's somber colors by the one who hears the melody and attempts now to "measure out wet wind upon the mountain."

We find our music where and as we can, alone in our rooms listening to the blues, in Haydn or Mozart or Beethoven, in a symphony hall in the nation's capital, alone, with a few hundred others. Or in a tenement, as I heard it earlier this summer at Jacob's Pillow, where the artist had captured something of the banality and violence of voices echoing up the stairs, counterpointing the vulgate with the precision of the woman and her partner, dancing without ever touching to a music inspired by our language pouring down and for a moment caught. The cadences of a vulgar New York speech so accurately rendered that I found myself laughing with relief. "Get him off me Harry. He's crushing me. Get him off me Harry," while the woman crossed her partner in a series of movements first frenetic, then as slow as underwater boxers caught in the idiom of ennui that had inspired the movements in the first place. "We got nothing Harry. Look at us. We got nothing. We got nothing but shit." And yet how beautiful, how electric the language, caught shimmering that night as the tall trees swaying in the light bent to listen.

You find your music where you can. So Philip Levine, in a complex crossing with Wordsworth, remembering a time when he worked the nightshift at Detroit Transmission, when he and the others sang in the cold dawn above the racket of machines and tried to keep warm. Now he evokes the bloody head and the foul mouth of Stash's music,

> addressing us by our names and nations.
> "Nigger, Kike, Hunky, River Rat,"
> but he gave it a tune, an old tune,
> like "America the Beautiful." And he danced
> a little two-step and smiled showing
> the four stained teeth left in the front
> and took another suck of cherry brandy.

An old tune, neither parody nor sentimentality, remembered there in the fallen city of man, "where your Cadillac cars get manufactured." And though the men he worked beside are dead, they still sing, Levine imagines, in heaven, though now "River Rat" and "Hunky" have been changed to the strains of "Time on My Hands" or "Begin the Beguine." What persists is the memory of those nameless men and women, their broken music, made up of the sounds of the street and factories, the curses and raucous laughter and cries, translated into the music of memory.

"Dove moans," the poet hears from among the Jewish graveyards somewhere in Italy:

> Dove moans,
> or something like them, from under
> the low, scorched pines, and farther
> off the laughter of other birds,
> and beyond the birds, the hum
> of a distant world still there.

Still and still there. "For most of us," Eliot wrote,

> there is only the unattended
> Moment, the moment in and out of time,
> The distraction fit, lost in a shaft of sunlight,
> The wild thyme unseen, or the winter lightning
> Or the waterfall, or music heard so deeply
> That it is not heard at all, but you are the music
> While the music lasts.

You hear it in the way the poet approaches the music: shy, assertive, terrified, or eager, on strong feet or on halting, warming to it. If we wait on it, sooner or later it may, just may, volley through until we hear it, Williams comforts us, until it is all about us, the verb detaching itself, "seeking to become articulate" until we wonder at the brain's ability to hear that music "and of our / skill sometimes to record it."

Sometimes to record it. I take this to be Stevens's argument in "The Creations of Sound," with Eliot's sense of the music of the poem. The poem, Stevens insists here, comes from a place we do not understand and rises in a music beyond ourselves,

> intelligent
> Beyond intelligence, an artificial man
>
> At a distance, a secondary expositor,
> A being of sound, whom one does not approach
> Through any exaggeration.

The poem must make "the visible a little hard / To see," he tells us, must reverberate along our pulse and "eke out the mind / On peculiar horns, themselves eked out / By the spontaneous particulars of sound." It must lead us out of ourselves until

> We say ourselves in syllables that rise
> From the floor, rising in speech we do not speak.

Except that of course we do speak it, surprised that we can, at least in isolated moments. Let Stevens, that sleight-of-hand impresario, have the penultimate word, tendering us a music we hear in and behind his syllables in the richest of blank verses scoring itself across the exquisite Blank:

> And out of what one sees and hears and out
> Of what one feels, who could have thought to make
> So many selves, so many sensuous worlds,
> As if the air, the mid-day air, was swarming
> With the metaphysical changes that occur,
> Merely in living as and where we live.

Reflect too for a moment on two athletes who died young: Hopkins and the even-younger Crane. Six weeks before his death at forty-four, Hopkins wrote what would become his final poem, a poem addressed to his old friend, Robert Bridges, who would live another thirty years and become England's poet laureate. Hopkins knew he had disappointed his friend on many scores, knew as well that Bridges blamed the loss of Hopkins's lyric gift on his having become a Jesuit. What matter now, Hopkins answered. It was too late to argue. He too had known in his time what immortal song had sounded like, knew the ecstasy of inspiration and felt along his pulse the tremors of the annunciation of the word. Now, at the end, he laughed out of his desolation, making of the dark itself a music. The very breath hisses from him in this, his final poem, knowing some of his music must be lost on his listener:

> if in my lagging lines you miss
> The roll, the rise, the carol, the creation,
> My winter world that scarcely breathes that bliss
> Now, yields you, with some sighs, our explanation.

And Crane. Knowing that he had glimpsed his own fate in the giant turtles he had seen writhing from bloody iron hooks along the wharves, he fairly wept. "Let not the pilgrim see himself again," he wrote, remembering the irresistible music he had followed in the calyx of his mind at what terrible cost, seeing himself in those crucified terrapin:

> Each daybreak on the wharf, their brine-caked eyes;
> —Spiked, overturned; such thunder in their strain!
> And clenched beaks coughing for the surge again!

This is the work of poems, to catch whatever music the scored net can. The rest lies in waiting until the tides carry that music back to us.

"Tides bring the bodies back sometimes, & not," Berryman wrote. He meant the ocean, remembering his dead father as he swam out

into the Gulf, attending to a music he alone could hear. But Berryman
meant too the tides of sound haunting his ears:

> The bodies of the self-drowned out there wait,
> wait, & the widows wait,
> my gramophone is the most powerful in the country,
> I am trying, trying to solve the andante
> but the ghost is off before me.

That seems often to be the problem: to find a music that will lift our
own lines, a music heard in fits and phrases only, until we are lifted
up by it even as we are cast down. An *Oh*, an *Ah*, a word, a phrase, a
melody. Sighs elongated and drawn out, the whole complex amassing
harmony calling after, until salt sand fills the unstopped ear at last.

1988

Kinnell's Legacy

On "The Avenue Bearing the Initial
of Christ into the New World"

IT'S ONE OF THOSE quicksilver pieces, Galway Kinnell's poem with the impossibly long title, "The Avenue Bearing the Initial of Christ into the New World." A poem whose parts seem to continually slide through your fingers as you try to hold them in the cup of your hands. A young man's poem: brash, sardonic, hard-bitten, overreaching, vulnerable, earnest, vital. He was thirty when he wrote it—"En l'an de mon trentiesme aage"—and the length of the rhythms like the length of the poem together make several important announcements, not unlike Whitman at the beginning of his own poetic career.

For one thing, the poem rejects Kinnell's earlier formalism to pursue a new rhetoric. Whitman is the key figure here. Whitman and Hart Crane . . . and Villon. And so the use of lists and a plethora of images, and—unlike Whitman but very much like Villon—the suppression of the poetic self to let more of the world into the poem. Like Lowell and Ginsberg, Kinnell knows the mystical union Whitman hoped for America is no longer possible. Such optimism was a pre–Civil War condition, and one Whitman himself rethought after Shiloh and Antietam.

Nor can Kinnell accept Whitman's lifelong desire for a vision of sane and sacred death. The voice of the Jew, Isaac—Hebrew for "he who laughs"—that son of Abraham, who in our time has been consigned to the flames of the Holocaust. More specifically, the Chicago-based writer Isaac Rosenfeld who, reading Whitman's vision of the sacredness of death, had dismissed it with the words, "Oi, what shit!" Death is death: mean, nasty, and inevitable, and Kinnell—who lost his own brother when he began writing this poem—knows this as much as anyone.

So too with Villon, three lines of whose poem "The Legacy" are evoked near the end of Kinnell's poem by way of counterpoint to Whitman. And why a medieval French poet from the streets of Paris, and a criminal at that? Because Villon's vision of death and old age and his vivid and realistic sense of medieval Paris chime so well with Kinnell's own sense of death, which is why Kinnell has twice now translated Villon's poems into an increasingly spare and vigorous American idiom. Consider Villon's sense of impending death brought home in images of corpses burning on Paris's cobbled streets in the wake of the Black Death, and Villon's premature aging (he disappeared from history at the age of thirty-two) after being confined, tortured, and sexually debased in the dungeons of Meung and Paris. Then superimpose on the image of burning corpses from the Black Death those grainy black-and-white film clips of the dead at Auschwitz and Buchenwald bulldozed into mass graves. The Holocaust seems very much on Kinnell's mind as he reads the history of mankind along Avenue C in the decade following the war. A once-teeming, vigorous Jewish quarter of Manhattan: one of the cities of the modern Diaspora, along with Paris, Damascus, Jerusalem, all "scattered over the lonely seaways, / Over the lonely deserts . . . / [hiding] In dark lanes and alleys."

About the origins of the poem, Kinnell has said that it began for him in Jerusalem in the mid-1950s, when he followed the stations Jesus walked as he was led off to die, staggering under the weight of the cross on which he would be nailed outside the gates of the city (GK to PM, 1 May 1985). Fourteen stations, beginning where Pilate condemned Jesus and ending at the tomb where Jesus was buried.

And where are the holy cities of the New World to vie with those of the Old? New York? "When I did settle on Avenue C, living on 5th

Street between C and D," Kinnell writes, "I noticed that the street had 14 blocks, and that recalled my Jerusalem thoughts. The stations of the cross exist in those 14 sections [of "The Avenue"], but barely, and could be called the [poem's] vanished skeleton." So, then, the origin of the poem may lie just here, in an attempt to deal with the big issues of love, death, empathy, and redemption. Looked at in this way, it reveals its affinities with "The Bear," *The Book of Nightmares,* and the poems remembering his dead mother and brother in *Mortal Acts, Mortal Words.* Kinnell's Christian background seems to stand behind this poem like an early irritant, for the poem holds together best if read as a meditation on death and the renewal poetry affords.

In *The Book of Nightmares* Kinnell laments Christian man's complicity in the death of his fellow Jews, for it was a Christian society—however Christianity may have been subverted—that, either directly or by standing by and doing nothing, abandoned the Jews. This sense of collective shame stands behind one of the most troubling images in "Avenue" as well. It is the figure of Christ the Jew nailing fish to a plank and scraping the scales from them as he turns them—in a parody inversion of the Resurrection—into "flesh for the first time in their lives." For the community living along Avenue C, the remnants of one of the largest Jewish communities in the New World, mixed now with blacks and Puerto Ricans and others, is not unlike the communities Kinnell mingled with—Jew, Arab, Christian—in Jerusalem. Kinnell knows too that the Jews have just survived the worst threat to their survival in the history of the race. That tenacity—of having passed through the fire and been transformed—is a source of both consolation and inspiration for the poet who would raise the world along Avenue C to the level of the imagination.

Moreover, as Kinnell understands, the locus of his poem is central to anyone aware of American place names and the history of American poetry. Situated in a tenement room a few blocks from the East River and the place where the Brooklyn ferries once docked, Kinnell cannot help but recall Whitman's "Crossing Brooklyn Ferry" and Hart Crane's *The Bridge,* and thus to a reconsideration of the failed promise of both poems.

Among the catalog of New World sounds Kinnell uses to announce his poem is a tugboat on the East River, chuffing by at dawn as it "blasts the bass-note of its passage, lifted / From the infra-bass of the sea." Those who recall "The Tunnel" will remember the tugboat lunging past on the East River at midnight at the close of Crane's poem, "wheezing wreathes of steam" and giving its "one galvanic blare" as it disappears into the night. So too the bums, those misplaced modern-day Daniel Boones, the romantic pioneers and adventurers who populate the "River" section of Crane's epic. In *The Bridge* Crane records seeing one such derelict in the guise of Rip van Winkle as he walked down Avenue A on his way to work, the derelict in turn reminding Crane of the rail-hopping hoboes he saw as a boy:

> Behind
> My father's cannery works I used to see
> Rail-squatters ranged in nomad raillery,
> The ancient men—wifeless or runaway
> Hobo—trekkers that forever search
> An empire wilderness of freight and rails.
> Each seemed a child, like me, on a loose perch,
> Holding to childhood like some termless play.

By contrast, Kinnell gives us the panhandlers and winos along Houston, who gob into their handkerchiefs and wipe your windshields as you wait cursing under your breath for the light to turn. The only thing that's changed since Crane's time is the language the bums use:

> You stood once on Houston, among panhandlers and winos
> Who weave the eastern ranges, learning to be free,
> To not care, to be knocked flat and to get up clear-headed
> Spitting the curses out. "Now be nice,"
> The proprietor threatens; "Be nice," he cajoles.
> "Fuck you," the bum shouts as he is hoisted again,
> "God fuck your mother."

From 1956 to '57 Kinnell taught American literature at the University of Grenoble, France, including *Leaves of Grass*. It was the year Ginsberg published *Howl*, the poem Kinnell says announced "Whitman's return to American poetry after an absence of a century." Any American writer who has worked abroad and been forced to speak in another tongue will understand the impact Whitman's fresh and concrete language must have had on Kinnell as he taught it to a French audience.

What does Whitman mean for Kinnell? Nothing so large as transcendentalism or philosophy, but rather music: a particular man's voice alive on the page long after the man himself is gone. Like James Wright and Philip Levine, Kinnell speaks "of a life far within. In this double character, of intimacy and commonplace, [Whitman's poetry] resembles prayer" (see Kinnell's 1971 essay, "Whitman's Indicative Words"). In fact, the curve of "Avenue" moves from street sounds to an attempt at transcendence.

It is night and it is raining. It is a night whose correlative is the East River rushing toward the North Atlantic. The poet looks down the avenue where he sees a lone wildcat cab trying to make time crosstown on Seventh. And then he notices the traffic lights:

> You knew even the traffic lights were made by God,
> The red splashes growing dimmer the farther away
> You looked, and away up at 14th, a few green stars;
> And without sequence, and nearly all at once,
> The red lights blinked into green,
> And just before there was one complete Avenue of green,
> The little green stars in the distance blinked.

If there is a light in that darkness, Kinnell tells us, it is merely the "feverish light / Skin is said to give off when the swimmer drowns at night."

"The Avenue Bearing the Initial of Christ into the New World" reads like a prelude to Kinnell's *Book of Nightmares*, for both are filled with Bosch-like images of death, like the twelve goat heads for sale in the market in Damascus, lips pulled back as if laughing. Or the mass-produced impersonal letter from the Nazi camp commandant addressed to the relatives of the deceased: "Your husband, _____, died in the Camp Hospital on _____. May I express my sincere sympathy on your bereavement." And, finally, the would-be suicide caught in the searchlights of the fire engines, prepared to jump from the top-floor window, and—in an image recalling the crucifixion—"nailed in place by the shine."

The more one reads this poem, the more one feels a sense of strangulation. It is everywhere, from the image of the old man wading toward his last hour, to the sun shining down on the New York ghetto like some jellyfish, to the pigeons who fan out from a rooftop. We live in a world cut off from the light, Kinnell suggests, and know the light only obliquely and in isolated moments. And yet, toward the end of the poem, Kinnell hears the solace of bells,

> The bells of Saint Brigid's
> On Tompkins Square
> Toll for someone who has died.

Lines followed by three more from Villon's "Legacy"—

> J'ois la cloche de Sorbonne,
> Qui toujours à neuf heures sonne
> Le Salut que l'Ange prédit,

which Kinnell himself has translated as

> I heard the bell of the Sorbonne
> Which always tolls at nine o'clock
> The salutation the Angel foretold.

What Villon says he did in "The Legacy" at precisely this juncture is what Kinnell also attempts to do: "So I stopped and wrote no further / In order to pray as the heart bid." It is one of the darkest moments in the poem, and the suicide surely recalls the figure of the suicide at the beginning of *The Bridge*, tilting from the edge of the Brooklyn Bridge before dropping into the river below.

Kinnell too waits, lying awake in his bed, "expecting the vision," and hearing the "dead spirituals" of blacks singing outside his window as the songs become prayers. But there is no response, except for the sound of garbage cans in the early morning hours being emptied into garbage trucks.

In the harbor at the head of the river that is East there is a woman. She has stood there for a century beckoning the teeming millions from around the world. "Give me your poor," she says. But the promise of the New World is more problematic now than it was then, the avenue

> A roadway of refuse from the teeming shores and ghettos
> And the Caribbean Paradise, into the new ghetto and new paradise,
> This God-forsaken Avenue bearing the initial of Christ
> Through the haste and carelessness of the ages,
> The sea standing in heaps, which keeps on collapsing,
> Where the drowned suffer a C-change,
> And remain the common poor.

"God-forsaken." The word occurs in the fourteenth station of the poem, parallel with the burial of Christ. "Behind the Power Station on 14th, the held breath / Of light, as God is a held breath, withheld." Thus the poet, before a silent God, while the river of history flows on, and the masses dissolve and die like fish, "pale / Bloated socks of riverwater and rotted seed, / That swirl on the tide . . . and on the ebb / Stream seaward, seeding the sea."

But there is another side to all this: the light that flares all the brighter for the darkness. What is the nature of the delight we feel in Rembrandt's painting depicting a side of beef, or those French *natures mortes* of dead fish and poultry? Kinnell suggests two answers: the answer Rilke gives in the ninth Duino elegy, and which Kinnell describes as "the resurrection of the world within us":

> Sind wir vielleicht *hier*, um zu sagen: Haus,
> Bruke, Brunnen, Tor, Krug, Obitbaum, Fenster,—
> hochstens: Saule, Turin aber zu *sagen*, verstebs,
> oh zu sagen *so*, wie selber die Dinge niemals
> innig meinten zu sein.
>
> [Perhaps we are *here* in order to say: house,
> bridge, fountain, gate, pitcher, fruit-tree, window—

at most: column, tower. . . .
But to *say* them, you must understand,
oh to say them more intensely than the Things themselves
ever dreamed of existing. (Stephen Mitchell's translation)]

The other is Whitman's answer: the ability of words to restore what they describe, something possible because poetry is not only a Virgilian elegy for what has been, but a way in which words "rescue things and creatures from time and death." Even "unspeakable" things can be redeemed if they can be accurately named. Which is why Kinnell can delight us even with the detritus of the world—dead fish, burnt mattresses, the stores along Avenue C, the derelicts—and why we return to them to celebrate what otherwise would have long emptied into oblivion. Consider the splendid and distinctive catalog of fish that Kinnell gives us at the eleventh station, so that we see them as if for the first time:

Porgies with receding jaws hinged apart
In a grimace of dejection, as if like cows
They had died under the sledgehammer, perches
In grass—green armor, spotted squeteagues
In the melting ice meek-faced and croaking no more,
Mud-eating mullets buried in crushed ice,
Tilefishes with scales like bits of chickenfat.

Just prior to this scene Kinnell had evoked the fire in Gold's junkhouse that had destroyed the detritus of a thousand lives in its own destruction. The alchemist's fire, in which baser materials are refined into gold. We know what made up that fire: love, human passion, the "bedbugged mattresses, springs / The stubbornness has been loved out of . . . / Carriages a single woman's work has brought to wreck." A world alive and shimmering in the words of the poem that revives them for an instant again. Like life itself, the poem is rife with tensions and cross-purposes. But what joy Kinnell finds in the words, even as he questions the efficacy of those words, spilled out from lungs that

    put out the light of the world as they
    Heave and collapse [while] the brain turns and rattles
    In its own black axlegrease.

In spite of our "nighttime / Of the blood," in spite of the murderous darkness, the words seem to laugh on. It is what saves them. And us.

1987

Lowell on Berryman on Lowell

❧

FIVE A.M. MAY 11, 1964. Another night of insomnia for John Berryman, still reeling from Lowell's maddening review of his *77 Dream Songs* in the *New York Review of Books*. But now, having ingested that bitter aspic, he sits down at a table in his Washington, D.C., apartment to compose himself by composing another Dream Song. He feels angry, betrayed. He has waited twenty years to hear what Lowell will say in print about him, and surely he expects something closer to the praise he—like Randall Jarrell—had lavished years earlier on Lowell. Well, Berryman has his answer now, misprintings and misreadings there on the page in black and white before him.[1]

Has he not just returned from five weeks of convalescence at Abbott Hospital in Minneapolis, still exhausted, his body toxic with alcohol, the result—he has tried to convince himself—of working so hard on his *Dream Songs*? It is while recovering in the hospital that the first copies of *77 Dream Songs* have reached him, along with a few welcome but scattered letters from poets amid an otherwise thundering silence. Then he hears from his publisher that Lowell is reviewing the book, though why, Berryman ponders ingenuously, someone of Lowell's stature should take on the chore of reviewing *his* book is beyond him. Remembering how Jarrell, Lowell's old friend as far back as Kenyon College, had run a rapier through his—Berryman's—first book of poems sixteen years before, he grows afraid, then anxious, indifferent, huffy, imperious.

When he receives an advance copy of Lowell's review, Berryman's heart sinks. After briefly surveying Berryman's strange career as a poet, Lowell concludes that 77 *Dream Songs* has turned out to be "larger and sloppier" than any of his previous work. "At first," Lowell admits, "the brain aches and freezes at so much darkness, disorder, and oddness." And though "the repeated situations" (the book's plot) and their "racy jabber" (the book's multileveled styles) have with rereading "become more and more enjoyable," even now he doesn't think he can "paraphrase accurately" even half of what he's read.

Still, Lowell *does* manage to praise certain passages, singling out—not surprisingly—Dream Song 29 as "one of the best and most unified" in the book. And yet, he has had to put the book down as "hazardous" and "imperfect," its "main faults" being its mannerisms and, "worse—disintegration." For a long time now he has felt that disintegration is the chief mark of Berryman's life, but now he feels he must apply the term to include Berryman's poems as well. How often, he complains, "one chafes at the relentless indulgence, and cannot tell the what or why of a passage." So here it is again: the same old bugbear of anacolutha—radical disjuncture of syntax and narrative—that Lowell had been warning Berryman against since the late 1940s. Compared to his own work in *Life Studies*, for instance, there never has been enough logical sequencing in Berryman's lyrics, and now he watches—appalled—as the individual Songs disintegrate again and again "into three or four separate parts."

In noting the lack of sequence in *The Dream Songs*, Lowell means to draw attention to the difficulty he as a reader has had in following almost any of the poems from start to finish. His own work is far more Flaubertian, far more linear and unified, both in terms of plot and consistency of metaphor, each part careful to connect with every other part. *His* poems at least form parts of a larger thematic unity.

Reading the review there in his hospital room, Berryman takes Lowell's strictures to mean that the book is merely a jumble. Sick though he is, he spends the better part of the next twenty-four hours reviewing the complex ways in which the Songs advance upon each other, opening up theme by theme from one song to the next. At last, exhausted, he reassures himself that the various orders he has worked so assiduously to create are really there. So the problem, then, lies with Lowell and not with himself. Still, there it is: Lowell's first public—and largely negative—assessment of Berryman in print. And *this* by an old friend. Could Jarrell himself have done worse, Berryman wonders. No doubt about it: Lowell, the man Berryman thinks of—now that Frost and Williams are gone—as America's chief poet. The public arbiter of poetic taste, intent—it seems—on keeping Berryman out of the spotlight he believes he has a right to share now with Lowell. Have not others, especially in England, already named Berryman as Lowell's chief competitor for the number-one place among American poets? Hasn't the British critic Tony Alvarez already implied as much by allowing only these two Americans into the first edition of his anthology of British poetry, called, simply, *The New Poetry*?[2]

So now, on this May morning in the nation's capital, Berryman sits down to compose what will eventually become Dream Song 177. (One up on the 77.) Talk about indirection! In this poem, Lowell figures as Addison. Why Addison? Perhaps because Addison had been for the early eighteenth century what Lowell surely is on his way to becoming for the 1960s: the apotheosis of the public poet. Perhaps too because Steele is remembered as the drunken buffoon in the Addison-Steele equation. Perhaps, considering the way Berryman's mind seems to work, Addison also suggests both the offspring of a poisonous snake— adder's son—as well as Yeats's famous incubus, Robert Artisson, who appears in that apocalyptic sequence, "Nineteen Hundred and Nineteen." Perhaps for all these reasons.

"Am tame now," Berryman begins, composing himself on the page:

> You may touch me, who had thrilled
> (before) your tips, twitcht from your breast your heart,
> & burnt your willing brain.
> I am tame now. Undead, I was not killed
> by Henry's viewers but maimed. It is my art
> to buzz the spotlight in vain,

fighting "at random" while Addison wins.
I would not war with Addison. I love him
and Addison so loves me back
me backsides, I may perish in his grins
& grip. I would he liked me less, less grim.
But he has helpt me, slack

& sick & hopeful, anew to know what man—
scrubbing the multiverse with dazzled thought—
still has in store for man:
a doghouse or a cave, is all we could,
according to my dreams. I stand in doubt,
surrounded by holy wood. (DS, 177)

No one—including Lowell himself—seems to have suspected that
this song, buried among hundreds of others, was aimed at Lowell. After all, as Berryman warned his readers in the very first of his Songs,
Henry had long been a master at hiding the day. Still, there it is: Berryman's anguished, comic, and veiled perception of Lowell's betrayal,
leaving Henry in doubt as to the worth of his long poem. No, Henry
has not been killed by the reviewer anymore than Keats had been by
his. But he has been maimed, accused of "fighting" (i.e., fitting, composing) his Songs "at random." And *this* by the very man who would
benefit most from keeping his friend under, in a "doghouse or a cave."

Those "dreams" in the penultimate line are of course Berryman's
Dream Songs. And the reference in the last line to "holy wood" evokes
not only the legend of the one priest who may sing at any time in the
Sacred Wood (an image Eliot had evoked forty-five years before in his
first volume of essays), but suggests too that Lowell (the man Berryman used to quip had such Hollywood good looks) still wants to hog
the spotlight, while poor Henry, true priest of the imagination, must
stay lost in the woods.

As for Lowell, he really does seem to have been puzzled and upset by the *Dream Songs*. Ironically, the same day Berryman composed
his attack on Lowell, Lowell was writing Jarrell that he'd just finished

a review of Berryman that he—Lowell—was sure Jarrell would find positive. "I've always felt he threw all he had into writing," Lowell defended himself, "and more and more as time went on," so that writing the review Lowell found himself throwing in "all my larger, more enthusiastic impressions." True, the *Dream Songs* didn't quite come up to the Bradstreet poem, and Berryman would probably read the review and feel Lowell had "hemmed him in with barbs."[3]

Three weeks later, however, reading Adrienne Rich's very positive assessment of *77 Dream Songs* in *The Nation*, Lowell wrote her to say that he'd been harsher on Berryman than she'd been because the poems had affected him so much. Such "smash and vehemence," such "unleashed power," had been too much for Lowell. Besides, there was something in Berryman's character so close to his own that for Lowell to look on Berryman "even in the imagination" was to feel as if he were drowning. Encountering him was rather like a blast of "oxygen coming into one's lungs and then failing."[4]

Months later Lowell was still trying to analyze the weird effect Berryman's Songs were having on him. Writing to William Meredith in October, he summed up what he had tried to accomplish in his review. Perhaps, he said, it had "some value as a record of a man's struggle"—he meant his own—"with the text, a climbing of barriers." He could see now more clearly that with *The Dream Songs* Berryman had actually remade himself into "a new poet, one whose humor and wildness make other new poets seem tame." But he was still reading him "with uncertainty and distress and quite likely envy," though to read with envy was itself a "tribute." And yet, if he still read Berryman "only here and there . . . with the all-out enjoying amazement" he reserved for Bishop, Plath, Larkin, and Roethke, there was still that handful of Songs to contend with that *no* one else had equaled.[5]

By the time Lowell wrote his review, he and Berryman had known each other for nearly twenty years. In the summer of 1946 the two had spent two heady weeks together—they and their first wives, Lowell's Jean Stafford and Berryman's Eileen—at the Lowells' summer place in Damariscotta Mills, Maine, thirty miles north of Bath. There, in a spacious, newly redecorated early-nineteenth-century clapboard farmhouse, the men wrote and discussed Browning and Spenser and Leontes's choppy, disjunctive syntax in *The Winter's Tale*. It had been a high point for Lowell, and those two weeks would remain for him— even after Berryman's death—a pastoral philosophers' circle where he and his Scholar Gypsy had talked poetry until time itself had seemed to stop.[6]

That September, Lowell—separated now from Stafford and living in a run-down apartment in lower Manhattan—went with Randall Jarrell down to Princeton to visit with the Berrymans again. Alas, it proved to be an ill-fated visit, for Jarrell, suffering from a spoiled canapé, lay on the Berrymans' couch, making up cruel parodies of Lowell's poems and—for added spice—contradicting almost everything Berryman had to say.

A year and a half later, when Berryman came down to Washington at Lowell's invitation to record his poems for the Library of Congress, the two went to visit Ezra Pound at St. Elizabeth's Hospital. Berryman kept good notes of this visit, but he did not see fit to record one incident, which Lowell, however, with some sangfroid, did describe in a letter to Peter Taylor. At some point during the visit, Berryman had wondered out loud if piety, taken to an extreme, might not itself become a vice. "That," Pound roared, "sounds like a survival from the time when you believed in saying things that were clever."[7]

In 1954, by which time Berryman was separated from Eileen and in desperate need of a job, Lowell made room for him at the University of Iowa by transferring to the University of Cincinnati for a term as Elliston Professor of Poetry—a position Berryman had held the year before. When one or the other was down, as often they were because of alcohol or depression, they wrote or phoned to offer each other a shoulder. Yet somehow, for nearly ten years—from late 1953 until the spring of 1962—the two did not see each other, though Lowell kept hoping he and Berryman might find a way to replicate their Maine talks.

During those years, of course, both poets continued to develop. Lowell had gone from the Catholic visionary phase of *Lord Weary's*

Castle—a phase that had won him a Pulitzer at the age of twenty-nine—through the clotted period of *The Mills of the Kavanaughs*, and on to the ground-breaking *Life Studies*. Berryman's development, though less spectacular, was every bit as significant. After publishing his first full-length book of poems, *The Dispossessed*, to faint and scattered praise in 1948, Berryman turned briefly to prose with a critical biography of Stephen Crane and half a dozen brilliant essays on Shakespeare. In 1953 he wrote his powerful and gnarled *Homage to Mistress Bradstreet*. And then—for five years—he published almost nothing. In 1958 he assembled a thin small-press pamphlet of new poems called *His Thought Made Pockets & the Plane Buckt*, containing all the verse he thought worth publishing since *The Dispossessed*. But by then he had found *The Dream Songs*.

He was also teaching full-time, writing new essays and introductions, and putting together a literature anthology for undergraduates. In the summer of 1955 he began writing the *Songs*, but only after spending most of the previous year analyzing on paper the complex levels of nearly two hundred of his dreams. (He had uncovered seventeen distinct levels, he crowed, for one of his dreams alone.) Four years later he began publishing the *Songs*, beginning with several in a single spread in the London *Times Literary Supplement*. Soon others began appearing in the American quarterlies and magazines. Some of these Lowell saw in print, others in manuscript. Others Berryman read to him over the phone at four in the morning.

One of those calls came late on the night of September 18, 1959. Suicidal with insomnia and living a seedy bachelor's existence in a run-down apartment in the notorious Seven Corners section of Minneapolis, Berryman phoned Lowell at his brownstone on Boston's "hardly passionate Marlboro Street." As it turned out, when Berryman called, Lowell had just been released from the hospital after suffering his own breakdown.

He too had just been through hell, Lowell wrote Berryman the day after Berryman's call, but he'd managed to make it back. In time things would even lighten up again, he consoled Berryman. The "dark moment comes," he explained. "It comes and goes." He congratulated

Berryman on his new Songs, this time getting even Henry's name wrong. "The new poem about Harry in its sixty parts must be a deluge of power," he wrote. "It will be exciting to see the parts you are about to publish. . . . You must believe that it will reach its finished form."[8] Yet, though he sounded positive in his letter, Lowell still had serious reservations about Berryman's opaque and difficult style. Some of these reservations he had already mentioned to Berryman over the years.

Back in the fall of 1947, for example, after the two men had spent what Lowell thirty years later would remember as "a very companionable weekend" together in Washington, they had exchanged poems. But while Berryman was enthusiastic about Lowell's work (the poems that would eventually appear in *The Mills of the Kavanaughs*), Lowell was uncertain about the poems that were about to appear in *The Dispossessed*. "I guess I must get used to reading my friends' poems, and not having them read mine," Lowell would remember Berryman writing him at this time. The tone of Berryman's letter, Lowell would recall four years after Berryman's death, still uneasy with the memory, had been "too lighthearted to be a whiplash." And yet Lowell had "felt rebuked particularly as I had done my best." In truth, Berryman's "jumpy style (later to soar)" had made him "stumble, and reveal my reserve." Lowell wrote these words in the summer of 1976, shortly before his own death, and they seem to express his mature opinion of Berryman's earlier work. Thinking back to their beginning as poets— his and Jarrell's and Berryman's beginnings—he felt that Berryman had been, "compared to other poets," "a prodigy." But compared with Jarrell (and by extension himself), he'd been "a slow starter."[9]

When *The Dispossessed* appeared in the spring of 1948, Berryman sent Lowell a copy, then waited for his response. When, after four months, he had not heard so much as a whisper, he wrote Lowell, asking if he'd ever received the book. Sheepishly, Lowell wrote back. It could not have helped oil Berryman's ragged nerves that Lowell should now misremember even the book's title. "Many apologies for not thanking you for *The Possessed*," he wrote, before praising what little in the book he could. "The new difficult poems" were what?

"The most wonderful advance anyone has made." He was simply at this point repeating what Jarrell had already written in his guarded review of Berryman for *The Nation*.

Lowell also had to agree with Jarrell's assessment that the poems existed rather as "bits and passages—so many breaks, anacolutha etc. that the whole poem usually escapes me." No doubt Berryman had the ability and the "equipment to do almost anything." But the clear implication remained that he hadn't yet done so, though—Lowell added—all that was needed was for Berryman to "dock" himself "in some overwhelming and unifying object." In short, all Berryman needed was a large-enough subject into which he could pour his energies.[10]

And yet a decade later Lowell was still wondering when his friend was ever going to find his subject. Going through Berryman's new poems in *His Thought Made Pockets* in the spring of 1959, Lowell asked Berryman if he really did need "so much twisting, obscurity, archaisms, strange word orders," ampersands, and the rest of it. Well, perhaps he did. At least, he added, "here as in the Bradstreet," Berryman had found, if not a subject, then at least a style and a voice, one that "vibrates and makes the heart ache."[11]

In April 1962 Lowell visited his—and Berryman's—old mentor, Allen Tate, in Minneapolis, where he gave a reading at the Walker Art Center and managed to spend a few days with Berryman. It was the first time Berryman and Lowell had seen each other since December 1953, and they had much to talk about. By then Berryman (forty-seven) was married for a third time, this time to Kate, a "girl of twenty-one" whom Lowell described as possessed of a parochial Catholic background, "innocent beyond belief," and pregnant. The Berrymans were at the moment living in a dull, two-room cinder-block apartment on Erie Place (Berryman had taken to spelling it Eerie), very near the university, where Berryman had been teaching for the past seven years. Lowell would remember Kate asleep in one room, "getting through the first child pains," while he and Berryman talked among Berryman's thousand books in the other.

Berryman, he told Elizabeth Bishop afterward, was now in "the 7th year" of a "long poem that fills a suitcase," the pieces of which had refused to yield themselves to his scrutiny. Confused by his "Berryisms" and twisted baby talk, Lowell thought *The Dream Songs* were written in the voice of Berryman's five-year-old son, Paul, from his second marriage. The effect was a "spooky . . . maddening tortured work of genius, or half genius, in John's later obscure, tortured, wandering style, full of parentheses, slang no one ever spoke, jagged, haunting lyrical moments etc." One shuddered, Lowell added, "to think of the child's birth."[12]

But it was also Lowell who had suggested to Berryman as early as 1959 that he publish a group of seventy-five or so of the *Songs* as a sort of dry run. That, he explained, would whet the appetite of Berryman's audience until he was ready to publish the *Songs* as a single book. But it was to take Berryman five more agonizing years, with much Hamletizing and interminable revising, before he could allow himself to publish even those seventy-five, expanded to seventy-seven. And it was the publication of the first selection, ironically, that was followed by Lowell's rejection of the ugly child he had asked Berryman to deliver.

So deep was Berryman's hurt when he read Lowell's review, in fact, that he nearly begged off from accepting the Russell Loines Award from Lowell at the American Academy of Arts in New York three weeks later. But accept the award he did, grasping Lowell's too-huge hand in both of his, before retiring back to Washington, unable to do much of anything for several weeks after except hide in his cave, drinking and commiserating with himself.

In February 1966 Lowell and Berryman met again, this time at Yale at a memorial service for Jarrell, who, four months earlier, had walked into the side of a moving car. Those present at the memorial included Jarrell's widow, Mary, Peter Taylor, Adrienne Rich, Richard Wilbur, Stanley Kunitz, Richard Eberhart, John Hollander, William Meredith, and Robert Penn Warren. Berryman, the great elegist for his generation, responded brilliantly to Jarrell's loss with several new Songs, eulogies as much as elegies, for the man he had both feared and admired for the past twenty years. In a drunken, inspired voice he read several of the new poems to the astonishment of those present. Yet, inspired though his reading was, Berryman was clearly in terrible shape, so much so that Rich and Lowell both wrote him afterward, pleading with him to take better care of himself.

"This is really just to say that I love you," Lowell wrote Berryman two weeks later. "And wonder at you, and want you to take care. Your reminiscences of Randall were the height of the evening, and seemed for a moment to lift away all the glaze and constraints that dog us, and yet it was all in order." Then he added, without equivocation, that he, like so many others, was pleased by what Berryman was doing in the new (post-*77*) *Dream Songs*. In fact he had shown Lowell—and all poets, really—brand new resources for poetry if only "we had the nerve."[13] And six months later, having read Berryman's *Opus Posthumous* sequence—book IV of *The Dream Songs*—he wired him at once in Dublin that the new poems constituted nothing less than "a tremendous and living triumph." A month later he wrote Berryman again to say that the sequence, which included a song in which Henry meets Jarrell in hell, was in fact "the crown of your wonderful work, witty, heart-breaking, all of a piece." "Somehow," he added, "one believes you on this huge matter of looking at death."[14]

At the same time that he was congratulating Berryman, however, Lowell was writing Philip Booth to say that Berryman's new poems were the product of a man living on the thin edge between life and death. They were, in fact, Berryman's "own elegy and written from the dirt of the grave." It was clear that Berryman was "very sick, spiritually and physically," and that his poems revealed "personal anguish everywhere." But then he and Lowell were poets and "couldn't dodge the fact." And poets by nature were "uniquely marked and fretted and must somehow keep even-tempered, amused, and in control. John B. in his mad way keeps talking about something evil stalking us poets. That's a bad way to talk, but there's truth in it."[15]

Still, Lowell's enthusiasm for the *Opus Posthumous* sequence remained bright. Writing to Bishop months later, he was still speaking of these "marvelous" poems as somehow having been written "ex humo, from beyond the tomb." By then he could add, with a sigh of audible relief, that Henry's imaginative descent into hell, with its comically grotesque return Lazarus-like to life—surrounded by the inevitable television reporters and tax collectors—had in fact "resurrected" Berryman once again.[16]

That was in February 1967, by which time Berryman had returned to his drinking with a suicidal vengeance. In May the wildly drunk, Irish-bearded poet flew to New York to receive an award from the Academy of American Poets. Immediately after the ceremonies, he was admitted to the French Hospital on Manhattan's West Side, suffering from alcoholic toxicity. It was there Lowell and Meredith visited him. What "a chaos and a ruin and a trial" Berryman seemed, Lowell wrote Meredith afterward. And yet underneath it all the man was "in much better shape than anyone dreamed, so that after three days in the hospital, all the shouting and eccentricity had gone."

He'd seen Berryman like this in Minneapolis in 1962, when Berryman had staggered through the halls of the university to teach before collapsing and taking a cab back to Abbott Hospital. Now, again, Berryman had found the strength to resurrect himself, rather like some bright, disheveled phoenix. "He's quite an actor," Lowell continued. "As soon as he has an unfamiliar audience he becomes three times as odd, then alone with him or with two or three friends, he becomes delightful."[17]

A month later Lowell was in Castine, Maine, furiously writing the blank-verse sonnets that would make up *Notebook 1967–68*, followed by *Notebook*, followed in turn by *History* and *For Lizzie and Harriet*, each book rising from the dismembered remains of the earlier. Like *The Dream Songs*, the notebooks are extended, open-ended sequences whose distant precursors are the Elizabethan sonnet sequence, but—as with Berryman's *Dream Songs*—modified and made contemporary. Like Pound's *Cantos* and Williams's *Paterson*, each has a fluid protagonist and incorporates both autobiography and the history of the tribe from its beginnings to the present. Obviously, the reservations Lowell had felt on reading the early Songs had by then disappeared, and

he read Berryman's lengthy sequel—*His Toy, His Dream, His Rest*—
on its publication in September 1968 with unmixed astonishment and
admiration. Afterward he wrote Berryman to compare his own just-
finished *Notebook 1967–68* with Berryman's epic, noting especially how
Berryman had incorporated so many different elements into the poems: history, "learning, thought, personality."[18]

But even after publication, both Berryman and Lowell continued
to work on the long poems each had thought he'd finished, writing
each other in undisguised triumph and glee about their respective obsessions. Berryman considered adding his new Songs to the published
volume as an appendix, while Lowell added new sonnets by the hundreds, even as he revised his old ones. In 1969 he published a new and
much-expanded edition called, simply, *Notebook*, and then revised his
revisions—often massively—over the next four years. When he wrote
Berryman in September 1969 to congratulate him on *The Dream Songs*
at last appearing under one cover, it was to emphasize their kinship:
"I think anyone who cared for your book would for mine. Anyway,
we're accomplished beyond jealousy. Without your book," he wrote,
then enlarged what he meant by changing that to read, "without *you*,
I would find writing more puzzling."[19]

The two men saw each other for the last time in December 1970. By
then Lowell was separated from Elizabeth Hardwick and living with
Caroline Blackwood in London. He had just returned to New York to
see Hardwick and their daughter, Harriet, for the first time in nine
months. For his part, Berryman had just completed a drunken reading tour of the Northeast, and the two men met at the Chelsea Hotel,
where Berryman was in the habit of staying when he was in New York.
Between them, Lowell could not help feeling, lay the shadow of that
other roaring boy, Dylan Thomas, who seventeen years before, in one
of the rooms of the Chelsea, had lapsed into the coma from which he
had never regained consciousness.

Now the two men sat over lunch, drinking in an empty cafeteria-
bar near the hotel. By then, Lowell would later recall, both were feeling
"high without assurance." Shortly before Lowell got up to go, he asked

Berryman when he would see him again. He'd meant in the next few days, before he flew back to England. "Cal," he told him, "I was thinking through lunch that I'll never see you again." "I wondered how in the murk of our conversation I had hurt him," Lowell would write, "but he explained that his doctor had told him one more drunken binge would kill him."[20]

Two days after Christmas, Lowell wrote Berryman for what turned out to be the last time. He had just read Berryman's post–*Dream Songs* volume, *Love & Fame,* and was stunned by the beauty and power of the "Eleven Addresses to the Lord." Thinking back to his own early, Catholic poems, Lowell could sense the "cunning" of Berryman's sequence, how it embodied the Corbière-like skeptic's point of view, while still sounding "like a Catholic prayer to a personal God." "It's one of the great poems of the age," he saw now, "a puzzle and triumph to anyone who wants to write a personal devotional poem." If the first three sections of the book did seem "a little casual and shaggy," what a closure he had provided. Then he added: "You write close to death—I mean in your imagination. Don't take it from your heart into life. Don't say we won't meet again."[21]

A year later Berryman jumped from the Washington Avenue Bridge in Minneapolis to his death. By then Lowell was living in an eighteenth-century country house in England, with a new wife and a new son. There's a story—apocryphal, as it turns out—that Berryman left a suicide note for Lowell. It is supposed to have read, simply, "Your move, Cal." No one seems to know for sure how that story got started, though the finger is often pointed at Auden. The truth is that Lowell was deeply affected by the news of his friend's death, even more than he let on.

A month after Berryman's death, Lowell wrote Frank Bidart that Marianne Moore had just died at the age of eighty-five. And yet, he noted, her death had made "little stir, unlike Berryman's—on whom each English week[ly] or arts page has a bad elegy." Berryman had been doomed, he saw now, at least since the time they'd taken that last meal together in New York. "Then it was drink, later he must have died from not drinking." Moore of course had been the more "inspired of the two" poets, he believed, but Berryman had done what few poets ever achieved by taking such enormous risks with himself. After so many years of agonizing apprenticeship, he added, Berryman had leapt "into himself in his last years bravely."[22]

In his memoir of Berryman, printed in the *New York Review of Books*—the same publication that had carried his assessment of the early *Dream Songs*—Lowell corrected what he'd said eight years before. He knew that his own late style, with its unexpected turns, its fits and starts and anacolutha, owed too much to Berryman to let his early assessment stand, for by 1970 Berryman had forever altered the poetic landscape. A style takes a lifetime to develop, and now that Berryman's arc was complete, Lowell could see where even the earlier jumps and fits had been tending, even if at times they seemed jammed and crowded to the point of confusion.

"Rattled by their mannerisms," Lowell admitted now, he had misjudged Berryman's first seventy-seven *Dream Songs*. Later the Songs had become clearer and clearer until, finally, "they had seemed as direct as a prose journal, as readable as poetry can be." And yet, and yet. In the long run those first seventy-seven probably revealed the "clearest" Berryman, "almost John's whole truth." Once Lowell had taken Berryman's style "for forcing." But, he conceded, "no voice . . . or persona sticks in my ear as his. It is poignant, abrasive, anguished, humorous. A voice on the page, identified as my friend's on the telephone, though lost now to mimicry. We should hear him read aloud. It is we who are labored and private, when he is smiling."[23]

In the last year of his own life, Lowell came across Berryman's real suicide note, printed at last in *Henry's Fate*. The note, Lowell could see, had also turned out to be Berryman's last Dream Song. Weirdly, it was also Berryman's last comic leap, even now mocking itself with its final "catlike flight / from home and classes— / to leap from the bridge." And yet, in spite of the crushing impact of that death, Lowell could still take comfort from his friend's spirit, catching himself praying "*to* not *for*" his friend, thinking of Berryman and smiling as he drifted off to sleep.[24] Smiling. It was what Lowell had noticed about himself as well in his obituary piece for Berryman. "I somehow smile," he wrote there, "though a bit crookedly, when I think of John's whole life, and even of the icy leap from the bridge to the hard ground. He was springy to the end, and on his feet."[25]

In the weeks following Berryman's death, Lowell was invited to come up to London for a BBC program remembering his friend. The focus of the evening was the BBC interview between a very drunken Berryman and the critic, Tony Alvarez. It had been shot five years earlier in Dublin, when the Berrymans were living in Ballsbridge, filmed half in Berryman's rented house and half in the local pub, which had served as Berryman's study. "John, close-up, just off drunkenness," Lowell wrote Hardwick that March, misreading Berryman's drunken brilliance for a kind of manic sobriety. There was Berryman, larger than life, in dramatic white and black, mad beard wagging. Like Henry, Berryman was "mannered, booming, like an old-fashioned star professor. His worst." And then once again he was thinking back to those impossibly innocent days along the Damariscotta River in high summer, when he and Berryman had discoursed happily on the stark, crabbed syntax of *The Winter's Tale*, when Berryman was still Lowell's own Scholar Gypsy, a brilliant presence amid the whispering trees and lakes. "I think of the young, beardless man," he wrote now, "simple, brilliant, the enthusiast . . . buried somewhere with the older."[26]

1992

NOTES

1. Berryman frequently dates his poetry manuscripts down to the hour. The original manuscript for Dream Song 177 is one of those so dated, as if Berryman had left a clue as to the poem's personal significance (JB Papers, Special Collections, University of Minnesota). As for the unfortunate misprints in Lowell's review, including turning Dream Song 29 into prose, the *New York Review of Books* printed a "correction" in the following issue. Lowell's review, called "The Poetry of John Berryman," appeared in the *New York Review of Books* for 28 May 1964, 2–3. The correction appeared in the issue for 11 June.

See "John Berryman," in Robert Lowell, *Collected Prose*, ed. Robert Giroux (New York: Farrar, Straus and Giroux, 1987), 104–18.

2. Tony Alvarez, *The New Poetry* (London: Penguin Books, 1962). When, three years later, he expanded his anthology, Alvarez included two more American poets: Sylvia Plath and Anne Sexton.

3. Robert Lowell to Randall Jarrell, 11 May 1964, Henry W. and Albert A. Berg Collection, New York Public Library.

4. Lowell to Adrienne Rich, 3 June 1964, in the Schlesinger Library at Radcliffe College. See also Berryman's letter to Rich thanking her "for such insight, sensitivity & generosity that you make me wonder" (qtd. in Mariani, *Dream Song* 408). The review, he noted pointedly, was in fact "the most remarkable American verse-review . . . since Jarrell's study of *Lord Weary's Castle.*" The implication here seems to have been that Lowell had missed the chance to do for Berryman what Jarrell had effected for Lowell nearly twenty years before.

5. Lowell to William Meredith, October 1964, Berg Collection.

6. For a fuller account of the Berrymans' stay with the Lowells at Damariscotta Mills, see Mariani, *Dream Song*, 175–77. For an extended firsthand account of that stay, see chapter 6 of Eileen Simpson's *Poets in Their Youth: A Memoir* (New York: Random House, 1982), 115–46.

7. Lowell to Peter Taylor, 18 February 1948. Quoted in Ian Hamilton, *Robert Lowell: A Biography* (New York: Random House, 1982), 130.

8. Lowell to John Berryman, 19 September 1959, JB Papers.

9. Lowell to William Meredith, summer 1976, Berg Collection.

10. Lowell to Berryman, fall 1948, JB Papers (see Mariani, *Dream Song*, 212ff.). As for misnaming books, Berryman himself does not escape blame. In the same letter asking Lowell if he'd ever received *The Dispossessed*, he added, "Best to the Kavanaughs of the Mills." Berryman to Lowell, 28 August 1948, Lowell Collection, Houghton Library, Harvard University.

11. Lowell to Berryman, spring 1959, JB Papers.

12. Lowell to Elizabeth Bishop, 14 April 1962, Bishop Collection, Vassar College. Part of this letter is quoted in David Kalstone's *Becoming a Poet: Elizabeth Bishop with Marianne Moore and Robert Lowell* (New York: Farrar, Straus and Giroux, 1989), 223ff. Bishop confessed to Lowell that she too found herself "pretty much at sea about that book—some pages I find wonderful, some

baffle me completely. I am sure he is saying *something* important—perhaps sometimes too personally? I also feel he's next-best to you" (Bishop to Lowell, 1 October 1964, quoted in Kalstone, *Becoming a Poet*, 224).

13. Lowell to Berryman, 10 March 1966, JB Papers.

14. Lowell to Berryman, 5 November 1966, JB Papers.

15. Lowell to Phillip Booth, 10 October 1966, quoted in Hamilton, *Robert Lowell*, 351.

16. Lowell to Bishop, February 1967, Bishop Collection.

17. Lowell to Meredith, June 1967, Berg Collection.

18. Lowell to Berryman, September 1968, JB Papers.

19. Lowell to Berryman, September 1969, JB Papers.

20. Lowell, "John Berryman," 116.

21. Lowell to Berryman, 27 December 1970, JB Papers.

22. Lowell to Frank Bidart, February 1972, Lowell Collection.

23. Lowell, "John Berryman," 115–16.

24. Lowell, "For John Berryman," *Day By Day* (New York: Farrar, Straus and Giroux, 1977), 27–28.

25. Lowell, "John Berryman," 115.

26. Lowell to Elizabeth Hardwick, 19 March 1972, Harry Ransom Research Center, University of Texas at Austin.

Writing Lowell

℘

I FIRST CAME TO LOWELL in the fall of 1963, around the time of John F. Kennedy's assassination. I was twenty-three, just married, and completing my master's degree at Colgate in the flint-backed Chenango Valley of upstate New York. Having completed the Great Books tradition at Manhattan College the spring before, I knew a little something about the past but virtually nothing about the present, and nothing at all about contemporary poetry. One of my instructors, knowing I was a Catholic, and wanting to lessen my invincible ignorance, suggested I look at the early poetry of Lowell, particularly "The Quaker Graveyard in Nantucket," and so I went down to the library to find the poem.

I remember standing in the stacks with a cold rain beating against the windows, and reading those majestic opening lines, thinking they were like something out of Milton and Melville. "A brackish reach of shoal off Madaket," the poem begins, linking the ancient Hebrew Sheol—the place for hell—with the small village on the shifting edge of Nantucket, that pre–Civil War whaling center, which I had visited the summer before with my bride:

> A brackish reach of shoal off Madaket,—
> The sea was still breaking violently and night
> Had steamed into our North Atlantic Fleet,
> When the drowned sailor clutched the drag-net. Light
> Flashed from his matted head and marble feet,
> He grappled at the net

With the coiled, hurdling muscles of his thighs:
The corpse was bloodless, a botch of reds and whites,
Its open, staring eyes
Were lustreless dead-lights
Or cabin-windows on a stranded hulk
Heavy with sand.

We are all children of our moment, and I realize now that I had been shaped by my education to read this sort of poem—allusive, tightly rhymed and metered—playing itself out against Milton's *Lycidas*, against *Moby Dick*, against Hopkins's "The Wreck of the Deutschland," against the orphic utterances of Hart Crane, against the allusiveness of Eliot as well as against the latinity of Allen Tate and John Crowe Ransom, both of whom had been Lowell's teachers. Here, in this young Boston Brahmin turned Catholic—and a conscientious objector to boot—was the most likely (and unlikely) modern offspring of those poetic forces. Something in Lowell's poem sank into me immediately, and has remained there, in spite of all sorts of transformations, since.

I often begin my courses in contemporary American poetry with a reading of "Quaker Graveyard," though I have come to realize that Lowell's poem points backward into high modernism rather than forward into postmodernism. I like what Robert Hass, my contemporary, has said in his essay on the poem in the *Voices and Visions* episode devoted to Lowell on PBS: that somehow Lowell's lines capture the anguish of a young man who saw what World War II had cost those caught up in the war. His myopia might have allowed him to wait the war out on the sidelines as a 4-F, but the fiery young idealist (who had worked for the Catholic publishing house of Sheed & Ward and had insisted that his wife, the novelist Jean Stafford, volunteer to work with Dorothy Day in the Bowery) decided now to inform President Roosevelt that he would not serve, that he would go to jail rather than add to the mayhem he saw in the Allied bombings of German population centers like Hamburg and Dresden.

But besides the poetry, there are more personal reasons for my having chosen to write about Lowell. He is, among other things, my father's exact contemporary, and in writing of Lowell I would be covering the exact arc of my father's first sixty years. Twenty years ago I chose to write about William Carlos Williams, the author of *Paterson*, in part because my mother's family came from the towns around Paterson, some of whom had worked in the depressed silk mills of that city. It made all the difference for me knowing that someone had found such people actually worth writing about.

And so too, with Lowell. My own father was raised on 61st and First, the youngest of eleven children, five of whom did not survive childhood. In the spring of 1944, when my younger brother and my mother and I watched my father from the fifth floor of a tenement on East 51st Street march off in his Army uniform with his duffel bag slung across his shoulder, to serve as an instructor in the care and feeding of Sherman tanks, Lowell was mopping floors in Bridgeport, Connecticut, part of the year-and-a-day sentence he had been given for refusing to serve in the same war for which my father was now leaving us.

I often find myself making these sorts of historical comparisons, the more so since so much of my own early history is oral and half-mythical now, since so few letters or other written records of any sort have survived, whereas Lowell's life, and the lives of those he affected, being the lives of writers, have provided me with a gorgeous if still fragmented array of such records. I find it delicious, for example, that Lowell would actually write Roosevelt that he was declining the president's kind offer to serve in the Armed Forces, and find it even more delicious that such news would be picked up by the newspapers in both Boston and New York. Never for a moment could I imagine my own father writing the president to decline such an invitation, and the truth is that much of his unit died fighting in the Ardennes offensive. All that saved my father, perhaps, was his genius with machines, and the Army needed that talent. Once he was called up he went, in spite of two children and a third on the way, and that was that. Fate itself had thrown the dice, he would have said. In time I became fascinated with finding out all I could about this man who had lived in some of the same places I had and who, moreover, had lived through the same historical events as my father and myself. Even better, Lowell left an incredible written track behind him, not only in his poems but in his letters and essays, even in hundreds of brilliant comments and quips.

When I began my doctoral work at Hunter College in the fall of 1964, Lowell was living less than a mile away in a posh artisan's apartment on West 67th Street, though as for my actually meeting him at the time, he might as well have been living in Tibet. It was the class thing, obviously, that kept me from actually writing about Lowell until I was fifty. I remember going with my wife to the American Place Theater in midtown Manhattan to see a performance of *The Old Glory*, a play based on Melville's *Benito Cereno* and Hawthorne's *My Kinsman, Major Molineaux*. The first part dealt with the overturning of racial hierarchies, as black slaves overpowered their Spanish slave masters at sea and then threatened the American sailors who had boarded the ship to investigate. The second dealt with British rule being undermined in America in the 1770s, even as American involvement in the Viet Nam war was spiraling more and more out of control when I saw the play.

I had gone to the theater, really, with the hope of somehow catching a glimpse of Lowell. I did not see him that night, but I did see him (it would be the only time I ever did) at the Guggenheim on Fifth Avenue, where he had gone to introduce his old friend, Randall Jarrell, who that evening, as it turned out, was there to read from a selection of Elizabeth Bishop's poems. It was late October 1964. I stood in line after the reading to shake hands with the fifty-year-old Jarrell, already fragile, shaky, high-strung, and who would be dead within a year.

Alas, as for Lowell, I never heard him speak, since my Israeli cabdriver did not yet know the intricacies of New York traffic and drove all over midtown New York before depositing me at the Guggenheim, too late to hear Lowell's introduction. Still, there he was, forty-seven years old, unmistakable in his height and dark grandeur, silent, marmoreal, too-tall in his blue suit, introspective, a dark plush flame. I wanted to touch his sleeve, the hem of his jacket, anything. But of course I did not. And then it was out the door and back into the autumn air. I was excited, happy. Next time, I thought, next time I would be ready with questions to engage him. He would speak and I would listen. But in the twelve years Lowell still had left, I never saw him again. Instead, I have had to carry on my discourse with him through his letters and poems and in dreams. Perhaps for the biographer in me it is just as well that I did not come in contact with Lowell again. For—in the absence of firsthand knowledge—I would try instead to create something like a living portrait of the poet, inevitably, I suppose, inserting into the life something of the fictive that the telling of lives seems always to entail.

While still a graduate student at Hunter between 1964 and 1967, I taught open-enrollment students, stenographers, businessmen, and police officers at Lehmann College in the Bronx and John Jay College in Manhattan. The city roiled under the tensions of the Civil Rights movement, the feminist movement, economic unrest, and the escalation of the war in Viet Nam. During the student takeover of offices and buildings at Columbia in the spring of 1968, several of my police-officer students from John Jay College were dispatched there to maintain order. I remember hearing them complain bitterly about their having to stand there while students taunted or spat at them. I remember too a John Jay colleague, a fiery little Marxist and history instructor, with a bloody bandage around his head walking down the school corridor, telling us that he'd been clubbed by several policemen after he'd told one police sergeant to call off his Dobermans. Soon after, I opened the *New York Review of Books* to find these lines of Lowell's (wry, bemused, condescending) describing the restoration of Grayson Kirk, president of Columbia, to his ransacked offices by some of those same police officers, several of whom had been seriously hurt in the attempt to restore order:

> The old king enters his study with the police;
> it's much like mine left in my hands a month:
> unopened letters, the thousand dead cigarettes,
> open books, yogurt cups in the unmade bed. . . .
> The sergeant picks up a defiled *White Goddess*,
> or the old king's offprints on ideograms,
> "Would a human beings do this things to these book?"

I read and re-read Lowell's new work as it appeared, not only *Life Studies* and *For the Union Dead* but *Near the Ocean*, *The Old Glory*, and his controversial translations of Villon, Rilke, Montale, Baudelaire, and Rimbaud in *Imitations*. At the same time I was working in a basement stall at the Queens College Library on a new critical reading of the sonnets of Gerard Manley Hopkins, which would form the heart of my dissertation. Like most people, I did not then know that during these same years I was reading Lowell for sustenance and a sense of continuity with the great tradition (a tradition passed on from Eliot to Lowell, it seemed) Lowell's own shattered life was following closely the breakdown of our society. I did not know then that in the four years I was living and teaching in New York, Lowell suffered four manic episodes that left him, as he himself said, iced-over.

Then, at the end of the decade, as the war dragged on and Nixon took over, Lowell's poetry took another radical shift. Now, instead of the finely crafted free-verse poems that had appeared at spaced intervals, there came a veritable torrent of blank-verse sonnets. I first read these sonnets in the *New York Review of Books*, a magazine he himself had helped underwrite. Actually, it was his wife Elizabeth Hardwick's project more than his, begun to fill a void when the *New York Times* ceased publication because of a labor strike. Later, I read the poems in the collections that began appearing in 1969: *Notebook 1967–1968*, *Notebook*, *History*, *For Lizzie and Harriet*, *The Dolphin*, all but the last ransacked and re-invented from the earlier volumes.

Even today it is not necessary to defend Lowell's achievement in *Life Studies*, the collection that defined the direction in which postmodern poetry was headed. There it was: work far more openly autobiographical than anything yet seen, even as it maintained the modernists' aesthetic distance through irony, restraint, vulnerability, and literary allusion. Still, Flaubert's shadow remained: the precise image weighted with a transferred emotional tenor (Eliot's objective correlative lifted from the literary dustbin and repolished), technical craft, and the leaving of certain things unsaid, which icy good breeding demanded.

These distancing factors had already been dismantled by poets like Roethke, Ginsberg, Plath, and Sexton, and Lowell himself was already beginning to become dissatisfied with the still-life perfections of *Life Studies* by the time the book won the Pulitzer Prize for poetry in 1960. Likewise, much of the public and experimental work Lowell gave us in *For the Union Dead* still holds.

But by 1967, the year he turned fifty, Lowell had become a tireless and obsessive reviser of his own poems, as if he no longer trusted the finished artifact. And yet he could not quite locate just how much of a raw, quasi-journalistic surface he wanted to give his poems. The truth is that behind Lowell's new epic sweep and modern sonnet sequencing lay Berryman's *Dream Songs*, which had been appearing since 1959, and which were finally collected ten years later. Thus Lowell's *Notebooks*. But by 1971, dissatisfied with what he had written, yet unable to stop writing his dispatches from the front or his cameos of history, Lowell began splitting his books into the public and the private, placing the public sonnets into *History* and the private ones in a book dedicated to his estranged wife, Elizabeth Hardwick, and his small daughter, Harriet.

Having exiled himself by that point to England, he began working on a third sequence about his involvement with and marriage to Lady Caroline Blackwood. In July 1973 he published three new books of poetry: *History*, that Roman meditation on the inexorability of man's fate to struggle and to die, and the two domestic sagas: *For Lizzie and Harriet* and *The Dolphin*, dedicated to Blackwood. Fifteen years younger than Lowell, Blackwood, heiress to the Guinness fortune, had already been married to the British painter Lucien Freud and the British composer Israel Citkowitz, by whom she had had three daughters. Now, with Lowell, she gave birth to their son, Sheridan.

So much revision. Not only one or two versions, but sometimes, as when Lowell reworked even his early poems, three versions of the same poem. Had even Auden, living downtown from Lowell in New York, done more revising of his canon? And what did a canon mean in the midst of so much uncertainty and second-guessing? There are nearly four hundred sonnets in *History*, the first half of which move from the dawn of mankind to the year of Lowell's birth, the second half devoted to the half century since.

So many poems on so many subjects to overwhelm the reader the way *The Cantos* or *Paterson* can also overwhelm. And with their repeated emphasis on violence and death and fate, one poem often seems to fade into the next. On the other hand, they do seem the exact analogue of our ten-year engagement with Viet Nam. Discounting the failed *Mills of the Kavanaughs* he wrote twenty years earlier, *History* remains the dragon in the gate to Lowell's achievement, though there is still plenty of real poetry there.

As for *For Lizzie and Harriet* and *The Dolphin*, these two volumes are often more talked about than read now, the first having become notorious because of Lowell's decision to incorporate passages from Hardwick's letters into the text. Critics still get upset about this use of someone else's letters, though William Carlos Williams had already pointed the way by incorporating Marcia Nardi's letters into the fabric of *Paterson*. But Lowell had to get his wife's letters into the text if he was to get her perspective into the poem, or register the complex, fuzzy, tragicomic, and often self-serving reasons for the destruction of one marriage and the start of yet another, though we should note that both books understand that the new marriage like the old was doomed to failure from the start. Both books will serve as Pascalian warnings about the lengths to which an intelligent man can deceive himself. But, having made his choices, Lowell was at great pains—like Dante before him—to record the inevitable harm his decision cost himself—and worse—others. *Divorce*, Williams had already noted in *Paterson: the inevitable sign of our times.* So with Lowell writing a quarter century later, when nearly half of all American marriages were ending in divorce. Whatever else they are, his poems are by turns raw-edged, brilliant, stuttering, and heart-breaking, and read with the same inevitable downfall one finds in the *Oresteia*, which he was also busy then translating. And just as Lowell condemned Johnson there for escalating the war in Viet Nam, he condemned himself for leaving his wife for a dolphin: half woman, half the product of his fevered imagination. Finally there is *Day by Day*, Lowell's last book, which he wrote in a free verse closer to *Life Studies*, but looser, more resonant with the quotidian accidents of life, the grit and blood of the humbling experiences of his final years still stuck to them. It's a book, really, about the inevitable dissolution of his new marriage as the inherent weaknesses and illnesses both he and Blackwood suffered from became clearer: physical pain, his breakdowns in spite of the lithium he was taking, their alcoholism, and the inevitable cross purposes between a man and a woman belonging to different worlds and generations. At the end Lowell was left with the realization that it was he—not his wife—who was unwanted, as he had been unwanted at the start by his own mother. A king fallen from grace, noting at the end with resignation and self-knowledge that life is generous only "to the opportune, / its constantly self-renewing teams of favorites," even as he, like Nixon—that other overreacher—was left standing outside the charmed circle, looking in.

In the years I was writing Lowell's life I never tired of him, and, in truth, he was gentler on my psyche than the brilliant Berryman was. I know Lowell's faults and errors and can cite chapter and verse there. But that is not what made me want to write about him. Rather, having read Ian Hamilton's life of the poet, it was to try and set the record straighter, without standing like some recording angel passing judgment on the man. I owe a debt to Lowell and to the poetry that for a generation sustained so many readers—myself among them—and gave articulation to our troubled time. Lowell had much to say and he said it well, in a variety of styles that range from the one that echoed Milton and Eliot to one closer to Williams, Flaubert, Henry Adams, Berryman, and Bishop. Always, of course, Lowell remained Lowell. Some poetry reviewers today seem as obtuse, self-serving, ideological, niggling, and stubborn about Lowell as they were in Lowell's day. But it was not for them that I wrote this book. It may be that the reasons for Lowell's recent neglect are as much ideological as they are historical and aesthetic. No one book alone can recover a poet of Lowell's stature, but the necessary reassessment has now begun and will continue, and I hope *Lost Puritan* will be read as a marker in that direction. One thing seems certain. We cannot dismiss him without dismissing much of ourselves.

1994

The Hole in the Middle of the Book
Absence and Presence in Biography

A TRUE STORY. It's an afternoon in late August, years ago, and I'm sitting in the Barn up on the Bread Loaf campus of Middlebury with my friend, Bob Pack. He has this deadpan look on his face, a look that means trouble. It's the face he wears when he's about to spring a joke on someone, and—in the absence of anyone else around—I must be that someone. "I got a letter last week," he begins, "and this book company in Boston wants me to write up my life for them."

Silence, then he leans forward conspiratorially. "They're willing to pay a thousand dollars," he says. "And that's where you come in. I want *you* to write it. Then I'll sign my name." I protest that I can't just ghost-write his life like that. There's too much I don't know, especially about his formative years, and the years before I knew him. But he waves away my objections. "Don't worry," he says, "you can make the whole thing up. And the thousand's yours."

He must be joking, but he's just sitting there, looking at me. I begin to explain that to write his autobiography would go against the truth claims of the form, that autobiography may use the forms of fiction, but there's the tacit understanding that what is written is true, or at least true from the subject's point of view. But by then it's too late. Pack's getting into this thing, like a dog with a bone, and he's not about to let it go. "No rush," he says, "you got months to do it."

Once, years before, he tells me, he gave a reading at some college. In one poem he had spoken movingly of the loss of his brother. After the reading, as he was gathering up his books and talking to some students, a young woman approached him and took his hand. There were tears in her eyes. The poem had meant a great deal to her, she told him, and she could understand something of what he was feeling, having herself experienced a similar loss. She could feel his loss in the way he'd read the poem. "It was truly awful," he tells her. "Except that I never had a brother. That part I made up. But I did have a dog I lost once. I loved that dog." She dropped his hand at once, and the look of sympathy the poem had aroused in her turned slowly to one of disgust, and the sense that she'd been had. The looks she threw my way, he tells me, with a certain aesthetic perversity, made the whole reading worthwhile. Certainly, he adds, they both learned a great deal about the workings of the fictive imagination.

Now, Pack is a master of fictions, having created hundreds of them over a lifetime of writing. And what this story reminds me of is the poem's ability to move us, in spite of the fact that the poem can never duplicate exactly "what happened," for to *say* what happened is by its very nature a construct and a fiction. So what, the writer will argue. What matters is the truth of the feelings, a sense of communion between poet and reader, evoked by the machinery of the story, its syntax and language, its images and music, its dramatic buildup, the complexities and resolution of the plot, the authority of the narrator, the willing suspension of belief as the reader comes under the spell of the teller.

If poems have absorbed most of my life, the period since 1970 has also been taken up with the lives of the poets who wrote the poems. I have formed "special attachments," if you will, to perhaps a dozen poets. Some I have barely written on, though they have occupied a large part of my own work as a poet. I think of Yeats, Stevens, Eliot, and Crane in this regard. But there are four on whom I have written, perhaps obsessively, and I want to say something here about each of them. I mean Hopkins, Williams, Berryman, and Lowell. In each instance it has been the poetry that led to the life.

W. S. Merwin has a poem about an encounter with Berryman when both were at Princeton in the late 1940s, Merwin as an undergraduate, Berryman as his instructor. How did one go about writing poems, Merwin remembers asking Berryman, especially in a dry time? Pray, Berryman told him, get down on your knees and pray. One would not have thought of such advice coming from Berryman, at least the Berryman who has come down to us in legend. But there it is. What sort of life, then, did Berryman really live? Or the others?

What sort of life, for instance, led to a poem like "The Windhover" or "To Elsie" or "Sailing to Byzantium" or "The Moose" or "Final Soliloquy of the Interior Paramour" or "Skunk Hour" or Dream Song 29, which begins, "There sat down once a thing so heavy"? How is it that this poet found this subject, and these particular words, and this particular form?

I cut my critical teeth in the late 1950s and early 1960s on the New Criticism, a movement already twenty-five years old when I entered the dialog as an undergraduate at Manhattan College, and so I found myself attending to the text and to the dynamics of the language as if all we had *was* the text. And because Manhattan still held tenaciously to a belief in the value of the Western tradition, I also found myself reading history, linguistics, sociology, anthropology, psychology, art criticism, and theology—especially theology—in an attempt to better understand the poems I was reading. By "better understanding" I mean the underlying psychodynamics and ontology of the poem—the pressures the poet brings to bear on it.

Into the maelstrom, then. Into the flux, scouring letters, memoirs, the critical comments of other writers and other scholars in order to better flesh out the poem. I read the poets whom the poets themselves had read, I read whatever I could discover—no matter how fleeting the journal or the magazine—for evidence of the lived lives of the poets. All this I did in the exuberance of youth, when time seemed to have no limits, in order to arrive at a better sense of the psychogenesis of the poem, the fabled primal scene, the Ur text, call it what you will.

I read the poem the way New Testament scholars go over Philo and Josephus and Temple coins for any trace of Christ's Passion, which may well be where my biographical impetus comes from: the Sacred Text as paradigm for the poetic text. Where and when I could, I drove or flew to libraries around the country, or begged for photocopies, and waited, and studied whatever variants of the manuscripts of a poem I could locate, dating them, trying in this way too to track a living mind at work. Anything to get inside the mind of the writer.

When I began doing this sort of work, back in the early 1960s, I hardly questioned myself about the possibility of my undertaking such a project. Older now, and having come up against a critical climate that doubts not only the idea of a unitive self but even the idea of a self at all, a climate that speaks of the death of the author and of the cracked, cubist insubstantiality of the drowsy reader, a climate that insists on reducing the text to a linguistic alphabet soup, I wonder if such an endeavor as creating a "character" from a living poet was doomed from the start to remain a fiction. Who knows? You get five or six moves and then the game is over, and I have already made most of my moves.

Back in the summer of 1970, when I was still new at this sort of thing, I spent six weeks as a young assistant professor trying to unravel the elements that I thought had gone into the making of a single sonnet of Hopkins's. All of this was by way of preparation for a talk I would give at a conference at UMass on Victorian England in the 1870s. The poem was "Andromeda," which begins:

> Now Time's Andromeda on this rock rude,
> With not her either beauty's equal or
> Her injury's.

The sonnet had been composed, it appeared from manuscript evidence, on August 12, 1879, while the young Father Hopkins (just turned thirty-five) was serving as curate at St. Aloysius's Catholic Church on the outskirts of Oxford, whose university he'd attended as a respectable Anglican a dozen years earlier. In his last year at Balliol College, Oxford, he'd converted to Roman Catholicism under the impetus of John

Henry Newman's Oxford Movement. To complicate matters, a year later Hopkins entered the Jesuits, an order that until recently had been suppressed in England. Why, I wondered, had Hopkins written this uncharacteristic sonnet, this allegory based on the Perseus/Andromeda myth, a poem so unlike his other sonnets? And why had he written it while at Oxford—uncomfortable in his role there surely? What, in other words, might a careful reading of the poem tell us about Hopkins, returned to the university town that had shaped him, but an outsider now, a self-exile looking in?

When I asked myself these questions, Hopkins had already been dead for eighty years. But here I was, trying to recover the poem's DNA elements, if you will. And this in spite of knowing that, had I been around to speak to Hopkins himself about the poem, I do not believe he himself could have said—except in the most general way—what particular irritant or insight had initiated the poem.

Still, by rummaging through the dusty corners of libraries, I did discover that, if Hopkins did pick up the London *Times* that day (was there a pun on the *Times* in the opening line, as there might be another on "rock rude" as a doubling for the Rock, meaning the Church, and in rude/rood?), he would have been able to read about Pope Leo XIII's recent encyclical attacking the excesses of atheistic liberalism. Being a priest, and living in a place that did not especially care for Catholics, did that start Hopkins using the legend of Perseus—the myth that later gave rise to the figure of St. George—as Christ saving *his* Andromeda, the Church?

But then who or what was "the wilder beast from west" Hopkins mentions in his poem? Liberalism? American democracy? Was he thinking of the new poetry coming out of America—i.e., Walt Whitman's—which Hopkins had learned about from reading reviews in the British quarterlies, and which already had its strong adherents in England and especially in Oxford, among them Oscar Wilde and Swinburne, the latter's poems particularly attractive to Hopkins, even as he distrusted them? Perhaps. Especially as Hopkins had already confessed that his own poetry was more like Whitman's than any other poet then writing in English. And, since Whitman appeared to be "a very great scoundrel" in Hopkins's eyes, mostly because of Whitman's open advocacy of homosexual love, was "Andromeda" Hopkins's way of exorcising the direction his poetry had taken by wrenching his own poetry into a more restrained and classical direction, including the uncharacteristic use of allegory?

I soon discovered that other Victorian poets (Kingsley, Browning, Morris) had also used the Andromeda story to treat of various contemporary religious and political crises. And, while Hopkins distrusted the classical gods (gentlemen rakes, he called them, always watching the servant girls), and disliked the use to which Swinburne and his friend Bridges had put the gods, he did acknowledge that they might be suitably used as allegory. That is, if one properly clothed them in abstractions. So, in answer to Bridges and Swinburne, Hopkins, two years a priest when he wrote the poem, tried his hand at the Andromeda myth to address his own sense of the dangers to the Church of which he was now so integral a part.

From what we know of Hopkins, conservative politically, Catholic in sensibility, and thoroughly trained in Greek and Latin (including Ovid's *Metamorphoses*, where Andromeda and Perseus figure), such a reading makes sense. There's a certain satisfaction and pleasure in creating a character out of words, a character with depth and a certain complexity. But is this enough to say I captured a life, even the life of a poem?

But consider this. If a poet were to search into the psychogenesis of one of his or her own poems, what in truth would that poet be able to recover? I suppose one might do what Poe did in writing about the origins of "The Raven," and fictionalize the poem's creation from beginning to end, though Poe did so with a ratiocinative chutzpah impressive enough to fool some into thinking that what Poe said he did after the event was in fact what he actually did. In truth, however, words themselves take on character in any such drama, so that, if one is given to assonance or consonance or rhyme or punning or image clusters, or has a penchant for narrative, or for parallel syntactical units, these will, rather like the characteristic brushstrokes of a Vermeer or a Van Gogh, enter into the DNA makeup of the poet.

Something then may be recovered, but never anything like the entire process. Even if one trained a camera on a writer at work and watched the lines unroll on the page or the computer, the way a camera was trained on Jackson Pollock as he painted one of his action paintings, who would have access to the rapid transits, fine tunings, negations, rethinkings, which occur in nanoseconds and alter the consequent direction of any work of art? Certainly not the artist, who cannot sit back and observe at the same moment that he or she is creating.

And so, since much is inevitably lost, the re-creation of the artistic event, which is at the heart of who the artist is, must always remain a fiction. Our critical and linguistic nets are too gross, too primitive, to ever fully capture the life of the poem, except impressionistically. The biographer may generate a good fiction, and may even teach us something about the creative process (it had better do at least that), and we may even convince ourselves that something like what we are reading actually occurred. By analogy, think for a moment of a computer-generated reenactment of a crime or, similarly, of the final seconds of a plane crash in which there are no survivors. The crash scene will be reconstructed from the evidence of the black box and the debris from the crash site. The computer model will seem plausible, it may educate us as to what might have gone wrong, it may even give us a model for what to do and what to avoid. And so with the mystery of the creative act. But that is as much as we can hope for.

SOON AFTER Lowell composed "Skunk Hour" in 1957, a young critic asked several poets to comment on the poem's meaning. John Berryman offered one reading, in part psychological (but since he had known Lowell for a dozen years by then, he had something of an edge in creating a reading of Lowell's mind). Richard Wilbur, who likewise knew Lowell, offered another reading, one further distanced by the screen of good manners and the New Criticism. In his counter-response Lowell gave his own version of how he'd written the poem.

It had begun, he explained, with a stanza that was now buried in the center of the poem, and then moving to the end. Afterward, he had added the first half. The poem, then, had begun as a cry of anguish, a dark night of the soul, a mental crucifixion:

> One dark night,
> my Tudor Ford climbed the hill's skull;
> I watched for love-cars. Lights turned down,
> they lay together, hull to hull,
> where the graveyard shelves on the town. . . .
> My mind's not right.

These lines, however, had proved too direct, too raw a wound, too revelatory of Lowell's strained relationship with himself as well as with his wife, Elizabeth Hardwick, to remain at the beginning of the poem, and so he had stepped back from the scene behind a mask of social satire, which fell somewhere between Henry Adams's civilities and Hart Crane's harsher strains.

I have no reason to doubt Lowell's recounting, and the manuscripts bear him out on the issue of how he composed the poem, at least in its outline. But even Lowell's recounting tells us little of how he actually wrote the poem, or why he chose the images he did, or about the specific dramatic tensions that went to make up the poem. One can see why he situated the poem as he did—in Castine, Maine—where he was then summering. And one can believe that Lowell, seeing himself helplessly entering into another manic phase, cruising the streets of the village and the graveyard beyond the town, was looking for company. One can even believe there are nocturnal predators in the form of skunks who march on their soles down the town's one main street. But how did these images coalesce in the white-hot incandescence of Lowell's mind?

And what about Lowell's relationship with Elizabeth Bishop—to whom the poem is dedicated—and the disheartening realization that this woman whom he loved and admired, and whom he had wanted for years to marry, could not return that affection because she was devoted to another woman? That too is part of the hellish erotic drama of Lowell's "Skunk Hour," and helps us understand the poem's tensions on yet another level. For all its openness, finally, the poem is at pains to conceal its deepest wounds.

ONE OF THE major problems in writing the life of a poet will be the question of perspective, of what angle—or angles—the biographer is going to take in attempting to "get at" the essence of that poet. After all, the poet does many things besides write poetry. The poet gets born, is raised, goes to school, travels, plays sports, reads, dates, falls in and out of love, drives a car, smokes perhaps, drinks (often), works at a job (teaching, doctoring, writing ads, selling insurance, directing plays, raising children), lives in a particular locale or locales with streets and rivers and shores and mountains (many of which may find their way into the poems). Poets lie, give misinformation about themselves, cheat. They also do noble things, think (often profoundly), act (sometimes with surprising generosity). Some even pray. But it is the biographer's first duty to bring us closer to the poems themselves, which is why, after all, we read the lives of the poets.

To do this the biographer will have to show us the poem through a particular set of lenses as skillfully as possible. Always the lenses themselves, however various, will be verbal by their very nature. The most, then, the biographer will have to deal with in recreating the protean life of the mind will be a set of linguistic signs, word choices, word tics (noun-, verb-, or adjective-prone?) a cluster of images expanding into symbols, a tonal range. And so irony looms large with the New Critics, just as destabilizing elements are important for creating a deconstructionist reading, undermining the very thing the writer seems to propound.

There is also the question of a writer's musical signature: those airy elements that tend to recur in a given work, and which, after a certain amount of exposure to a writer, we recognize as signatures of that writer. These linguistic and tonal elements, "settled" on the page, are similar to the painter's brush strokes, or to the musician's recurring chords and melody lines. They help us determine how the artist actually got the work done. They can also help determine when an artist is doing original work or merely Parnassian—work characteristic of the artist, but without adding anything original, work that uses nothing but the "rotted names," in Stevens's formulation. And therein lies the problem, for tracking genius remains the most elusive element about the artist. It is rather like the Heisenbergian track that can follow the wake of an element, but not the element itself. We have the work of the creator, if you will, but never the creator. It is, in short, for this biographer the real hole in the middle of biography.

Often a writer does not want his biography told, and the biographer who attempts one, knowing that, enters dangerous waters. That the subject himself or herself will have already passed into history hardly matters, because there is often the living to contend with: a wife, a daughter, a son, a lover or lovers. Even other biographers. And always: those who believed that life was theirs to tell or not to tell. When the subject is a recent figure, as with Lowell or Berryman or Williams, the biographer can be sure of making—often unwittingly—as many enemies as friends. Often (alas) such individuals are drawn to write the reviews in the way carrion draws flies. Try as the biographer will to anticipate and even appease such shadowy figures, it is impossible to do so.

And there are other difficulties. One of the major ones is the way a writer will go to any amount of trouble to keep the biographer off the trail. With Gerard Manley Hopkins, who died in 1889, there is the problem of a largely hidden life. As he got older, he seems hardly to have expected his poems to survive, much less to see his life written, other than in the obituary notice Jesuits receive from their fellow Jesuits. When he died at forty-four, his letters were scattered, his poems unpublished and in various stages of revision in various hands. Some of his most important manuscripts—like the original of "The Wreck of the Deutschland"—were lost even during his lifetime. His journals and sermon notes were left in various drawers and might easily have been burned in the weeks following his death. Some papers, perhaps even the beginnings of poems, seem in fact to have been destroyed, including some at his own hands. He was leaving the matter of his literary remains, he said, in God's hands, his work to be saved or lost as God thought fit.

At least God seems to have been watching. As it turned out, it took thirty years for his poems to be published, and when they were, it was by his friend, Robert Bridges, who was by then poet laureate of England. And though he cared for his dead friend's work, he was more than a little embarrassed by the strangeness he found there. Hopkins left no last will and testament for his work, no arrangement by theme or subject, no project—as Yeats did—for a final text. And as for the life? Over the past fifty years there have been a number of biographies— short lives and fuller ones—though none of them has yet gotten it right, especially in terms of the brilliant fusion of the English Romantic and the Catholic Jesuit that makes Hopkins's poems so luminous.

Another problem for the biographer is that the poet may try to pre-empt the biographer by writing his own life, concluding that, if anyone is going to tell the story, it will be the poet. But there are problems here as well: the problems of what gets put in and what gets left out. If the writer is John Updike, he may reasonably feel he can do a better job than any professional biographer. If the writer is the late James Merrill, he may be at pains to provide us with a complex but partial bildungsroman, showing us the poet as a young man coming into possession of his own identity, and spelling out what that identity will be. Or the poet may give us a series of autobiographies, fragments of a life, as Yeats did and as Philip Levine has done in *The Bread of Time*, subtitled *Toward an Autobiography*.

If the writer is William Carlos Williams, he will order his story to present a certain picture of himself, a picture that will give us the public figure. In his *Autobiography*, written rapidly and in a matter of months when he was in his late sixties, Williams went out of his way to discount his relations with many of the women in his life. In electing to keep quiet about this part of his life, he tried to simplify what had in fact given much of his life and poetry its particular energy, drive, focus, and indirection, all of which did go into the complex tensions of his multifaceted epic, *Paterson.*

A far better barometer of Williams's chief preoccupations as a writer, in fact, will be found in the complex, cubist strategies he provides in the juxtaposed passages there about his wife, mother, and grand-mother—the central women in his life—with the other women he knew. In the ways in which he both reveals and conceals these rela-tionships, we come closer to the central issues that define a man ob-sessed with the feminine and with the myth of America. It is an im-age of an America debased and unappreciated, but an America that has proven, like his northern New Jersey rivers and towns, capable of rising renewed from its own ashes. What the *Autobiography*, in short, shows us is how a country doctor from New Jersey—unlike those ur-bane polyglot expatriates, Pound and Eliot—stayed at home and still managed to become an American classic like Walt Whitman. What *Pa-terson* shows us is a troubled, complex artist in search of a language, a country, and a self, in the process showing us how we too might come into possession of our world and ourselves.

IF, ON THE other hand, the writer is John Berryman, fully two thirds of the telling of that life will be taken up in an attempt to show how the poet concealed his past, as if it did not exist, or was of no interest to anyone. Only following extensive psychoanalysis and the discovery that he could not finally escape writing out of his deepest concerns, did he finally come out, as he says, from behind the shadow of his father (a suicide at forty) to talk. It is interesting that the masks he created for himself in *The Dream Songs* in order to begin talking—and he talked brilliantly—gradually became more and more transparent portraits of himself.

Berryman's first book of poems, *The Dispossessed*, published when he was thirty-three, is as obscure and opaque a volume of poetry as one is going to find in this century, and one must already be familiar with the poet's life and major preoccupations—and know how to crack the various linguistic codes Berryman was at pains to place between himself and the reader—even to begin to understand what he was saying in these poems. In truth, if these were all the poet had left us, the privacy and obscurity Berryman courted would have been his.

But *Homage to Mistress Bradstreet*, written in the winter of 1953, began to change all that. The poem is a brilliant and tortured tour de force, and reading it one is aware that it is as much about Berryman's bizarre and unresolved relations with his mother, his wife, and several other women—his various "mistresses"—as it is about his relationship with the poet Anne Bradstreet, dead three centuries when Berryman set out to seduce her.

In *The Dream Songs* that followed, Berryman changed his strategy, shifting from a dialogue between two characters and opting instead to internalize the dialogue with two versions of the self in black and white. These were Henry, a white American male in early middle age, and the ghostly black interlocutor who remains nameless but who may perhaps be described as a mix of Joban comforter, Ralph Ellison's Invisible Man, and Berryman's conscience. Slowly Berryman fused these two selves into one, and one much closer to Berryman himself. There are other voices—dream voices, baby voices, the voice of the professor, of the used-car salesman, of the woman, the lawyer, the voice of the dead, the voices even of animals—for Berryman is a master ventriloquist. But all of these are, as with James Joyce in *Ulysses*, or with Dickens (doing the police in different voices), or with Eliot, or with Shakespeare, aspects of the poet himself.

Only in the two years left him before he committed suicide did Berryman finally come out as much as he could to talk to us, though even the trope of naked honesty—given the fictive nature of language—could only begin to approximate the poet's own complexities. If what we have in Berryman's last phase is a figure not unlike St. Augustine in the *Confessions*, mixed with the ironic detachment of a Laforgue, a poet dear to that other possum-playing poet, T. S. Eliot—at least early on—that may be because irony has been and remains the sine qua non, the last face-saving resort, of so much of our literature.

FINALLY, THERE ARE the various Robert Lowells. There's the young apocalyptic Lowell, the Boston Lowell who converted to Roman Catholicism and became a conscientious objector during World War II, and who sounds like a mixture of Jeremiah, Blake, Milton, Hopkins, Eliot, and Hart Crane. He is a poet for whom all history came to be viewed through the emblems of his puritan forebears, who felt compelled to deal with the trauma of his own life through a mythopoeic frame, where history itself came to be read in terms of his own preoccupations and concerns. The Depression, World War II, Viet Nam, the Kennedy and Johnson and Nixon years: all of it was folded back into the poet's own life until, like the Southern Fugitives (who could not forget the long shadow cast on them by Appomattox) or like Walt Whitman in "Song of Myself"—Lowell became the prophet of a deeply troubled America.

But, as large as Lowell's shadow was, the shadow of history proved even larger. History was unwieldy, indifferent even to the poet's Emersonian eye, more an ocean with its own countercurrents than merely an idea concocted by the poet. Eventually Lowell's apocalyptic vision of the end time gave way to a more cyclical sense of things unfolding blindly, a view closer to the one shared by Hardy and Yeats. After a series of bruising mental breakdowns in which he learned that he could not even control the domain of the self, Lowell's poems finally came to acknowledge that he was a diminished thing, bowed and frizzled by time.

In *Life Studies* he turned to history under the species of his own family drama, attempting in his forties not so much to explain God's ways to man as to explain the strange mystery of who he himself was, and how it was—given his progenitors and the currents of history— he had gotten that way. By then he had the Eliot of *The Waste Land* to show him what history could tell him about the human condition, and so, by extension, about himself.

To do this he learned to stand back, with several layerings of ironic distancing, to watch himself as he moved through history. He was an inveterate student of Freud, Thucydides, Gibbon, and Macaulay, and struggled to see where he was in light of his own complex moment. Before he was forty, he had turned away from the prophetic voices of Milton and Whitman to Flaubert and Baudelaire. Flaubert provided the detached and diagnostic view; Baudelaire helped him to turn inward and downward. Both provided the detachment he needed if he was to survive his own depression. In the poems he wrote between his fiftieth and fifty-fifth years, he layered his own historical moment in a manner closer to what Pound had done in the *Cantos*, employing a broader canvas, except that where Pound modulated between a prose-like line and highly wrought epiphanic moments, Lowell decided on a flatter, elliptical, and experimental syntax—like, one realizes, New York jazz in the late 1950s and 1960s.

In his long sequences, he learned to replicate something of Berryman's rapid transits from idea to idea. Otherwise, his is an East Coast language, closer to Frank O'Hara's and John Ashbery's New York monologues, though different from either. More studied, more allusive, like the language of a very intelligent, hip, and bookish man. He was no longer after the certainties of a Henry Adams. That belonged to his Boston years. Rather, he wanted to capture something of the dizzying, heady, sophisticated, urbane, overheard quality of words that the vortex of New York provided in the tumultuous decade that gave us the Kennedys, King and the Civil Rights movement, the women's movement, Johnson, Nixon, and the Hundred Years War unfolding in Viet Nam.

Finally, his last work, written in the three years before his death, cuts away much of the marmoreal quality of history to focus on a much reduced Lowell, a man in a new marriage that, in spite of its brilliant early promise, and in spite of a new son, had already come apart. *Day by Day* is Lear *redivivus*, a testament by turns comic, winning, heartbreaking, and heavy with retrospection and loss. It is an autumnal book, and it was Lowell's last. Here, finally, Lowell takes responsibility for the mistakes he has made: what he calls harm to others, harm to himself. Somehow he managed to convince himself that he could break free of American history and begin again with a new marriage, a new family, a new country (England), even a new style of poetry. Instead history followed after, and he had to watch as fate caught up with him again in pastoral England. What *Day by Day* recounts is Lowell's final tragic act: the insistent recurrence of mental illnesses, a heart attack, several hospitalizations, the loss of a country and then another country. The loss too of his Anglo-Irish wife, and—finally—many of those who had been closest to him.

STILL, READING the thousands of fragments we call the evidence of a life, and then shaping these into a "life" are among the greatest pleasures afforded the biographer. Why else spend so much of one's own life writing the lives of others? The pleasure of writing biography is like the pleasure of writing any story, of getting words down on the page in an order that will make a lasting impact. How satisfying it is to find a form that will explain why X or Y did this or that. How delightful to go through often contradictory testimony to arrive at what seems the most plausible motive for an individual's actions. And, as a portrait begins to emerge, it comes as a happy surprise to the biographer as well.

One question I'm often asked is why I have worked with such difficult lives as I have. Hopkins, a Jesuit priest—a celibate who remained faithful to his vows but who had to struggle with an overwhelming attraction to beauty, including the erotic, and who on the other hand experienced bouts of severe depression that left him feeling as if he were going mad. Or—to simplify—there is Williams the lover, Williams the faux naïf, Williams the creator of the antipoetic, Williams the democrat who was the friend of Ezra Pound. When I started out pursuing Williams in 1970, he was still considered by many a minor writer. Or there is Berryman the roaring boy, the raging alcoholic, the womanizer, the suicide. Or Lowell, with his seasonal manic-depressive bouts and drinking and troubled marriages. It is the sort of reduction that occurs in the reviews, the soap-opera quotient that in the public's eye overrides the unique genius of each of these poets. But that is not what interests me. What I have tried to do is give what Lowell called the rightful name to each picture in the landscape, to give as full and balanced a picture of each of these poets as might be done within the constraints of a book. If I too could only flinch at some of the things Williams and Berryman and Lowell did, I also came in time to understand why they acted as they did, and tried to show the reader the underlying heroism—the centrality, if you will—of each of these lives for the times in which they lived. Poets, after all, are primarily thinkers who shape their times in ways it is the biographer's task to elucidate. Shelley had it right when he called poets (those worthy of the name) the unacknowledged legislators of the world. They certainly interact with history at its deepest linguistic reality in ways their more powerful Washington counterparts can never hope to do.

But biography is only a beginning. For no biography can tell the whole story or represent fully the poet's achievement. Impressions can be made, a taste of what the artist did can be indicated. If biographers have done their work well, they will send the reader back to the poetry again, and so back to the source, to return to someone whose voice and gestures readers have come to recognize and perhaps even love. We may even find ourselves returning to a friend, forgetting for the moment the essentially elegiac nature of the biographical act: that, since the subject we are writing of is always already in the past tense, there must always remain a hole in the middle of the book.

1995

Staring into the Abyss

Robert Pack's Later Poems

ONE OF THE pleasures of reading any of Bob Pack's later sequences—
Faces in a Single Tree (1984); *Clayfeld Rejoices, Clayfeld Laments* (1987);
Before It Vanishes: A Packet for Professor Pagels (1989); and Pack's *In-
heritance: Reflections in a Gene Pool* (published in *Fathering the Map:
New and Selected Later Poems*, in 1993)—is watching how a single poem
contains so many of Pack's interlocking themes, images, and tropes. So
many of the same motifs played again and again, but with consummate
skill and exhilarating variety. No wonder this poet loves his Mozart.

But there's also the way Pack—now sixty-five—continues to stare at
the darkness until he makes it shine. He's like some Yiddish comedian,
filled with outrageous and subtle puns, playing the language. Consider
"The Black Hole," one of the poems in *Before It Vanishes*, to which I
am particularly attracted, even though it's a troubling poem. Pack begins his comedy routine by letting Professor Pagels have the first word.
Pagels is the articulate scientist, and he articulates here the old Science
vs. Art controversy made popular for the past one hundred and fifty
years by Darwin, Huxley, Freud, Einstein, and (more recently) C. P.
Snow, all of whom can be said to represent the scientific imagination.
"Imagine [that] the whole mass of the sun is crushed down to a radius of a few kilometers," Heinz Pagels writes in *Perfect Symmetry*.
"The gravity and space curvature near this compacted sun is enormous. . . . Since light cannot leave this object, it 'appears' as a black
hole in space. . . . An observer who fell into the center of a black hole

could see time slow down." But, he adds, "The falling observer can never communicate his strange experience to his friend outside."

Well, maybe the scientific imagination can't communicate such a subjective experience. But the poet is certainly willing to give the skeptics a run for their money. One of the best examples of Pack's willingness to arm-wrestle with his distinguished adversary occurs in "Pepper and Salt," where Pagels, in order to explain the concept of entropy increase—the way in which matter moves inevitably toward formlessness—suggests a simple experiment. "Take a glass jar and fill it up a quarter of the way with salt." If this sounds like an excerpt from a cosmic cookbook, all well and good, and Pack will play outrageously with that figure as well. Now, Pagels continues, add granulated pepper until it is half full. "There is a black layer on top of a white layer—an improbable configuration of all particles. . . . Now shake the jar vigorously. The result is a gray mixture, a disorganized configuration of the salt and pepper. If you keep shaking, it is very unlikely that the original configuration will ever return. Not in a million years of shaking will it return." A million years? Who you kidding, Professor Pagels? Pack retorts, even as he hurls a rubber chicken at his white-coated straight man. "With just two shakes of the glass jar—voila! / the scattered pepper / organizes to the top; / salt burrows underneath." It's all in the flick of the wrist, says Pack.

So here in "The Black Hole," where Pack once again does what Pagels suggests, this time imagining the sun compacted to a radius of a few kilometers. Where has he seen such a thing, Pack asks himself. Why, in the sun's brilliant reflection caught in the blue surface of a Maine woods lake. Or—again—the sun reflected in the dark hole of his own mind, as he sits at his desk writing his lines. So Pack begins his poem simply enough, using an easy, ambling, level narrative line to get underway. The narrator and his brother plan to meet at their old campsite in Maine and fish for rainbows, playing back old times together and renewing their covenant of brotherhood over some trout and a few cold beers. The speaker hires a bush pilot to fly him out to the lake, and it soon becomes clear that the pilot is not only psychotic but—playfully or not—bent on his own destruction. The plane with its heavy pontoons doesn't even look as if it could ever get "its ass" off the ground, any more than Baudelaire's albatross could, and the pilot keeps staring "queerly" into the sun, drawn toward it like some "modern Dedalus."

Now Pack begins sketching a series of ever-increasing circles as his double is piloted into the wilderness. From this height he can see the circular path swathed through the woods by a tornado ten years before. Next, he experiences two of the pilot's "lucky loops," a smaller one first, then a wider one that kills the plane's engine and sends it hurtling toward "the evening sun / reflected in the lake" below, where his brother—his double—watches him hurtle (in terrifying slow motion) toward his death.

"An observer who fell into the center of a black hole could see time slow down. But the falling observer can never communicate his strange experience to his friend outside." Thus Pagels. And Pack, his *o—os* of terror giving way to *os* of wonder—filling the page in the moment before his speaker crashes forever into the sun disked in the lake:

> Oh, I was falling
> through my mind's black hole, the one
>
> curved space to float me home,
> so slowly I had time to think that I
> alone had nothing left to know
> except the circle of the sun within the sky
>
> inside the water, blue advancing
> bluer into brighter blue—

Oh, hole, float, home, slowly, alone, know. The o-sounds themselves form a shorthand of the final knowledge of our flight into the fiery black hole of our extinctions.

But just here—in this final moment—Pack continues to slow time down. His brother, the fictive self who watches the self, cannot, *will not* believe what he is witnessing as the speaker plummets to the earth, and so must hide his eyes. At this moment, Pack turns to his other brother,

Professor Pagels, bidding *him* to stare into the tiny *os* of his—Pack's—
eyes to see if he cannot see reflected there what Pack imagines himself
to be staring at when the moment of his own extinction is upon him.
Will he see the sun reflected there? There, within the black hole at the
center of the pupil? Will he feel

> the unresisted pull into the perfect heart
> of orange light, the last surprise
>
> of pure acceptance that can never pass
> beyond itself?

And though that communication with the other at the point between
life and death is framed by a question mark, it is nevertheless a clear
and terrifying communication. In spite of the crack-brained pilot and
the fishing expedition and the rest of it, Pack has given us a leap into
the terrifying Sublime.

Then, suddenly, a reprieve. The starved engine starts again, and the
plane—along with the poem's syntax—levels out again, and the moment of final acceptance of the way things are gives way to terror and
shaky knees and bruises and the ground-hugging that follows such terrible ascents and descents. Pack's narrative leaps forward in time now
for just a moment, and we learn that the pilot, Joel (Hebrew for "Yahweh is God," i.e., "God is God," another circle or blinding tautology
suggested there), has finally killed himself "flying home." What "flying home" finally means is left for us to puzzle, for the meaning of
Joel's death is beyond the ability of Joel's neighbor to communicate,
although Pack has already allowed us to imagine what Joel's final moments must have felt like before he finally vanished.

The poem ends back in the Maine woods, the two brothers—as yet
unaware of the pilot's death—sitting around a campfire after a day of
fishing, cooking up their mess of rainbow trout. It is a "covenant of
brothers" Pack celebrates here, all the more precious because one of the
narrator's brothers (Joel) is already dead and the speaker himself has
just barely escaped the fate he knows he must one day meet. The sign

of the Biblical covenant is, of course, the rainbow sent by Yahweh to Noah after the flood. And now here it is again, in the rainbow colors of the fire—"orange-red" and "green-blue"—themselves recalling the orange of the dying sun and the blue of the terrifying oncoming waters—and, paradoxically, at the center of that welcome rainbow fire, the sacrifice of a "sizzling rainbow trout,"

> its smeared red stripe surrounded by black dots—
> collapsed suns lost in their trapped light.

Reminders, then, of death and loss even in the midst of a mortal beauty so rich and dappled it can bring tears to one's eyes. It is our own fate we stare upon as we stare at the trout. "Heartbreaking beauty must suffice," Pack sums up, "the brotherhood of sharing what we lose, / the rainbow in warmed ice."

As the fates would have it, however, the Tambo and Bones whizz-bang scientist vs. poet comedy routine was to take an unexpected and tragic turn with the death of Heinz Pagels in a mountain-climbing accident on July 24, 1988, shortly after Pack had completed his poetic sequence. Ironically, at the close of *The Cosmic Code*, Pagels too had stared hard into the sun, imagining the moment of his own death, a death he saw as occurring almost exactly as it did—in a fall while mountain climbing. Pagels's obituary in the *New York Times* quoted the following passage: "I dreamed I was clutching at the face of a rock, but it would not hold. Gravel gave way. I grasped for a shrub, but it pulled loose, and in cold terror I fell into the abyss. Suddenly . . . I realized that what I embody, the principle of life, cannot be destroyed. It is written into the cosmic code, the order of the universe. As I continued to fall in the dark void, embraced by the vault of the heavens, I sang to the beauty of the stars and made my peace with the darkness."

What was Pagels thinking of when he wrote that passage? Lucifer, the light bearer? Surely "dark Void" and "vault of heaven" and singing "to the beauty of the stars" belong to an altogether different linguistic universe than the one we usually think of in conjunction with the scientific imagination. And in fact they are closer to Blake's and Shelley's reading of the Miltonic Sublime. Whatever, Pagels would seem to have upped the ante on Pack. After all, if Pack's alter ego did plummet toward the abyss of the lake, he also leveled off to return to the embrace of the human family and the covenant of a shared meal over an open fire. Pagels, on the other hand, fell singing into the abyss, arms forever outstretched to embrace the stars. Having originally intended to end his sequence with a first *hello*, a reaching across to Pagels in a meeting (which actually did occur when Pack called Pagels and was subsequently invited to read some of his poems at a gathering of the Reality Club in midtown Manhattan, at which Heinz Pagels presided), Pack, though ten years older, is the one who must now say good-bye.

Did Pagels somehow choose his death, Pack wonders, in order to "keep true" to his "wide-eyed vow to live / in touch with your abyss?" As a longtime student of Freud, Pack cannot help wondering if indeed we all somehow rehearse beforehand the occasion of our deaths. Pagels too must have rehearsed the final act of his life, hoping "to find the right last thought that might / contain eternity." Now Pack replays Pagels's death a final time, rehearsing it as he had rehearsed his own death in "The Black Hole," searching for some final insight into that death. The gravel giving way, the shrub's roots pulling free, and that terrifying moment, "before acceleration starts," when the self realizes it is about to die. What did it feel like, that final free-fall through space, by a mind performing its final act of consciousness before plunging into oblivion?

But this is no replay of the final grand gesture Pagels had written into the script for himself. For the poet, that sounds too much like grand guignol, pure theater. No, Pack says, rewriting Pagels for the last time. No, the terrible moment of realization must have been otherwise than Pagels had written of it. In that final moment there was still time to feel alive:

> time to feel your heart
> push forth a surge of blood;
> there's time to feel a gasp leap out,
> expanding from your lungs,
> a cringing whisper first, and then a shout,
> embodied as a scream.

Not a yes, then, to fate, as Heinz Pagels had thought, but rather a no, "a full, involuntary *No!*" as if—as if—"from someone else." From whom then? From Heinz's father, crying out helplessly as he saw his son fall Icarus-like to his death? From us, who—like the brother in "The Black Hole"—would have turned away from the tragedy? Or from Pack, whose "decomposing voice" as he moves toward his own death dares now to reenact Pagels's death, and who now cries out—helplessly— against this death?

In a final gesture of communion with his lost friend and brother, Pack tries to follow Pagels into that terrifying final abyss. Now it is the poet who is falling, trying "to dream your liberating dream / of the encompassing abyss," when Pagels had imagined himself singing to the cold, indifferent stars. From the perspective of aeonic time, which both he and Pagels have been playing with throughout the entire sequence, Pack knows all too well it will not matter soon just "who preceded whom." But for this brief, precious interim, safe for the moment in his own home with those same stars shining brightly overhead, Pack admits that he cannot—will not!—follow his adversary/mentor into "the indifferent air." Instead, he repeats his good-bye once again, choosing instead, like Frost before him, to remain earthbound. Yes, there is a terrible beauty in the starlit heavens, but Pack is not willing to go into the abyss one precious second before his time, since he does not know where things are bound to go better than they do right here.

In many of his poems Pack seems to have repeatedly rehearsed his own death, armed with his headset tuned to his beloved Mozart. But not yet, he keeps saying, like Augustine. Not yet. There is too much beauty everywhere around one, even if that beauty is an indifferent, heartbreaking, mortal beauty. Besides, there are one's family and one's friends. And those are the subjects and themes fit for this earthbound Romantic as he stands outside on a winter's night, under the shadow of his own roof, a snowman marveling at the shagged brilliance of the distant stars before he goes inside again.

1994

Hardy's Heartbreak

☙

THOMAS HARDY: an old ghost who has haunted me now for forty years. Call it a lover's quarrel that goes back to my time in graduate school, when it took the form of an interior monologue with that immensity, Irving Howe, my professor at Hunter, who was then in the midst of his own extensive meditation on Hardy. How deeply this question of literature goes. How one's dialogue with a particular figure will surface and go underground and resurface again years later, like those rivers in the American Southwest, the questions and answers changing as we ourselves change and are changed by the encounter with a larger-than-life presence over a lifetime.

At twenty-six I remember admitting to another professor, Allen Mandelbaum, how much the poets of the moment were on my mind. He, who had spent his early years translating Ungaretti, Montale, and Quasimodo, as he would spend his later years translating Virgil and Dante and Homer and Ovid into an English worthy of the originals, told me that within a few years the terms of my debate would shift away from living contemporaries toward the great presences who inhabit the philosophers' circle, eternally discoursing on poetry and language. When that happened, he added, the concerns of the present would settle into their proper dimension as I assumed a more philosophical approach to things. He was right.

An example. Recently I read an article in the *New York Times Book Review* about Hershel Parker, Melville's biographer, becoming so incensed by a report that Melville was a wife beater that he'd gone running to cool off and then fallen, breaking his wrist. Wife-beating was a serious accusation, he insisted, and in Melville's case totally unfounded. Besides, the charge had been brought by an upstart out to make a name for herself. Melville himself had died in 1891, so the issue probably matters little to him personally. But it does matter to his name, and the fallout from such a charge could well be enormous . . . or not. Someone may actually refuse to read *Moby Dick* now, and others will work to expunge—as the biographer said—one more "dead white male" from the canon. In this case that will be especially unfortunate, for it will mean expunging a dead white whale as well.

One would have thought the crime of which Melville stood accused had happened only yesterday, and in a very real sense it had, so large had Melville's presence entered his biographer. And to tell the truth, I have felt exactly the same way about those poets in whose lives I've invested. Three months ago, for instance, reading a newly discovered letter Hopkins wrote to three fellow Jesuits back in 1881, it was as if his words of greeting had been personally addressed to me, bringing me news about a man I have known as well as anyone for the past thirty-five years.

I BEGAN teaching modern poetry at the University of Massachusetts in Emily Dickinson's hometown in the fall of 1968. After a passing nod to Hardy as one of my protomoderns, I get down to business with Yeats. Every few years I offer a seminar on Hopkins and Yeats, but only once have I ever expanded that course to include Hardy. That was at the Bread Loaf School of English in the summer of 1984, and by the end of the first week I had to tell my students that, in spite of the extensive reading in Hardy I'd done to prepare for the course, including the novels and that mostly tiresome epic of Hardy's, *The Dynasts*, cover to cover, I had still not been won over by the poetry. Within minutes, of course, word got back to central administration about my disaffection. We laughed about it, but there it was, and there was little I could do about it.

The fact is that Tiny Hardy—John Berryman's epithet for the man—

did not touch me the way either Yeats or Hopkins did. He seemed old-fashioned not only in his intellectual concerns (Comte, Hegel, Spengler) but in his diction and in his concerns for a provincial world, a world in many ways closer to Shakespeare's than to ours, but that—thanks to Darwin's theories of evolution and the eroding skepticism of the new German Higher Criticism—was already coming under fire and would soon be blown to hell by the events of World War I and the new technology that included not only the bicycle but the motor car, the Spad, and the radio.

But there is something more: a matter of temperament and constitution. My own proclivities have been with Williams, Pound, and Eliot: the modernist experimenters out to reinvent poetry, beginning with breaking the back of the iambic pentameter, the dominant master beat. (Williams in fact came to call it the masturbate, so obsessive did he find its dreamlike systole/diastole lullings.)

Somewhere in the middle of all this were of course those practitioners who still used a gorgeous blank verse in the service of the modernist revolution—poets like Wallace Stevens and Hart Crane. But then even Hopkins and Yeats had employed a modified blank-verse line with variations: sprung rhythm for Hopkins to escape the draw of Milton; packed spondees for Yeats to escape the tug of Shelley and Tennyson.

The second half of the twentieth century has seen the waning of the modernist experiment and the resurgence of the "new" formalism, a formalism chopped and jazzed up, but with the essential DNA of formal verse and blank verse still shoring it up. Of course there is also the Blakean/King James line of Whitman alive and well in Ginsberg's seminal *Howl*, as in the later poetry of Adrienne Rich and C. K. Williams. And there is the musical amalgam of Tennyson and Provençal we hear in Pound's *Cantos* operating in Charles Olson, Robert Duncan, and Charles Wright.

Moreover, Bishop and Berryman and Lowell and Strand and Simic and Levine and Walcott have all written a wonderful formal verse, roughed up and counterpointed and made purposely irregular, but there for all that. It's a technical strategy for writing verse in English,

and it has been going on in English since Chaucer learned to negotiate between the courtly finish of French and Italian poetry and the
rougher, more native meters of the English countryside. It's a tension
one finds likewise in the ways in which Wyatt and Surrey brought Pe-
trarch's hendecasyllables over into English.

In Hardy, it's a question of working with and against the Latinate
smoothness of the Keats / Tennyson / Swinburne line by purposely
roughing the surface to bring his measures into closer proximity with
the language of the Dorset countryside—his Yoknapatawpha, his Wes-
sex. In observing this tension between the smoothness of Swinburne
and the *rim ram ruff* of the local shepherds and tavern keepers, he
did for the language of Victorian and Georgian England what Larkin
would do for post–World War II England, or what William Carlos
Williams would do for American poetry.

In this country the past forty years have seen a major turn in poetic
practice toward free verse, in the tradition of Williams, with Whitman
often invoked as the founder. One thinks in this connection of Ginsberg, Creeley, Olson, Levertov, Kinnell, Levine, James Wright, C. K.
Williams, Bill Matthews, and Lowell's *Life Studies*. But once a revolution has succeeded in taking over the presidential palace, as I think
Williams's did in the 1950s, it eventually becomes mainstream, and in
time grows old, itself needing a new infusion of blood.

ON MY DESK these past three months has rested the wrist-numbing
one thousand-page edition of *The Complete Poems of Thomas Hardy*,
edited by James Gibson. The volume contains 947 poems, written between 1865 and 1928. That's a period of sixty-three years, during which
time Hardy also wrote half a dozen and more splendid novels, among
them *Far from the Madding Crowd*, *The Return of the Native*, *Tess of
the D'Urbervilles*, and *Jude the Obscure*. He began in his early twenties
as a poet, and then, realizing he could not make a living that way, put
his poetic vocation on hold for the better part of thirty years, until he
could return to it full time.

By 1895 this faux provincial, this player of fiddles at weddings, this worker in stone and restorer of old churches, a man who because of the accident of his birth had had no chance to attend either Oxford or Cambridge, was moving among the foremost literary circles of England, a well-known novelist who could command large sums for his serializations, a shy man much lionized and sought after. Then, with the brouhaha that attended the reception of his "pessimistic" portrayal of contemporary life in *Jude the Obscure* (one wag of a critic called it *Jude the Obscene*), Hardy turned his back on fiction to devote himself from then on to his first love, poetry.

A thousand pages of poetry means that each of us can create our own Hardy. I've been amused and edified by the different takes different poets and critics give us of Hardy. Joseph Brodsky, for instance: the late Russian poet who distrusted free verse but who remained endlessly fascinated by the formal dimensions of English and looked to Hardy (as to Auden and Frost and Yeats) for the play of sound and language. Or John Crowe Ransom, with his particular fascination for Hardy's theological fables. Or Donald Davie, who twenty-five years ago saw in Hardy the real fountainhead of poetry written in England in this century and who saw in modernism an American import via Pound and Eliot, a movement that for all its bustle never really took root in England. Hardy's true heir, he believed, was none other than Philip Larkin who, after an early flirtation with Yeats, had turned decisively to Hardy for inspiration and direction. Larkin's England turns out in fact to be Hardy's writ small, an England of drab tenements and lowered expectations, yet still capable of hearing the tragic withdrawal of the Sublime.

THERE IS A particular philosophical coloration about Hardy's mind established early in the poetry that remained a constant, except that it darkened with age. It became a settled way of viewing the world, absorbed from his family background. Call it fate, necessity, determinism with a dollop of free will operating perhaps, but there it was: a way of seeing by those born into hard times who of necessity learn early to make their own way. You see it in those who have gone hungry when they were young, or who were burned by bad debts, so that no amount of security acquired later ever makes up for that initial sense that fate is a large cat that plays with you before it kills you. No matter how much money Hardy acquired later in life, he seems to have remained a tight-fisted peasant in his dealings with his wives and relatives. No matter how much the sun shone and the spring rains came, he believed, there was always disaster waiting just around the bend. Just when the crops were ready to be harvested, lightning or wind or some other pestilence struck.

A frequent churchgoer who read the lessons from the pulpit and who pored daily over the Bible for news of the human condition, marking and dating passages that seemed to have relevance to his own life, Hardy early on lost his faith in God, perhaps at the hands of one of the new liberated women he knew and for whom his character, Sue Bridehead, was the model. At least faith in a God his fellow Christians would have recognized. The gods, if they existed at all, he was sure, cared nothing for us. Or, as wanton boys to flies, killed us for their sport. At best they were indifferent. At worst, they actually seemed to have it out for us.

After his closest friend cut his own throat in a moment of severe depression in the mid-1870s, Hardy's belief in a malevolent will ruling the universe hardened, shaping all of his subsequent fiction. Thereafter his heroes and heroines never had a chance. The odds were so against them it seemed as if the gods themselves had loaded the dice. Given his background and his reading, Hardy ought to have become an old-fashioned conservative. But in fact he saw himself as a liberal humanist, so much so that he was genuinely surprised and depressed when, at the ripe age of seventy-eight, he learned that—in spite of the horrors of the Napoleonic wars a century earlier—Europe was about to repeat the horror on an even more massive scale in the wake of the assassination of the archduke at Sarajevo.

Hardy was obsessed by the unfolding of time and history, and there is never—as there is in Hopkins or Eliot because of their faith—a sense of the possibility of human transcendence. True, Hardy used what Philip Larkin called the old myth kitty, but you never feel for a moment that he believed it might better the human condition. If there is hope, it is always a hope defeated, and his conditionals make Wallace Stevens look like a Billy Graham.

There is also something—as Donald Davie wrote incisively—of the Victorian engineer about Hardy, marching his fables through to their inexorable close. A few Gothic finials here and there, perhaps, but a streamlined precision and masterful execution of the verse lines slipping smoothly into place and locking. It is important to remember when we think of rustic Hardy that no one—no one—was more varied in his use of the formal elements of English poetry. If the form exists, Hardy probably used it somewhere among his nine hundred poems. His will is in this like his own impercipient will—Fate, Ananke, Necessity—and his poems move always toward their one inevitable fatalistic close. Yet having said this, it is also true that again and again he strikes a chord, a note of authentic heartbreak as he touches on the human condition. It is a chord as old as Aeschylus and the author of Job, which is why I find myself returning to him again and again. Reading him I touch again something very old and permanent in the English psyche, older than the Gothic cathedrals he pored over so lovingly, older than the druid stones of Stonehenge.

Consider for example Hardy's ability to engineer a particular poem through to completion: "The Convergence of the Twain," written in late April 1912, following the sinking of the *Titanic.* When I saw pictures in the *National Geographic* a few years back of what still remains of the *Titanic*—its two halves lying on the ocean floor a mile down in black, icy waters, I could not help but think of Hardy's poem. I remember the undersea camera moving along the ocean bottom and coming across two shoes lying side by side. There was no longer a trace of the person who once inhabited those shoes, for every bone had long since been ground down to dust. In this chilling world of cold currents the human seemed inconsequential and irrelevant.

I have said that Hardy the confirmed agnostic read his Bible constantly, using it as a talisman against which he might register the events and shocks of his own life. It is no wonder, then, that this poem reads like a gloss on Ecclesiastes: "Vanity, vanity, saith the Preacher. All is Vanity." If it is the Pride of Life that built the *Titanic*, Hardy reminds us, remembering that the ship had been billed as unsinkable, there is surely Something out there that laughs at our boasts. And so, as the poem opens, all that promise is past. The ship's remains lie in a solitude beyond recovery, and we have all the time in the world now to examine this wreck. Thirty-five years separate the wreck of the *Titanic* from the wreck of the *Deutschland*, and there is a world of difference between Hopkins's transcendent cry to God and Hardy's meditation on eternal stillness.

A ship, an iceberg, and—uniting them—a third: the Immanent Will. And so Hardy builds his poem triad by triad, rib by rib, weighted iceberg by iceberg. Here is the pattern of the poem: a three-stress line, followed by another like it, and then a weighty hexameter, all linked together by a single rhyme. There is an inescapable heaviness to each of these triads—two light threes, followed by a heavy six, the last line made even longer by internal pauses and thick, consonantal clusters. As in this line: "The sea-worm crawls—grotesque, slimed, dumb, indifferent." This is not your garden-variety worm, but it will do for general dissolution. The effect of skimming and drag in these stanzas is inescapable, and Hardy repeats the effect with subtle modulations eleven times, marking each of his stanzas with a roman numeral, as if they were chapters in a book or verses from the Bible. Or as if each were a separate meditation, which indeed they are. One thinks, for example, of Stevens's "Thirteen Ways of Looking at a Blackbird," with its similarly numbered stanzas, written a few years after Hardy's meditation.

Here then is Hardy the engineer at work. In the first five stanzas he focuses on the eternal present. Here all is absence: the absence of those salamandrine fires in the engine room that once powered the ship, those engines become now steel burial chambers moved by more elemental forces. So too with those opulent mirrors that once showed off those beautiful people, many of them claimed now by sea worms.

The jewels—symbols of human success and worth—now lie lightless, returned to the earth from which they sprang. In a world of darkness visible, Hardy has his moon-eyed fish ask the very question the author of Ecclesiastes had asked, a question one identifies with the sacred Sublime rather than with fish: "What does this vaingloriousness down here?"

Now, in the sixth and midmost passage, Hardy shifts to answer the fishes' query. While this *Titanic*, "This creature of cleaving wing," was being fashioned with the most up-to-date technological advances of 1912, the same technology that was building the Suez and Panama Canals and New York's skyscrapers and London's subway system and Germany's new railway system, the Immanent Will "that stirs and urges everything" was busy preparing a wedding for this lovely ship. Hardy calls it a "welding," of course, a word that brings to mind acetylene torches and arc lamps and steel ribs being assembled, but one cannot help but hear "wedding" as well.

And who is the *Titanic*'s mate? A Frankenstein, if you will, a Shape of Ice growing by increments somewhere out there in the North Atlantic, dissociate, still a thousand miles away. And now the last five stanzas of the poem shift to the past tense, but a past tense that moves inexorably toward the fictive present, until the ship and the iceberg become— at the command of the Spinner of Years—"twin halves of one august event." Note too how superbly crafted the last stanza is. Here Hardy welds past and present—the past tense of "said" juxtaposed to the Spinner of the Years' command that the moment is "Now!" And suddenly we are shifted back to the terrible moment of collision, forced to relive it every time we read the poem: the awful union of the fair ship with its monstrous mate waiting out there in the fog. A nightmare present, where "consummation comes, and jars two hemispheres."

Those two hemispheres, those twin halves—which recall in a perverse manner Plato's fable of sexual union in *The Symposium*—are not only the ship and its phonetic twin Shape—but also England, the *Titanic*'s point of embarkation, and America, its destination: Old World and New, both caught in this inexorable tragedy. Note too Hardy's brand of humor—muted of course—in having those moon-eyed creatures address us in the language of the Bible. He seems to have derived a certain comfort and distance from the tragedy by creating this poem, with—as he names them in the poem itself—his own "rhythmic tidal lyres" to counter the yawing ocean.

But if pity—the way we look at the world—and irony—the way the world seems to look back—are characteristic signatures in Hardy's poems, there is also a superb elegiac strain in the man, as in his late paean to life's bounty in the poem "Great Things." Here the music is masterful and subtle. It reminds one of those old footstomping reels played at country dances in fields and farms and granges, the sort of music Williams would catch in his poem "The Kermess," based on Breughel's depiction of a peasant wedding. Listen to Hardy as he recalls a country world gone these fifty years. This is not your lounge-lizard scene in downtown Prague or some smoky jazz bar on 53rd Street, but something older, a place where Clym Yeobright or Falstaff might have come to spend an evening, a place you might still find, say, on the Dingle Peninsula or at Land's End in Cornwall:

> Sweet cyder is a great thing,
>   A great thing to me,
> Spinning down to Weymouth town
>   By Ridgway thirstily,
> And maid and mistress summoning
>   Who tend the hostelry:
> O cyder is a great thing,
>   A great thing to me!

The effect is rollicking and exuberant, a celebration, quite simply, of life itself. The second stanza continues and heightens the celebration, as Hardy remembers those all-night dances in midsummer, breaking up finally only as the sun came up. And so from maid and mistress to a fit dancing partner and on to love itself in the third stanza, with its memory of a sweet assignation out under the night sky of Dorset, where a young woman moves "Out from the nearest tree" at midnight to meet her lover. Who is this woman, the biographer wants to know, anxious to give her a name and an airy destination. But of this the old man himself is silent. Enough that he was there. And she. And then, in the final stanza, Hardy bows once more to Time. True, all of this has ended or will end, we know, because there is of course the One who will one day call, and soon now: "Soul, I have need of thee." What then, when your time is up? What then? And what does Hardy do? Why, he repeats again what he has already enumerated: expectation, wine, woman, and song, and "Love, and its ecstasy." It is a more human and more satisfying consummation surely than what we find in "The Convergence of the Twain," though he knows that all of this—the fact and even the memory of it—must someday roll on into the distant past. And yet he allows the last line to continue sounding a lingering musical note. How great to have tasted such pleasure at all, he insists. How few of our modern poets have touched that note of joy, poignant and fleeting. And yet it is also true, Hardy tells us, that as long as we can recall it, we can relive something of its joy. And when we cannot, it will no longer matter.

A final poem. Part of a series of poems Hardy found himself writing in the weeks and months and years following the death of his first wife, Emma Gifford. He first met Emma, the poems tell us, in rural Cornwall while doing restoration work on a parish church, and it seems clear that Emma and Hardy felt a strong mutual attraction from the first. As Hardy came to know Emma and she him, it is true, each became increasingly more disenchanted with the other until finally they were like two ghosts inhabiting the same house, barely speaking to each other. What had seemed at first whimsical and fresh and worldly in Emma came in time to pale as Hardy met more and more sophisticated women from the middle and upper classes. These he pursued in letters and fantasies, sometimes finding a response in return, more often not.

In time Emma of course came to feel these rebuffs, turning more and more to her fundamentalist brand of religion and to food and other consolations, even as her husband immersed himself in his writing, his contacts, and in gray philosophy. That is, when he wasn't fantasizing the perfect woman. As Emma became heavier and alas more grotesque looking, she began dressing in a younger and younger style, until in her late sixties she was wearing white wide muslin dresses and blue sashes in the fashion of a Victorian schoolgirl.

For his part Hardy became thinner and harder and more bitter. Often one could see the two of them riding their newfangled bicycles past the houses where Hardy's relatives lived, though neither Emma nor Hardy any longer acknowledged them. Slowly, inevitably, the two of them became "Two golden gourds . . . splashed with frost, / Distorted by hale fatness, turned grotesque / . . . Washed into rinds by rotting winter rains," as a much younger Stevens would write of his own strained marriage a few years later.

And then, suddenly, Emma was gone. On a late November morning in 1912, she turned to the wall and breathed her last, leaving Hardy— as she had become accustomed to doing in life—without so much as a good-bye. Only this time she would not be back. Informed by the maid of his wife's death, Hardy was dumbstruck. Worst, and most unexpectedly, despite all the disappointments he had suffered in his marriage, he began remembering Emma now as he had first known her: a beautiful, vivacious young woman riding a horse over the cliffs of Beeney in far-off Cornwall in that splendid summer of 1870. Within months the seventy-three-year-old Hardy took his brother back to Cornwall to revisit the places where he had first met Emma: the inn where he'd stayed on his way west, the parsonage where she'd lived with her sister and her sister's husband, the caves and cliffs and other Cornwall landscapes. He became haunted by his wife as he had known her then, when the world was young and he unknown, with the best of life still before him, and a woman riding a horse with abandon, her hair blowing across her flushed cheeks.

The twenty-one poems Hardy called, simply, "Poems of 1912–1913," make up one of the most moving love sequences in the language, though the actual number of poems recalling moments with his wife that he wrote over the last fifteen years of his life is closer to one hundred. By then he was married to his second wife, a woman who'd been his secretary and who was half his age. Let us look at one of these poems. Not one of the 1912–13 sequence, but one clearly related to it in theme and subject. It's called "The Shadow on the Stone" and was begun in the months following Emma's death, though not completed for another three years.

The place is Max Gate, the brick house with turret that Hardy designed and built and where he and Emma lived for the last thirty years of their married life. The setting of the poem is simple enough. The poet has gone out to the old Druid stone behind the house. Obsessed by old things English, the England of the druids, of Stonehenge, of the Roman occupation, the England of Arthur and Camelot, he notices the shadows playing on the stone from the trees behind him as they toss in the autumn wind. The scene is wintry and the poet alone. In another time, he thinks, his dead wife would have been outdoors gardening.

Then he wonders. Is the shadow he sees playing on the druid stone possibly her shadow? And if so, is she standing at this moment there behind him? So great is his desire that she be there that he begins speaking to her, the way an old man will, though he is unwilling to turn, lest he discover what he fears: that she is not there after all. It is because his mind *knows* she cannot be there that he is tempted to turn and confirm the stark truth. And yet he cannot do this because he needs her to be somehow, impossibly, there for him.

The story is as old as Lot's wife, who—when Lot turned to see if his wife was there—saw her changed to a pillar of salt for his presumption in turning. It is the story too of Orpheus turning, only to see his dear Eurydice fading back forever into the depths of hell. And so Hardy refuses to turn. Instead, he walks softly from the glade, unwilling to "unvision" a shape he knows cannot be there, but hoping, as he said in "The Oxen," another poem of lost faith, that "it might be so." These poems to a lost wife and a lost opportunity to love broke my heart when I first read them thirty years ago, and they go on breaking my heart whenever I read them now. I am sure they also broke his, even as they helped him face the growing darkness. Few poets have given us anything like this sequence and its aftermath. Frost, perhaps, in one or two poems written in the years following his wife's death. But who else?

Hardy is an extraordinary figure, in large part because he seems to stand off to the side and to expect so little from us. Here are the poems, he seems to say. Take them or leave them. Or come back to them in ten or twenty years, when you are ready. If this one doesn't speak to you, no matter. Try another. After all, the world is deep and varied enough. Here, look them over, he seems like Frost to say, and drink, be whole again, beyond confusion.

1995

Hart Crane

"Clenched Beaks Coughing for the Surge Again"

❧

UNDOUBTEDLY EVERY POET has at some time experienced it and most have written of it: a dry time, when words refuse themselves, a time when everything seems dust. Hopkins, in the last months of his life, calling on God to send his roots rain. Yeats, nearing the end, cataloging the myths that had sustained his poetry for fifty years, only to watch as his circus animals—his high subject matter and his themes— one by one began deserting him. Williams, broken by a stroke, wondering if the shadowy deathlike figure curled up on the bridge between Texas and Mexico—"interjurisdictional"—wasn't after all the mirror image of himself.

So, too, with Hart Crane, in his powerful lyric "O Carib Isle!", standing before a graveyard on the Isle of Pines (off the southern coast of Cuba) in the late summer of 1926, having just turned twenty-seven, and wondering—as Whitman sixty years before him had in "As I Ebb'd with the Ocean of Life"—whether the whole project of poetry—including his long project, *The Bridge*, envisioned as the positive to Eliot's despairing vision in *The Waste Land*—would ever amount to anything more than a futile exhalation of air.

It's a poem about poetry, questioning the efficacy of language and metaphor to transform the quotidian bread of existence into something more. And so it begins by questioning Emerson's idea of a correspondence between nature and meaning, including the very notion of meaning itself. It opens with a hostile nature, feverishly hissing:

143

> The tarantula rattling at the lily's foot
> Across the feet of the dead, laid in white sand
> Near the coral beach.

The lines are like blank verse, but more irregular, flatter, even disso-nant. That lily may be there to remember the resurrection of the dead, but it is the tarantula that dominates the scene. It and the white sand and the coral beach made up of the remains of millions upon millions of once-living creatures reduced now to this white death.

There are fiddler crabs too to contend with, which likewise seem out to subvert the poet's attempts to create an order out of words. Instead, they merely leave illegible markings in the sand as they "side-stilt" across the beach. More, they actually seem intent to "shift, sub-vert," and "anagrammatize" Crane's name, and with it, his very iden-tity. More, they mock his attempts to order the world, rewriting his script and the traditional power of the poet to call things by their liv-ing names. Even Crane's name is reshuffled here, anagrammatized into "Nacre"—mother-of-pearl. By providing us with the adjectival form of "nacre" in the ninth line—"nacreous frames of tropic death"—Crane sees that all life is eventually metamorphosed into white death: limestone, coral, bone, the "Brutal necklaces of shells" that frame and mock these graves. At the same time he provides an image of poetry's ultimate entropy. Poetry does, after all, come down—as the title of his first book of poems, published that fall, reminds us—to a series of "nacreous frames of tropic death." In other words, the ultimate "white buildings" of gravestones. Keats's empty urns.

Nothing mourns the passing of life here in the tropics, Crane feels. And beyond there is also the undifferentiating sea always somewhere near to swallow one. In Crane's negative Mallarméan syntax, "neither" is actually the unspoken first word of the poem, the stripped syntax reading, "Neither the tarantula, . . . nor the zigzag crabs . . . mourn." In fact, nothing mourns the passing of life here, nothing "Below the palsy that one eucalyptus lifts / In wrinkled shadows." Even the euca-lyptus seems whitened by ague and fever, as it shimmers in the intense noonday heat, itself become an image of hell (hell: backformed on the

Greek *kalyptos*, meaning something hidden, concealed, like its cousin, crypt, *kryptos*, later in the poem).

Against nature's gargantuan pressure to white out all human meaning and human feeling, Crane has no recourse but to either surrender to or answer that pressure with the pressure of the human imagination. Recall Stevens's concluding words from "The Noble Rider and the Sound of Words": "The mind has added nothing to human nature. It is a violence from within that protects us from a violence without. It is the imagination pressing back against the pressure of reality . . . help[ing] us to live our lives." Like Adam in the garden making the world in his own image, Crane too will name, though to be sure he no longer has Adam's assurance that there is any correspondence between the things he names and the names and music at his disposal. Words, he has been warned by the philosopher Oswald Spengler, whom he has just read, have become strangers to the world beyond. And yet to name—to utter "Tree names, flower names" deliberately, in the teeth of indifferent nature—is all the poet can do to "gainsay" for a little while "death's brittle crypt," which is also "death's brittle script."

Crypt, kryptos: something hidden. A key concept for Crane, as for all the Romantics. Bodies hidden, meanings concealed. The dead tell no secrets, Crane knows, though—as he had already noted in "At Melville's Tomb"—they maddeningly intimate them, much as seashells, washed up on the beach, hint at the secrets of the great sea and so of our origins and of our destinies. Against our feeble utterances, our little namings, our tiny exhalations of clicking syllables, our beating of the gums, Crane places a version of the vast Sublime in the tropic wind that, like some great serpent, "knots itself in one great death— / Coils and withdraws."

A great wind preparing to strike, then striking, then withdrawing. *Ananke* (fate, necessity). Hurricane season in the tropics. When Crane began writing this poem in late August, the hurricane that would render unlivable the house where he was staying was still two months away. But when the cataclysm struck, Crane spent the night under the bed with "Aunt Sally" Simpson, the elderly caretaker of the estate, along with her parrot, Attaboy, while above them the ceiling plaster buckled and caved, the roof screamed as it peeled loose, and two-by-fours were wind-hammered six feet into the ground at a single stroke. Next morning Crane would watch horrified as a donkey, near death, staggered blindly out of the jungle and collapsed. That one night was enough to remind him that nature could reduce even the strongest to ruin. A force not unlike the vast and terrifying aurora borealis in Stevens's late "Auroras of Autumn," or the eruption of Mt. Pelée that, Williams recalled in his poem "Catastrophic Birth," had wiped out his mother's French relatives.

Indeed, Crane's hurricane doubles in the closing lines of his poem *as* a volcano, leaving the poet and his words mere shells cast up in the aftermath of its demonic passing:

> Slagged of the hurricane—I, cast within its flow,
> Congeal by afternoons here, satin and vacant.
> You have given me the shell, Satan,—carbonic amulet
> Sere of the sun exploded in the sea.

But if these are the poem's final words, at least the poet is a living witness to nature's violent passing, and in the process he has managed to hear—and even to record—something of the glory of the Sublime. He sees in nature no "Captain," no God, no ordering principle on "this doubloon isle / Without a turnstile." For really there seems no way in, no way of reaching a deeper understanding of the world. This world belongs finally not to him but to those "catchword crabs" scuttling about in the underbrush, repeating the same, unvarying sounds ad nauseam, until the crabs themselves become anagrammatizations (crab/Carib) for the experience of the place itself. What vision is possible, he laments, where his own eyes have been "webbed," "baked," and then "ambushed" and where his ideas of order, shaped by images of Ohio and New York, have been rendered void.

And yet something in Crane continues to cry out. "Let fiery blossoms clot the light," he prays now, and "render my ghost." The phrase is suggestive, and means not only a melting down and transformation, but a delivering of one's spirit over. In fact, it recalls—a favorite with

Crane—Christ's final agonizing cry from the cross to be delivered into the Father's hands. Crane's spirit, then, "Sieved upwards . . . Until it meets the blue's comedian host." In spite of the absence of any captain, Crane's prayer—the cry of this prisoner in his "black and white" uniform in a black-and-white world—strikes us all the more for that with its force and vulnerability. We want that cry of utter destitution, I think, to be answered. And, in fact, it is.

For now Crane gives utterance to five of the most powerful lines in all of modern poetry. These lines—four of which rhyme on a single note—are the cry of the pilgrim, a prayer, a petition, a striving for eloquence, a desire to hear the mighty strain of the Sublime again. Longer than blank verse, these epic lines interlaced with stately spondees. Marlovian lines now, as Crane sees himself like those sea turtles, pulled up from their hidden sea world to be bound, spiked, eviscerated—crucified—along the wharves of the world's marketplace each morning, their eyes caked by bitter salt, reminding him of their—and his—lost world.

"Such thunder in their strain," the poet cries, marveling as these strange visionaries strain, like Crane himself, to sing in an otherworldly strain of music something of what they have seen and lost, their "clenched beaks coughing for the surge again!" Though they cannot tell us what they have seen, Crane makes us feel something of the unearthly music these creatures have heard, and which they manifest now in their stifled cries. It is something of what we, too, must feel here, in the majestic music Crane has managed to render in these lines, even as the poet too is slowly eviscerated by self-torment and an indifferent world. It is the trembling, electric surge and majesty of a vision toward which the poem, made up of clenched words, can only gesture. A hint, then, of that unheard music Crane somehow heard, this "nacreous frame" of words called "O Carib Isle!" netting something of that thunder in the strain of his own haunting lines.

1995

Skyscraper Soup

Two Views of Twenties New York

❧

SKYSCRAPER SOUP: John Marin's watercolors of lower New York, Alfred Stieglitz's Flatiron Building and the canyoned high rises of midtown Manhattan, Georgia O'Keefe's white skyscrapers against a nightblue sky. Langston Hughes's blues and jazz-drenched 125th Street, the Greenwich Village of Mina Loy and Marianne Moore, of Lola Ridge and E. E. Cummings. Wallace Stevens applauding the Dadaesque vision of the Baroness Elsa von Freytag Loringhoven, before she chased him up past 14th Street, so that he avoided the Village for years, as William Carlos Williams remembered with a laugh four decades later. Dos Passos's *Manhattan Transfer* and F. Scott Fitzgerald's Gatsby and Edmund Wilson's urbane *New Yorker* prose and García Lorca's salute to the teeming democracy of the city. George Antheil at the Carnegie, all-night jam sessions at the Cotton Club. Images in paint and music and words that make up our idea of New York seventy-five years ago.

Add to the mix the poems and prose of William Carlos Williams and Hart Crane, the poet from Jersey and the wonder boy from Cleveland, who saw two New Yorks from widely differing angles. Call it the East and West of it. Two competing visions and the two languages by which these two musicked the impossible city, the white anemone (roots and gutters and all) rising out of the two rivers that encircle the island. Williams across the Hudson in the Meadowlands fronting his hometown of Rutherford. Hart Crane inhabiting a half-dozen brownstones in the Village, or later, across the East River, over on Columbia Heights, both men gazing, each from his own perspective, at the brilliant white buildings erotically charged in the shimmering distance.

Each knew the existence of the other as far back as 1916, when the precocious Hart Crane—then seventeen and still living in Cleveland—sent the thirty-three-year-old Williams some poems for a new magazine Williams and Alfred Kreymborg and Maxwell Bodenheim were putting together over in Grantwood in a group of cottages on the New Jersey Palisades, a magazine meant to rival *Poetry* (Chicago) and called—simply—*Others*. Williams liked Crane's stuff, but—he'd had to explain—the magazine itself had fallen on hard times (as most of the little magazines had, or would), and so no chance there for publishing.

There was one other early moment of contact between Crane and Williams, which came a few years later when Crane convinced Williams to buy a painting by a local artist from south of Cleveland whom Crane was championing: Bill Sommers. Williams liked one of Sommers's paintings: a quirky landscape that had somehow gotten—as he phrased it—under his drawers. And soon it found its way into Williams's study, alongside work by Charles Demuth and Charles Scheeler, two of Williams's pals.

But the real exchange between Williams and Crane did not occur until after the publication of Crane's first book of poems, *White Buildings*, published in late 1926. Then Crane became not just another poet, but a New York poet, and someone—as Williams's New York friends reminded him—to be reckoned with. Of course by then Williams and Crane had been watching each other for several years. Crane had read and enjoyed Williams's experimental prose poem *Kora in Hell* when it was published in 1920, then *Spring & All* in 1923 and—two years later—*In the American Grain*, a book that, in spite of Crane's denials, helped shape *The Bridge*, his epic of America. He was also following Williams's work in the little magazines, much as Williams was following Crane's: magazines on cheap paper often, some published sporadically, in New York, Paris, Berlin, London. And as the 1920s wore on, it became clearer that the two men were lining up in opposing camps, each bent on creating a very different kind of poetry. Each used

Whitman, that other New York poet, as a club with which to beat the other over the head. Reading Whitman, Crane told Yvor Winters in late 1926, one sensed one was in the presence of a poet destined for the ages. Reading Williams, on the other hand, one too often felt in the presence not of someone who wrote poems addressed to the Sublime but, rather, to the household gods only. Though he could see that Williams was a generous man who could appreciate "the best that is given him," he was also a poet who managed only to dramatize "trifles in the classic manner of the old Chinese poets . . . occasionally giving a metaphysical twist to his experience." But, Crane wondered, was that enough?

The story of these two men taking each other's measure—and of what that portended for the direction American poetry would take—is a fascinating one, and it is a story I have tried to tell from the two sides in two different biographies written two decades apart: *A New World Naked* and *The Broken Tower*. And as a biographer you learn that it makes all the difference which side you choose to approach your subject from. To begin with, as Whitman's heirs, both wanted to become—like Frost, Pound, and Cummings—the quintessential American poet.

With his painter's eye, trained to see not only as Scheeler and Demuth and Marsden Hartley saw, but as Picasso and Braque and Juan Gris had rearranged the world, Williams focused on the shimmering edges of the world around him. His language is the language he heard about him, but heightened by measure and shaped by the inherent music of what he called the American idiom, a music different in rhythm and tempo from the English language of the schools. For all its apparent simplicity, Williams's idiom is complex and polyphonic, full of hundreds of little surprises in its typographical makeup. It would have its own complex of allusions, many of them so subtly placed that most readers are still not even aware that the plain language he employed can carry so much literary resonance.

Because he saw himself as Whitman's disciple, Williams would focus on the specific weight of the multifoliate catalog of discrete things that made up his world. And he would write about them in a language far less overtly rhetorical and closer to the living speech of his own corner of America: New York City and northern New Jersey. Yes, he would use symbols, though he continued more or less to distrust them, viewing them as washing over the things of the world and staining them with a quasi-religious weight. For the same reason he feared Eliot's Prufrock and especially *The Waste Land*, with its six languages, including Greek and Sanskrit, and its heavy symbolic allusiveness, which netted everything into its lines from the Bible to Petronius to Dante to jazz, and seemed to demand a world of footnotes to be explicated and referenced. Williams knew that what Eliot had done with *The Waste Land* was to make of poetry a kind of academic cottage industry and, in doing so, had become the darling of the universities. And in large part Williams was right. His own strategy would be instead to use a kind of radical metonymy, where the specifics of a scene—random though they might appear—would point to a larger design and, beyond that, to a brave new world.

Which is why Williams also distrusted and feared Hart Crane. Crane, he was convinced, was—finally—Eliot's American disciple, even as Eliot was a disciple of Mallarmé and the nineteenth-century French *symbolistes*. And *that* way, Williams was convinced, spelled the death of an indigenous American poetry. The analogy between American jazz and European music is not irrelevant here. Worse was the transcendent strain Williams heard in Eliot and Crane: a real churchgoing organ music underlying the lines—many of them blank verse lines, which properly belonged to Shakespeare and the Elizabethans but not to the realities of twentieth-century America. Such music, Williams and his sometime friend and compatriot Ezra Pound were convinced—no longer belonged. Didn't Crane understand there was a revolution in the arts going on below (and above) 14th Street? As problematic as Cummings might be as a poet, at least he was trying to break the old poetic lineup with every typographical trick at his disposal (though, thanks to a classical training at Harvard, somehow the blank-verse virus seemed to stick to his poems in spite of himself).

In his thirties Williams had had to reimagine himself. In the decade between 1910 and 1920 he went from the pale Romanticism of *Palgrave's*

Treasury to become a disciple of Pound, imitating Pound's Brown-ingesque phase, then his Chinese phase and Imagist phases. For a solid year—from the fall of 1917 to the fall of 1918—he wrote furiously in a kind of automatic style, pounding away at his typewriter to get down on the page whatever came into his head, only editing the mass of words afterward. The book that resulted from that experiment was *Kora in Hell*, his prose improvisations, a book Pound dismissed as little more than a pastiche of Rimbaud, served up forty years late. Still, the experiment had freed up Williams, making him aware that what you did when you wrote was to use words—so many paint daubs or lin-guistic counters moved about here and there as freely as the imagina-tion dictated. It was a strategy that led directly to his real breakthrough volume, *Spring & All*, published in Paris in 1923 in a princely edition of three hundred copies by his friend and sometime collaborator, Robert McAlmon.

But what a book it was, this celebration of the imagination, and in it Williams tried on many styles, the fractured and the classical side by side, doing with words what Gertrude Stein had done before him, herself taking her lead from the Cubists. Something was happening, Williams knew. He too had been swept up in a vortex of energies, a cold March wind whipping "dashes of cold rain" about, providing an energy not unlike what Marianne Moore had described in "The Fish," an energy at

> one with submarine vistas
> purple and black fish turning
> among undulant seaweed—

Yes, there was a revolution going on, a revolution Williams was happy to be involved in. Yet even Pound often slipped back into the past, as he had in his classic renditions of the ancient Chinese poetry, which now Williams questioned:

> The grief of the bowmen of Shu
> moves nearer—There is
> an approach with difficulty from

the dead—the winter casing of grief
How easy to slip
into the old mode, how hard to
cling firmly to the advance. . . .

Which was why Crane—who for his part had turned resolutely *to* the past—remained so anathema to Williams. Walking across Brooklyn Bridge hand in hand with his sailor lover, Crane had envisioned his overleaping bridge as a rainbow, a harp, a tower, a zodiac, a ship, a score of music written on the heavens, a sign, finally, of God's promise of eternal love. Having glimpsed all this, Crane found it necessary to create a language commensurate with his vision. And where else to locate such transcendence in language but in a return to the language's golden age, which Crane—with the help of T. S. Eliot—would locate among the linguistic marvels of Marlowe and Shakespeare and the other Elizabethans. No matter that the higher consciousness had been revealed to Crane along with the laughing gas he'd been given in a dentist's chair in Cleveland. What matter the specifics of the occasion? What *did* matter was that he had managed to touch the heavens and—having glimpsed a new world—he meant to get back there with whatever it took, whether through love, sex, alcohol, or poetry. And for a time all of these seemed to work.

Though he repeatedly denied it, Crane was essentially religious in his feelings, and he managed to get into his lines something of the intense and exalted feelings he'd experienced crossing his bridge with the wind whispering through the bound cables, the white buildings of lower Manhattan gleaming in the morning sun or winking like Christmas parcels on winter nights. To capture something of this rapture, he would employ a blank verse line that echoed Marlowe's, the name he gave himself when he was on the prowl for sailors over on Sands Street in Brooklyn, in the bars near the Fulton Fish Markets, or as far away as Hoboken:

> Through the bound cable strands, the arching path
> Upward, veering with light, the flight of strings,—

Taut miles of shuttling moonlight syncopate
The whispered rush, telepathy of wires.
Up the index of night, granite and steel—
Transparent meshes—fleckless the gleaming staves—
Sibylline voices flicker, waveringly stream
As though a god were issue of the strings. . . .

And through that cordage, threading with its call
One arc synoptic of all tides below—
Their labyrinthine mouths of history
Pouring reply as though all ships at sea
Complighted in one vibrant breath made cry,—
"Make thy love sure—to weave whose song we ply!"

Here was a vision of New York rendered transcendently, and for one
three-day stretch, while he got his vision of New York as the new Atlantis down on paper, Crane forgot time itself. For three days, he reported afterward, he'd been transported in a way he would never be
again. Years later he would look at what he'd written then and wonder
at what he must have felt to have achieved language of that musical and
symbolic complexity. Something like it—less intense, perhaps—but
lengthened across a three-month stretch—would come again on the
Isle of Pines off the southern coast of Cuba in the summer and fall of
1926, when he wrote—among so many other extraordinary poems—
his "Proem: To Brooklyn Bridge":

How many dawns, chill from his rippling rest
The seagull's wings shall dip and pivot him,
Shedding white rings of tumult, building high
Over the chained bay waters Liberty. . . .

O harp and altar, of the fury fused,
(How could mere toil align thy choiring strings!)
Terrific threshold of the prophet's pledge,
Prayer of pariah, and the lover's cry,—

Again the traffic lights that skim thy swift
Unfractioned idiom, immaculate sigh of stars,

Beading thy path—condense eternity:
And we have seen night lifted in thine arms. . . .

O Sleepless as the river under thee,
Vaulting the sea, the prairies' dreaming sod,
Unto us lowliest sometime sweep, descend
And of the curveship lend a myth to God.

But he would also learn despair, a despair as deep as any Eliot had experienced in *The Waste Land*, the poem *The Bridge* had been meant to counter. "O Carib Isle!", that meditation on death and emptiness, provides one example, "The Tunnel" another. There, the poet would ride the New York subways alone at midnight. It became for him his own vision of hell, where he would discover, not Whitman this time, but Whitman's dark opposite, Poe, his disembodied head swinging from a strap, the mouth contorted in a cry of agony, the agate lights of the track signals reflecting off the subway windows a sign of the terrible emptying of the poet's vision. The ultimate fate, then, of the American visionary, a premonition of what was waiting out there for him as his life spun more and more out of control.

But Crane could also do the police in different voices when he needed, as he demonstrated in "Cutty Sark" and "The River" and again in "The Tunnel," imitating the speech he'd heard around him in the bars or among the drifters one constantly jostled up against in New York. Unlike Williams, who used the idiom to express the world of his Polish mothers, Crane used it for his gamblers, johns, and prostitutes. In "Cutty Sark" he encounters a drunken sailor in a South Street bar at two in the morning. It is something out of his friend Eugene O'Neill's world, the Ancient Mariner turned psychotic:

"It's *S.S. Ala*—Antwerp—now remember kid
to put me out at three she sails on time.
I'm not much good at time any more keep
weakeyed watches sometimes snooze"—his bony hands
got to beating time . . . "A whaler once—
I ought to keep time and get over it—I'm a

Democrat—I know what time it is—No
I don't want to know what time it is—that
damned white Arctic killed my time."

Or this, a numbers man overheard on the Lexington Avenue IRT, from
"The Tunnel":

Let's have a pencil, Jimmy—living now
At Floral Park
Flatbush—on the fourth of July—
Like a pigeon's muddy dream—potatoes
to dig in the field—travlin the town—too—
night after night—the Culver line—the
girls all shaping up—it used to be—

And this, streetwalker's speech at midnight on the Emperor's empty
pavement:

[W]hat do you want? Getting weak on the links?
fandaddle daddy don't ask for change—IS THIS
FOURTEENTH? it's half past six she said—if
You don't like my gate why did you
swing on it, why didja
swing on it
anyhow—

Still, such language is more the exception, a bow toward Cummings
and Williams. For Williams, on the other hand, such speech was central to his insistence on raising the idiom to the level of the imagination. It is, after all, our language: raw, undisciplined, but full of radiant
promise in the hands of the right poet. Speed, energy, the rapid transfer of light from line to line, image to image, thought to thought, the
resonances coming from the intersection of words at white heat, without rhetorical connectives. Here is a comic meditation from *Spring &
All*, on the crossover from life into easeful death, likened to a trip up
to the pastoral Bronx, replete with maps and subway ads:

Somebody dies every four minutes
in New York State—

To hell with you and your poetry—
You will rot and be blown

through the next solar system
with the rest of the gases—

What the hell do you know about it?

AXIOMS

Don't get killed

Careful Crossing Campaign
Cross Crossings Cautiously

THE HORSES   black
                             &
PRANCED   white

Outings in New York City

Ho for the open country

Don't stay shut up in hot rooms
Go to one of the Great Parks
Pelham Bay for example

It's on Long Island Sound
with bathing, boating
tennis, baseball, golf, etc.

Acres and acres of green grass
Wonderful shade trees, rippling brooks

     Take the Pelham Bay Park Branch
     of the Lexington Ave. (East Side)
     Line and you are there in a few
     minutes

Interborough Rapid Transit Co.

A little false, Williams would write, dreaming of Manhattan from
the Jersey side of the Hudson, those white buildings gleaming in the

afternoon sun, promising love, fame, poetry, and the illusion of freedom. The great buildings across the river, life below 14th Street, the
New World's cultural Mecca beckoning, and just a car or train ride
away. He'd gone to school there—the Horace Mann School on the upper West Side—travelling there from Rutherford. He'd been part of
the Village scene, had acted opposite Mina Loy down on Macdougal
Street—in the same theater that housed Eugene O'Neill's Province-
town Players—in a weird one-act play called *Lima Beans* that Alfred
Kreymborg had put together, a farce satirizing married life.

Once, a few blocks away, he'd been transfixed by Mayakovsky's Russian poetry at one of Lola Ridge's soirées. He'd visited Marianne Moore
and E. E. Cummings here, seen Wallace Stevens and Marcel Duchamp
and made love in an apartment to Evelyn Scott, novelist and erstwhile
mistress of Thomas Merton's father. In his fortieth year he would think
back to his younger self at twenty-four, working long hours as an intern
at the French Hospital on 34th Street, when he'd had an affair with a
young nurse by the name of Margaret Blake Purvis. A girl, he would
remember with regret, whom he had loved and then lost touch with,
the memory of her become now part of the skyscraper soup that was
the city he carried in his head:

> Wrigley's, appendicitis, John Marin:
> skyscraper soup—
>
> Either that or a bullet!
>
> Once
> anything might have happened
> You lay relaxed on my knees—
> the starry night
> spread out warm and blind
> above the hospital . . .
>
> In my life the furniture eats me
>
> the chairs, the floor
> the walls

which heard your sobs
drank up my emotion—
they which alone know everything

and snitched on us in the morning . . .

breasts to see, white and blue—
to hold in the hand, to nozzle

It is not onion soup
Your sobs soaked through the walls
breaking the hospital to pieces . . .

           I   watched!

Clean is he alone
after whom stream
the broken pieces of the city—
flying apart at his approaches

but I merely
caress you curiously

fifteen years ago and you still
go about the city, they say
patching up sick school children.

Like Crane, Williams's poems can also break your heart. It is the city that lures, that promises, and then smashes those promises. Besides, Williams came to see, New York was just too big, too great for any one individual to make his or her own, and so he would turn to the local once again, to the streets of Rutherford and Garfield and Passaic and the city of Paterson and its language, whose falls haunted him all his life as if they were God whispering to him.

It is part of the record what the two men thought of each other. If on several occasions Crane sought Williams out, Williams usually stayed shy, in part because of Crane's reputation as a tough homosexual, a damaged archangel who was not adverse to getting into bar fights. But the real issue was that each had his own idea of what American poetry should be, and neither believed the other was on the right track. For Crane, Williams was forever beginning again, the quickchange artist who picked up and discarded styles with dizzying speed, alternately playing the war-whooping tough and the hairshirt sentimentalist.

For Williams, Crane had gone wrong practically from the start. If Crane was right, Williams told Pound in 1927, then his own search for an American idiom was wrong. Not that he believed for a minute that he was in the wrong. Besides, he had longevity on his side: the 1930s and 1940s and 1950s in which to develop and add to his sizable body of work, and very impressive work at that. Soon after Crane jumped to his death from the stern of the S.S. *Orizaba* in April 1932, Williams offered his assessment of Crane's work. There were marvelous things in the poetry, Williams was willing to acknowledge, as in those poems in *White Buildings* where one heard "the sound of continual surf" running through them ("Repose of Rivers," perhaps, or "At Melville's Tomb," or the "Voyages" sequence), with the "alternate peak and back rush of waves in them." Still, Williams could not help feeling that here was poetry put together as much to please the editor of some New York Sunday supplement as for anything else. Mostly the poems were a "direct step backward to the bad poetry of any age but especially to the triumphant regression" of the French *symbolistes* who had followed Whitman, by whom Williams meant Mallarmé. It was a style that had come to a head in the work of the one poet Williams disliked and distrusted more than any other: T. S. Eliot.

The result—Williams believed—was that by 1930, with the publication of *The Bridge*, Crane had come to a dead-end in his life as in his writing. Crane had tried it all ways, Williams summed up, writing his poems "right and left, front and back, up and down and round in a circle both ways, criss cross and at varying speeds," until he'd exhausted his options, and himself in the process. By the time Crane had hit thirty he'd depleted the possibilities of his elevated idiom. It was a language that had given out just as the 1920s themselves had given way to the Depression. The way New York's glimmering Woolworth tower had bowed to the Empire State Building, and the quaint gothic towers of Brooklyn Bridge had in time been dwarfed by the modern steel towers of the George Washington Bridge, which now bound New York not to Brooklyn but to Williams's home territory. "A petal, colorless and without form," Williams wrote the same year *The Bridge* was published, watching *his* bridge go up along the northern end of Manhattan:

> The oblong towers lie
> beyond the low hill and northward the great
> bridge stanchions,
> small in the distance, have appeared,
> pinkish and incomplete—
> It is the city,
> approaching over the river. Nothing
> of it is mine, but visibly
> for all that it is a petal of a flower—my own.
> It is a flower through which the wind
> combs the whitened grass and a black dog
> with yellow legs stands eating from a
> garbage barrel.

No transcendence there. No ideas but in things themselves. "This / is no more a romance than an allegory," Williams closed his own poem. There it was: the sheer necessity to write, to get it down, his flower, his bridge, his world, without benefit of Hart Crane, or the bridge over on the East River Crane had tried to turn into a myth of God. "I plan one thing," the exasperated, bull-headed poet from New Jersey ended, not yet there but unwilling to quit:

> That I could press
> buttons to do the curing or the caring for
> the sick that I do laboriously now by hand
> for cash, to have the time
> when I am fresh, in the morning, when
> my mind is clear and burning—to write.

Still, would we not be the poorer without them both, for between them have they not managed to give us two compelling images of New York? There is the city's transcendent aspirations glimpsed in those wintry seagulls swirling high above the Brooklyn Bridge, a sense of wonder that, in spite of the thousands of images television and the movies offer us, the bridge still manages to summon up for us.

On the other hand there is too the city's swirling demotic energies, its Yiddish and African American and Spanish and Italian and Polish and Arabic and Chinese all mixing with the basic English staple. Stir in the painters and appendicitis and Wrigley's Spearmint, and Broadway and the Battery and 14th and 125th and the jazz clubs, and you have something of the skyscraper soup Williams's poems capture. And these too offer their own heady momentary lift, their own glittering grasshopper transcendences.

1999

Frost among the Poets

꧁

"People who read me seem to be divided into four groups," Robert Frost summed himself up in 1958, when he was already in his mid-eighties and concluding an extraordinary career as the most popular poet this nation has yet produced. "Twenty-five percent like me for the right reasons; twenty-five percent like me for the wrong reasons; twenty-five percent hate me for the wrong reasons; twenty-five percent hate me for the right reasons. It's that last twenty-five percent that worries me." Well, here it is, the 125th anniversary year of Frost's birthday, and I am here to tell you that it is also possible for one person to contain all four groups in one bifurcated and divided self.

I came of age in a time and in a place when Frost's reputation seemed already to belong to the past. One could, it seemed, relegate the old man to a status at once literary and historical: a regional New England poet who wrote of a farming world long since in decline. It was a world that seemed to have little to do with the mean streets of New York City and the sprawling, freshly minted suburbs of Long Island, places where I grew up in the 1940s and 1950s. When my family moved from a New York tenement to Levittown fifty years ago, I watched the last of the old potato farms, along with their houses and barns, go under month after month to omnivorous bulldozers, to be replaced in rapid order by thousands of cape cods and ranch-style homes.

By the time I graduated high school in 1958, Frost had long been apotheosized into the best-known American poet in our high-school curriculum, a curriculum that in any case was never very strong in poetry. The other presences were Whitman and Dickinson and one whose reputation has since slipped into near-oblivion: Longfellow. Everyone of course had by then at least heard of Frost. I can still recall the blue-backed textbook in my sophomore English class, and Frost's "Birches," which I read with interest, especially its description of those trees bent permanently by the long weight of snow, their tops trailing the ground like girls washing their hair. Until then, I'd never thought of those gracefully bent shapes in that metaphorical light. Even my father, who had grown up in New York's Little Italy, could quote a few lines from him. Somehow Frost attracted huge audiences wherever he went, having given us a fistful of poems where they would not be easily dislodged.

When I went on to Manhattan College in the Bronx, Frost had to contend in my imagination with the modernists, whom I had not read—or read in any systematic way—until then. Now he jostled with Yeats and Stevens, Pound and Eliot, Marianne Moore, Williams, and Hart Crane, as well as the younger poets who had come into their own since the war: Dylan Thomas, Auden, and the Beats.

In the winter of 1964, at Colgate, I took a cozy seminar in Hardy and Frost that met once a week, and spent that spring reading Frost's *Collected Poems*, including the Parnassian self-parodic work, as well as the boring and unworkable later masques. Our instructor was Russ Spears, an elderly, white-haired professor who wrote outrageous letters to the local newspapers under the pen-name J. Alfred Spenalzo, and who pretty much let his small class say whatever they pleased, provided the statement was general enough and inoffensive enough. Poetry was something to be enjoyed; it was certainly not to be overly scrutinized. Several times that semester we sipped our Frost with pale sherry. As usual, I was slow to pick up on the unspoken rule that poems were something that simply washed over one.

Once in particular, in the flush of my youthful inquisitorial mode, I crossed the line by questioning Frost's public persona, his Yankee chumminess, his "you come, too" stance, which did not sit easy with a New Yorker. It was at that point that Spears, peering over his glasses at me, suggested (very gently) that I relax. It was exactly the wrong advice for a twenty-three-year-old who had by then read *The Waste Land* and Joyce's *Ulysses* and who was out for blood. Or, if not that, to unravel the metaphysical secrets of the universe of literature as quickly as possible. Fresh from my courses in the Metaphysical poets and the modernists via T. S. Eliot, I was asking the wrong questions. Much of Frost's understanding of the human condition and of his vast indifferent universe did not register with me, and I—like others—mistook Frost's shuttlecock humor and slippery irony for solid ground. "I am never more serious than when I am joking," Frost had said on more than one occasion, and his speech cadences play over the lines, counterpointing them, like a current running against the main flow and creating a surprising dissonance of thought and expectation that can cut you off at the legs.

Here's the problem. I figured that if the woman in the clothing store who sold me chinos *and* the garrulous local postmaster could both think of Frost as the best poet they'd ever read, how good could the man really be? Besides, I could understand Frost. Good poetry, Empson and Tate and Eliot and Pound had drilled into me, was difficult. Good poetry meant far-reaching metaphor and classical allusions that required two-inch footnotes (the more the better). Good meant Greek tags and Sanskrit and Provençal, Li Po, Propertius, Flaubert. Good was the free-verse revolution, begun by Whitman and continued by Williams and Ginsberg until by sheer volume it had far outpaced formal verse in America by a ratio of ten to one. By the mid-1960s everyone, it seemed, had come over to the side of free verse. Only a handful of Americans seemed to write in rhymed forms anymore, a scattering of tall pines that had not yet succumbed to the tsunami of free verse.

I wrote a dissertation on Hopkins—that protomodern, as the thinking then went—which I revised and published. But of course the Jesuit Hopkins and the skeptical, self-questioning, self-lacerating Frost belonged to different universes, not only in temperament—the one undergoing a kenotic emptying of self, a self-effacement that might have left us no trace of his ever having been here, and Robert Frost, who thought hell a half-empty auditorium.

In 1967 I went looking for a teaching job. UMass-Amherst was expanding then, and the thought of moving from the gridlock of New York City vastly appealed. Once again, Frost's landscape of maple and birch and tobacco barn loomed, along with the idea of moving to the place that had provided so much of our classical American literature, from Anne Bradstreet to Emerson and Hawthorne, to Melville and Dickinson, as well as Lowell, Wilbur, Plath, and Sexton. And of course Robert Frost, who had once procured a very sweet deal with Amherst College, just down the road, where he taught the odd class, but mostly propounded to packed houses.

I taught the American modernists. That meant Stevens, who had attracted and puzzled me like some still-forming island glimpsed on the ocean's horizon for the past decade. It meant teaching the man who had championed so much of modern poetry, the controversial Pound. It meant Eliot and Prufrock and *The Waste Land*. It meant the dissociation of sensibility and tradition and the individual talent. It meant Hardy, Yeats, Auden, and Dylan Thomas, with a little Marianne Moore and D. H. Lawrence thrown in. Mostly, back then, it meant for me a comparatively new voice, about whom I knew almost nothing: Dr. William Carlos Williams of Rutherford, New Jersey.

But neither Frost nor Dickinson—those two Amherst presences— spoke to me as Williams and his epic, *Paterson*, did. Paterson—that New Jersey mill town fifteen miles west of the George Washington Bridge—had been a second home to me growing up. My relatives still lived there. My Swedish grandmother had worked there, my Polish grandfather had served as postmaster of Singac after returning, gassed, from the trenches in France, and my mother had been born in Clifton, which bleeds into Paterson. I myself had swum in the golden upper reaches of the Passaic under a canopy of maples. "The filthiest swill-hole in all Christendom," Williams had christened Paterson, and yet he spent a lifetime dreaming and writing about the place. Landscape is all, especially—I suppose—one's maternal landscape, as if that could be recovered. And yet here I was, having exiled myself from New York and New Jersey, hiking the hills of western Massachusetts in places like Wendell and the Quabbin Reservoir, with its second-growth trees reclaiming the old apple orchards and stone cellar holes on the outskirts of the five drowned towns. In other words, Robert Frost's world.

Thirty years ago, to follow Williams and the American idiom and the variable foot seemed to me at odds with what Frost was after. Frost (and I would have to add his Gardiner, Maine, neighbor, Edwin Arlington Robinson) came to look to me not like moderns but like protomoderns, poets who had come of age in an older time. Like Hardy they were the last proponents of formal verse, the worthy successors of Wordsworth and Shelley, of Browning and Tennyson. Frost was a pre-cubist. He had not shattered the surface, and for the most part he did not call attention to his liftings and borrowings from the classical and Romantic traditions. Like Robinson, he shaped well-made poems that seemed to explain themselves without the need of academic instructors such as I was destined to become.

Williams then was like found gold, his measure yet to be taken save by a handful of poets like Ginsberg and Lowell and Berryman and Robert Creeley. It meant a literary line that included Pound, Yeats, Eliot, Marianne Moore, Hart Crane, Gertrude Stein, Louis Zukofsky. It meant Cézanne, Juan Gris, Picasso, Mina Loy, Alfred Stieglitz, the Federalists, Washington, Burr, Père Sebastian Rasles. It meant too the dissonance of Georges Antheil, and fifty poets and writers who have all but disappeared from public consciousness. It certainly did not include Frost, who had summarily dismissed Williams as someone who wrote only "pips of poems," like "The Red Wheelbarrow."

But the two had far more in common than one might think: an intense interest in the nature of the poetic line, and of the way the spoken voice rides across the line, setting up a musical counterpoint. In Williams's case this was achieved (as with Whitman) by his phrasing— his New Jersey speech—with the shadow of the pentameter behind it. In Frost's it was achieved by a strong medial caesura that provides a signature tone in Frost, a kind of overriding idiomatic phrasing that we hear over and above the words themselves. This common music is a subtle thing, like language itself, often invisible or only semitransparent. But both poets possessed it, and each managed to make the American idiom his own.

Both their poems are filled with men and women: farmers and country folk in Frost (though his letters reveal his wide reading and wide travels, and his ability to catch the nuances not only of New Hampshire and Vermont but of New York and California and Virginia as well). In Williams it is the residents of northern New Jersey, of East Rutherford and Passaic and Garfield and Paterson, many of these people his own patients. But there are too the voices of Greenwich Village and Sutton Place and Harlem, the whole vast metropolis of New York. And then there are the immigrant accents of the Italian American community living south of him, or the Norwegian American accents of his wife's relatives.

Here's an example of the varieties of the American idiom. In the summer of 1946 Williams and his wife, Floss, vacationed in Shelburne Falls, a town twenty miles west of where I live. In letters and several essays, Williams talks about the language of the farmers he found in that area, a language so fresh and distinctive in its phrasing and idiom, so delicious, he found himself laughing with delight. And all this less than two hundred miles from his own home. When I was writing my biography of Williams, I asked a friend who had grown up in Shelburne Falls to accompany me when I went up there to try and locate exactly which landscapes along the Deerfield River Williams might have known.

My friend knew one old-timer who'd been farming up that way since the 1940s, and so we picked him up and began driving around, the farmer at the wheel and my friend up front with him. After a while they forgot all about my presence in the back seat and began talking in a kind of local shorthand that, try as I might, I could only follow by fits and starts. As I listened to the local dialect like Williams before me, I too began laughing with sheer delight at the inventiveness of what I was hearing, though afterward I could not for the love of me repeat what I had heard. It was like finding a fresh variety of the American idiom, as if one had recovered one of those two-hundred-plus varieties of apples that used to flourish in those ruined Massachusetts apple orchards and have since all but disappeared.

And yes, there is a downside to this search for the local idiom: a certain breathlessness, an exclamatory mode in Williams when he sees something that most of the rest of us do not see, and sees it with a kind of Zen clarity that catches most of us unawares. Williams really did catch the quotidian in this way, as if all creation were a constant surprise, unfolding before us in ways that were small Emersonian miracles. With Frost, it is a kind of down-home, subtly New England, dry and ironic voice, a half-playful, half-defensive mode that hides— often—an underlying insecurity and even fear, something Frost I think knew about himself. You know this voice. Pound has it too in a self-parodic way, as when, after twenty years in Europe, he tries on the American idiom in the *Pisan Cantos* and gives us at times his Idaho Ez voice. It is akin to the voice you hear in Frost's less successful, talky poems and masques, or sometimes in his letters, or often when he jokes before a packed auditorium. It is the voice of an intensely private man who has found a way of addressing a mob of strangers he must both entertain and keep at bay.

Most poets who have written about Frost have followed, not surprisingly, in his "formal" tradition. So, for instance, I have not found extensive comments on Frost by those in the free-verse camp, though this doesn't mean they haven't heard Frost. Ezra Pound may be the exception, but that is because Frost came to Pound at the very beginning of the poetic revolution, in London, approaching Pound (Frost's junior by eleven years) with hat in hand to ask for a favor at a time (1913) when Pound had influence with the British literary establishment and Frost did not. In short, Frost was hoping for a decent notice from a fellow American, and Pound managed to come up with a formulation that seems to have both appeased and enraged Frost. "Another American, found, as usual, on this side of the water, by an English publisher. . . . It's an old story." That was how Pound spread the news about Frost, in the process insulting his fellow Americans. Frost's first book—*A Boy's Will*—was, he noted, raw and filled with infelicities, and yet somehow it smacked of the New Hampshire woods. Where he most liked Frost, it seems, is where Frost sounded most like him.

Of Frost's second, groundbreaking volume, perhaps his finest book ever, *North of Boston*, Pound offered a comparison: Jane Austen's English backwater world and Stendhal's more cosmopolitan European grasp, where Frost stood in for Austen, and Pound for the Frenchman. "Professors to the contrary notwithstanding," Pound wrote, "no one expects Jane Austen to be as interesting as Stendhal. A book about a dull, stupid, hemmed-in sort of life, by a person who has lived it, will never be as interesting as the work of some author who has comprehended many men's manners and seen many grades and conditions of existence. But Mr. Frost's people are distinctly real. Their speech is real; he has known them. I don't want much to meet them, but I know that they exist, and what is more, that they exist as he has portrayed them." It is exactly the kind of comment that made Frost distrust Pound for the rest of his life, though he would be instrumental fifty years later in getting Pound released from St. Elizabeth's Hospital for the Criminally Insane, where Pound held a kind of madcap court for thirteen years. It is the kind of comment that would have made Williams—guilty of the same "so-called" provincialism—also want to smash his friend, Ezra.

An aside. It may simply be the times, but the phrasing "many men's manners" points to Pound's relative failure to portray women when measured up against either Williams or Frost. One has only to study the gestures and interactions of Amy, the wife in "Home Burial," cowering and defiant before her baffled and angry husband, the wife in "The Death of the Hired Man," or the broken wife in "A Servant to Servants" to begin to see how well Frost understood women. Once, fifteen years ago, a high-school teacher and extremely militant feminist—I do not know how else to describe her—argued in a seminar I was conducting (a class made up of secondary-school teachers) that male writers had no right to portray women in their work. History had showed that the attempt—which stemmed from a kind of colonial aggrandizement of the feminine—always ended in failure. I listened, and nodded, and we went on.

The following day I brought in a copy of "A Servant to Servants," told the class that the poem was spoken by a woman—I did not name its author—and then read it, excusing myself first for taking the liberty of aggrandizing the woman's voice, but that I had no choice, having only the one voice my mother had given me. I was afraid of course someone would recognize the poem right off, but luckily—for me, if not for American literature—no one did. By the end of the poem, several were in tears or near tears, and the woman who had insisted that no man could do justice to a woman's point of view was nodding sympathetically. We talked about the poem, about the entrapment of women, of how some have historically been mistreated, and then I told them that Frost had written the poem. Well, the militant feminist shot back, seeing I had misrepresented the poem by not saying straight out who had written it, maybe in that one instance a man had caught something. She never forgave me. A cheap shot on my part, I confess, but harried teachers teach as they can.

It may be of interest to note that Pound singled out for special praise in *North of Boston* "The Death of the Hired Man" as "perhaps the best" poem in the book, as well as parts of "The Housekeeper," "Mending Wall," and "The Black Cottage." He said nothing at all of the poem that has become for many Frost's signature poem, "Home Burial." And yet at least three poets have given us extended readings of this poem, a poem that takes place between a man and his wife speaking at cross, bitter purposes over the death of their infant son. The three poets are Randall Jarrell and two Nobel Prize–winning poets (one—interestingly—Russian, the other Irish): Joseph Brodsky and Seamus Heaney. Brodsky's comments seem to me to ripple off of Jarrell's, which predate Brodsky's by nearly thirty years. But all three have something important to say about the dramatic possibilities of poetry. After all, it is us you will find in Frost's poem, and not just the folks of rural New England at the turn of the century.

Surely the poem owes a great deal to the loss of the Frosts' own child,

their firstborn, a boy who died of cholera just short of his fourth birthday in 1900, when Frost and his wife were in their mid-twenties. Just to
say that is to break the heart, but Frost managed, a dozen years after the
event, to tell the story with the necessary detachment of a Greek trage-
dian. First, here's the man, whose act of digging his own son's grave has
rendered him in his wife's eyes an unfeeling monster who can't seem
to say or do the right thing, a theme that haunted Frost and to which
he would return. How precisely he captures the man's combination of
wounded pride, self-pity, suppressed rage, and bullying logic, a logic
that quickly goes wide of the mark, degenerating into something like
a barrage of axiomatic Yankee saws:

> My words are nearly always an offense.
> I don't know how to speak of anything
> So as to please you. But I might be taught,
> I should suppose. I can't say I see how.
> A man must partly give up being a man
> With womenfolk. We could have some arrangement
> By which I'd bind myself to keep hands off
> Anything special you're a-mind to name.
> Though I don't like such things 'twixt those that love.
> Two that don't love can't live together without them.
> But two that do can't live together with them.

To which the woman responds not with words but by moving the
latch of the front door, as if preparing to spring free of a trap. She is
overwrought, the husband feels, and she has succeeded in wedging the
child's death between them like a knife. He tries again with words, and
again he fails. But at least now he has released in her a tirade of words
in place of the silence that has grown up around the fact of the child's
death. "If you had any feelings," she comes back at him, and now we
see what she has been harboring against her husband all this time: the
image of his making the dirt around his dead child's grave furiously
gambol and leap through the air while the dead child lay in its little
coffin:

If you had any feelings, you that dug
With your own hand—how could you?—his little grave;
I saw you from that very window there,
Making the gravel leap and leap in air,
Leap up, like that, like that, and land so lightly
And roll back down the mound beside the hole.
I thought, Who is that man? I didn't know you.
And I crept down the stairs and up the stairs
To look again, and still your spade kept lifting.
Then you came in. I heard your rumbling voice
Out in the kitchen, and I don't know why,
But I went near to see with my own eyes.
You could sit there with the stains on your shoes
Of the fresh earth from your own baby's grave
And talk about your everyday concerns.
You had stood the spade up against the wall
Outside there in the entry, for I saw it.

The husband stands now, condemned by his own wife, the shovel that dug the grave the awful instrument by which he has committed the unforgivable sin, a transgression he had not known until this very moment he'd committed. What economy and precision Frost gives us here. Two voices, each with their own complex way of understanding, each with the full force of emotional truth on their side and this terrible loss between them, the loss of someone who should have stood as the guarantor of love between them. No wonder poets like Heaney and Brodsky have come back to this poem, finding in it the stuff of which indelible dramatic poetry is made.

In any case, Frost is with us to stay, regardless of the poetic weather. We each have our image of him, I suppose, some of them flattering, others less so. Seamus Heaney, who has farming in his blood, prefers the younger Frost, who knew farming and got the particulars of its world into so many of his poems. The sound of the scythe, for instance, in "Mowing," the sound of deep silence and the iambic swish of the blade back and forth, grounding the poet's very words:

There was never a sound beside the wood but one,
And that was my long scythe whispering to the ground.
What was it it whispered? I knew not well myself;
Perhaps it was something about the heat of the sun,
Something, perhaps, about the lack of sound. . . .

After all, poetry means work, means "earnest love," means facts, the particulars of existence, the thing seen, a thing made of this and this and this. It means a plan unfolding line by line, row after row, containing the surprises poetry brings in its very making: the "feeble-pointed spikes of flowers / (Pale orchises)," and that narrow fellow in the grass, "a bright green snake." The long scythe in Frost's double economy makes hay for the farmer as for the poet.

Derek Walcott sees an altogether different Frost, half Cincinnatus, half Seneca. For Walcott, having been brought up on the periphery of two empires—Britain and America—Frost is the white-haired octogenarian Roman senator reciting his poetry at John Kennedy's inauguration. Kennedy, "the young emperor," Walcott warily tells us, at that "sublime Augustan moment" when the power of the United States shimmered on a million TV screens in the January sun as both Republic and Empire, a world power passing itself off as "a homespun vision of pioneer values." It is Walcott, the Trinidadian outsider, who provides us with this darker image of America, invoking its slave past, its dispossession and colonization of Native Americans, in the lines Frost spoke that January day forty years ago—

The land was ours before we were the land's.
She was our land more than a hundred years
Before we were her people—

This "we" and "our" are certainly not as inclusive as Whitman's, but something more exclusive, "something as tight and regional as . . . a Currier and Ives print, strictly New England in black and white." And of course Walcott too is on to something. I remember one of my colleagues at UMass who had known Frost fairly well, saying one afternoon twenty years ago that Frost—whom Kennedy would send to Nikita Khrushchev's Russia as good-will ambassador in the summer of 1962—may have contributed to the Cuban missile crisis when he told Khrushchev that the fight had gone out of young Americans. In the States such a comment would have gone virtually unnoticed. But what Frost failed to realize was that even such offhanded comments as he was used to make might be taken seriously in Russia, where poets are watched far more seriously (for better and for worse) than happens here. Ironically, that October, in the midst of one of the largest gatherings of American poets ever assembled in the nation's capital, even as Jarrell was extolling Frost's centrality to the enterprise of poetry, Kennedy was preparing to bring the nation to the brink of Armageddon.

Frost the scrapper, Frost the cantankerous, jealous for his prerogatives, reminding MacLeish and Berryman and Williams and others that there could only be one heavyweight in the ring at a time, in boxing (which he loved) as in poetry. Consider Berryman's meeting with Frost at Bread Loaf that same summer of 1962, when Frost let it be known that Berryman—like Williams before him—had a reputation as a womanizer, which made the poetry itself suspect. Once the younger Berryman had paid the proper obeisance, however, letting Frost understand that Frost was still top dog (though barely, since Berryman was even then assembling his own knockout *Dream Songs*), the two men got along well enough.

The immediate upshot was three Dream Songs that Berryman wrote for Frost following the elder statesman's death the following January and that he read at Frost's memorial service at Amherst College. Now the old man belonged to the ages, Berryman wrote, making—as usual—a brilliant assessment of Frost's status not simply as an American poet, but as a world classic, who knew the Roman poets as well as Pound and Eliot, but who wore that learning far more lightly:

> Now he has become, abrupt, an industry,
> Professional-Friends-of-Robert-Frost all over
> gap wide their mouths

while the quirky medium of so many truths
is quiet. Let's be quiet. Let us listen:
—What for, Mr. Bones?
      —while he begins to have it out with Horace.

Or Robert Lowell, recalling a visit to Frost at his home in Cambridge in the late 1950s, prior to one of Lowell's manic episodes. Frost at midnight, he wrote later, slyly linking Frost with Coleridge's poem of the same title. A quiet poem, Lowell's, a blank-verse sonnet, the two poets alone, "the audience gone / to vapor," the whole edifice of the public Frost for the moment "laid on the shelf in mothballs," Frost listening as Lowell tells him twice that "he feels too full of himself." And Frost, warning him what such afflatus and fame as he had enjoyed came down to: a father's inability to stop his son from killing himself or being able to help his daughter. And Lowell, not yet understanding, repeating himself, "Sometimes I'm so happy I can't stand myself." And Frost, resignedly, remembering Wordsworth's "Surprised by Joy," saying "When I am too full of joy, I think / how little good my health did anyone near me."

Two final images of Frost, the first a story the poet Joseph Langland told me, an incident harking back sixty years now, when Langland was just starting out. It's a particularly haunting story for me, for I spent a summer at the Bread Loaf School of English years ago, living with my family in the Homer Noble Farm, and feeling Frost's presence there palpably, especially in the middle distance between the house and Frost's cabin, where so many poets and teachers had come over the years to see him. In the summer of 1940 Langland, then twenty-three, was an *Atlantic Monthly* scholar at Bread Loaf. That same summer the poet and New Critic John Crowe Ransom was teaching at Bread Loaf, and one day he asked Frost if he could bring two young poets over to the Noble Farm to meet him. Langland was one, David McDowell— who went on to become William Carlos Williams's publisher years later—the other. Frost told Ransom to bring them over after dinner. Ransom, being the southern gentleman he was, arrived in suit and tie, only to find the sixty-six-year-old Frost outside, dressed in overalls, waiting for them with a bat and a couple of softballs.

There was in those days, Langland remembers, a barn on the property off to one side of the house, with an old manure pile in front of it, covered with weeds. Frost told the two young men to get out in the field, then stationed Ransom closer in, in front of the manure pile. For the better part of an hour, Frost batted while the three men fielded, most of the balls bouncing out to Ransom, who several times had to wade into the pile to retrieve the ball. By the time Frost was finished batting, Ransom had his suit jacket off, his tie loose, and his shirtsleeves rolled up, and he was sweating. As dusk descended, Frost shrugged. Too late, he barked, for anyone else to bat, and with that he invited the men into the darkened house.

In the living room he took a Coleman lantern from a hook, lit it (there being no electricity then) and walked out into the kitchen, where he invited his guests to sit down. Ransom mentioned that both Langland and McDowell had brought a poem to read. Perhaps Frost would care to hear them? Frost mumbled his assent, and Langland went first. It was a musical piece with a ballad meter, and, after Langland finished, there was an awkward silence, at last punctuated by Frost's muttering a kind of noncommittal acknowledgment. The only other sound was the creak of kitchen stools.

Then it was McDowell's turn. McDowell had been Ransom's student at Kenyon and trained in the New Critical method of writing poetry, and now he read a long and complex poem. In the silence that followed, McDowell nervously broke in by explaining that the poem he'd just read was rather complex and that it used enjambment, varied caesurae, a double set of metaphors, and irony. As he went on, Frost's right hand slowly rose in time with the explanation, until at last his arm was level with his head. Finally, Frost brought his hand down. "Careful, young man," he said. "Or you'll *say* a better poem than the one you wrote." Frost's wry comment, no doubt, on the New Criticism that Ransom himself had helped invent.

A final image. The young Frost, writing by lamplight in the middle of a winter's night in a farmhouse in southern Vermont, his children and his wife asleep, the chores done, the house silent except for the creak of wood and the sound of the wind, his name still unknown to the larger world. He has been writing a long poem, but now—suddenly—he feels the stirrings of a lyric. The lamplight flickers across the page, and mercifully, like some unbidden grace, the night gives him first one line and then another. "Whose woods these are," he begins wryly, "I *think* I know." For who really owns the woods, except for the darkness and the elements? And then he is off, with a playful couplet to warm himself against the cold. "His house is in the village, though."

Then a third line, cutting across the play of the initial rhymes with an unrhymed third, "He will not see me stopping here." And then the initial rhyme picked up again, bracketing and end-stopping the stanza with its muffling oblivion: "To watch his woods fill up with snow." A form, *aaba*, repeated in each successive stanza and resolved only in the last. A sense of mystery and mastery, of serious play. A resonance, a small narrative drama that will, in succeeding stanzas, move to the high lyrical register of a line like, "Of easy wind and downy flake," before the poem settles back, repeating the last line, "And miles to go before I sleep." It is a devilishly simple line that has—over the intervening seventy-five years—raised as many questions as it has answered. Lines, lines sticking in the craw with their subtle iambic clipclop, lines that somehow have—like so many others of Frost's—proven impossible now to dislodge.

1999

Reconfiguring Flame
The Art of Biography

FIRST SOME DISCLOSURES. Thirty years ago, in the afterglow of the New Formalism, with its laserbeam exclusivity focused on the text, I began my first tentative steps toward writing biography by inserting historical and biographical facts into my commentaries on the poems of X. I would think back to the old "works and lives" the Victorians had offered us, or pore over Richard Ellmann's massive and instructive life of James Joyce. I was twenty-six, married, the father of two small boys with a third soon to arrive. Afternoons and nights I taught police officers at the Academy on New York's 23rd Street, and in between rode the elevated up to the Bronx campus of Hunter to teach my radical students who, armed with bullhorns, were already—in 1965— protesting the war in Viet Nam amidst a Vorticist flurry of mounted police. Into this world of radicals—dreamer that I was—I tried inserting Matthew Arnold's classical touchstones and Newman's *Idea of a University*. Compound this with adding to the world of tactical patrol officers and undercover officers Milton's *Paradise Lost* and Goethe's *Faust*, all with equal unsuccess.

One of my students, I remember, was a blue-eyed Dane who was in the habit of strapping a .357 magnum across his crotch and sitting in the front row. For comfort while he sat, he once explained. In the four months we read Plato and Aeschylus and the book of Job together he refused to crack a single smile. Twice a week—with unfailing regularity—he sat directly in front of me, arms folded, and stared unblinkingly at an imaginary point just beyond my head. Perhaps he was thinking of his class in firearms, which he taught immediately after my class. Perhaps he was thinking of targets. I didn't ask.

Another student in the same class was Frank Serpico, with whom I and my wife and he and his girlfriend—a New York City nurse—several times double-dated, Frank pointing out the apartments in Little Italy where the mob lived, or ordering homemade *grappa* for the four of us in the local pizza joints. Happily, the Knapp Commission and the disclosures on police corruption with which he was so centrally involved and which would result in his being shot in the face were still a year off.

Between classes and teaching I wrote each day doggedly at my *Commentary on the Complete Poems of Gerard Manley Hopkins*, mostly in a basement carrel at Queens College, a half mile's walk from my apartment. Otherwise I wrote at a tiny desk in our cramped apartment while my wife taught third grade and my oldest son slept or gurgled in a baby seat at my feet, my toes playing over his stomach, while I read him Hopkins's "The Wreck of the Deutschland," a scenario which, as I look back on it, may have had something to do with his becoming a Jesuit. Writing my commentary, I garnered what facts I could, hiding—like any proto-biographer worth his or her salt—the many gaps in my knowledge of the poet, then tied together as best I could all of his poems—the work of a quarter century—into the fiction of a coherent whole. It was my first attempt at reconfiguring flame.

Already I could feel fledgling biographer's wings sprouting. But in 1970 biography did not seem the sort of thing an assistant professor of English *did*. And so it was back to critical analysis, something I enjoyed doing. Still, it seemed such a small piece of all I wanted to know about my subjects. To complicate matters, there was also the fact that I wanted not only to teach poetry but also write the stuff. For ten years and more I'd studied it, analyzed it, parsed it. Finally, in my early thirties, as I began to lose the women in my family—first my grandmothers, then my godmother—I felt the need to honor those losses. I needed to write of what kept crashing over the falls and disappearing, and I had nothing but words to reconfigure the darting flames before they were pulled under by time's relentless rush. "It is time for you to cease being an altar boy at the altar of the Muse," the Milanese poet Giovanni Giudici, announced to me in my kitchen over coffee one March morning a quarter century ago. "It is time now for you to ascend to the altar as a priest of the imagination." It was a somewhat baroque way of conferring on me the mantle, but effective for all that. Henceforth I would write poems.

But because I had no community of writers on which I could call (that would come later), I would have to create my own pantheon of philosopher poets. I would study the lives of those poets who meant the most to me. I would seek—step by step—their lives and their papers, to determine how *they* had done it. As an assistant professor at the University of Massachusetts, I found my chance. Trained in the Victorian period, I was asked to retrain now as a modernist. I beamed. I flushed. The muses had smiled upon me. And so, in addition to Hopkins and the Brownings and Wilde and Meredith and Swinburne, I began reading in depth the moderns: Stevens, Frost, Yeats, and Williams. Especially Williams.

Williams intrigued me, though few of my colleagues knew anything about him thirty years ago. In fact, one of them had kindly warned me away from the poet for my own good, that is, if I ever expected advancement in the department. Three years earlier, browsing through a local bookstore in Queens, I had picked up a paperback with the intriguing title, *Paterson*. Paterson, New Jersey? I knew Paterson. My mother had been born in the next town over. Before my birth, my mother's mother had worked in the silk mills that ran along the Passaic. I had cousins living in Paterson, and had played along the cliffs above the Passaic with my brother, just where, in fact—as I discovered twenty-five years later—Williams, sitting with his granddaughter in the late 1940s, had been photographed by *Life* magazine. What kind of person in his right mind, I wondered, would write about a place like Paterson, and spend thirty years of his life doing it? But that afternoon, looking through the poem—which ran to 250 pages—I was struck by its alternate accessibility and density. I stared and stared, scratched my head, then put the book back on the rack where I'd found it.

When I picked the book up again, in 1968, it was because Williams's shorter poems had struck me immediately with their freshness and vitality, their approachability, their willingness to talk about the things of my world. After *The Waste Land,* after Pound's *Cantos* and Stevens's ideas of order, what was left, I wondered. Now, however, I found myself coming back to Williams and to his epic. It was a way, I understand better now, of coming in contact with the lost world of my mother, for even in my troubled dreams—now that she is dead—I keep returning to that landscape, to its mean streets and river and falls, hoping in that way to know her better.

Shortly afterward, I began ransacking the manuscript collections at Buffalo, Yale, Harvard, Texas, and some forty other libraries, trying to locate every letter related to and every scrap of manuscript of *Paterson* I could lay my hands on, in an effort to learn how Williams had actually composed his poem. Finally, in 1978, in typical byzantine fashion, I approached James Raimes at Oxford University Press with the idea of writing not a biography of Williams—*that* would have struck me as sheer bravado—but rather a biography of the stages of the making of an American epic. In that bizarre, oblique gesture, one sees the debilitating effects of too much time spent in academia. When Raimes called me, it was to say he simply wasn't interested in the project as I'd outlined it. But if I was willing to write a biography of Williams—say in the range of 600 pages—he was willing to offer me a generous $2,000 contract: one thousand up front, one thousand when the final manuscript was approved. A quick calculation tells me that I had signed on for about 0.4 cents per hour. I would have a week to decide my future.

Actually, only my own fears had stopped me from suggesting a biography in the first place. I would work toward that immensity, I calculated, by increments, writing my biography of Williams, say, at sixty. "Had we but world enough, and time . . ." But Raimes—bless him—pushed me into making my decision. And so, at thirty-seven, I took on the burden of my first full biography. I read everything and ransacked the libraries for everything. I had already—in '73 and '74—written a commentary on all the criticism available on Williams. This latter was a task I would advise against undertaking, unless you are a masochist, for it robbed me of two years of my life, years when I might have been doing something else—anything else—like writing deconstructionist criticism or learning to play the ukulele. What the exercise did give me—besides a new set of powerful enemies—was a thorough grounding in what three generations of critics had had to say about Williams, which in truth was not a great deal.

Finally, after a further year of research, I was ready to approach the Williams family for new disclosures, and drove down to Dr. Williams's house in Rutherford on the chance of meeting Williams's wife, Florence. When I pulled up to the substantial Victorian home where the Williamses had lived from 1912 until Williams's death in 1963, I couldn't believe my good fortune. There in the back yard I spotted a thin, trim, balding man in his mid-sixties, watching over the garden his parents had tended to for half a century. William Eric Williams, like his father a physician with a specialty in pediatrics, still worked out of his father's modest office attached to the north side of the house. I parked my car and introduced myself, knowing full well how much of a pain such intrusions can be, but burning with love for my subject.

Dr. Williams kept doing what he had been doing—watering the plants—while I kept talking. Doc—as I soon came to call him, and which he quickly warmed to—was used to this sort of intrusion, I soon learned, and even—I think—welcomed it. But I'd done a hell of a lot of homework, and even he seemed impressed that I knew as much as I did about his father. How was his mother, I finally ventured? He nodded to the second story. She was up there, he said, in her bedroom, and she was dying.

It had—that statement—the no-nonsense directness of the father, and it was enough, of course, to momentarily halt the conversation. All this time spent preparing to meet the legendary Floss Williams, only to arrive just too late. His mother had been O.K. just a few weeks earlier, he added. In fact, two flower children had knocked at the front door and said they'd read one of Williams's poems about a red wheelbarrow, and his mother had invited them in. Call it the adorable chutzpah of the young. Perhaps it was just as well that things had worked out as they had, for an earlier student of his father, an Englishman, had run afoul of Floss by asking too many questions of the wrong people, until she'd sent him on his way.

Finally, I was invited to come back down, at which time he promised to show me whatever stuff—letters, poems, photos—were still lying around the house. It was as casual as that. So, when the time came, I drove back down to Rutherford to stay in the poet's old study for a week. Doc Williams had found much good stuff in the interim, letters especially, crammed into old shoe boxes. Letters Pop had sent each week he'd been away at Williams College during the Depression, as later, when he'd served as an intern in one of the New York hospitals, and then as an M.D. assigned to the Navy Seabees in the South Pacific for much of the Second World War.

Williams had also written his younger son, Paul, though Paul had thrown many of *his* letters away. Paul was in many respects the classic younger son. Big, easygoing, he'd played football in high school, married right out of college, gone on to the Wharton School of Business, had two children—a boy and a girl—before being called up during the war to serve on a Navy destroyer in the North Atlantic. After the war, he'd gone on to work for Abraham & Strauss in New York, selling merchandise, and there he'd stayed until he'd retired. He too was helpful, saying what he knew, but otherwise he kept a kind of hands-off policy with regard to his father's life.

Bill Jr. was different. One sensed just how much he loved his father, though one also felt a reserve—a holding back—at some deeper level. In fact, what slowly dawned on me was that Doc and I had entered into some necessary symbiotic relationship, and that—as I learned about his father—he was also learning things about his father he'd never known, or only vaguely suspected. In short, there were disclosures and privacies to be understood and respected on both sides.

This direction in the relationship came to a head six months after

I'd read through the materials Doc Williams kept finding in drawers, bookcases and out-of-the-way file cabinets. I knew—because the curator at Buffalo had told me—that there was a substantial collection of materials Williams had given the University of Buffalo, but which—after his death—Floss had insisted be returned to her. Among these papers were letters Williams had written his wife, some of them dating back to the 1920s and some as late as 1954, when Williams—then seventy—had been institutionalized for shock therapy and psychoanalysis at Hillside Hospital in Queens, following a stroke that had nearly killed him. On a particular day I was to come down to Rutherford, Doc explained. No one except Floss and perhaps the curator at SUNY Buffalo had ever seen what was in these wrapped packages, not even the sons.

The day I was to see the papers at 9 Ridge Road arrived. There were drinks, dinner, some talk. I sat in the small living room, with the names of Pound, Stevens, Marianne Moore, Jarrell, and Lowell glancing at me from the glassed-in bookshelves behind me. To my left was the fireplace into which Williams had tossed the Christmas greens he'd burned some thirty-five years before. On the walls: an original Audubon print of a blue heron, together with original paintings by Ben Shahn, Charlie Demuth, Charles Scheeler. The room was palpable with presences. Doc Williams's wife, Mimi, had disappeared into the kitchen. I sensed that I was about to be tested.

All this talk about his father screwing around with other women, Doc suddenly asked—peering at me intently with that diagnostician's eye his father had also possessed—that stuff was all crap, wasn't it? I was taken completely by surprise. He had to know, didn't he, that much of it was true? From what I knew of Floss, of her tight-lipped dignity and her desire to save her sons from being hurt by certain disclosures, she would have kept her own counsel. But if I was to write and write honestly, some of these disclosures would have to be made. Otherwise my book would be a lie. In those milliseconds I felt a great weight descending.

Much of it *was* true, I told him, sweating, as I looked him in the eye. But he had my word that I would be careful to substantiate the claims I made wherever I could. And besides, I told him, adding what he must have already known and which his father's late poem, "Asphodel, that Greeny Flower," had already made abundantly clear, there was this countertruth to consider: that his mother had remained his father's only wife for nearly fifty years and that he had loved her, though how he chose to express that love would remain problematic to his generation and even more so to mine.

Something in me could feel the ten feet of metaphorical rope that lay between me and the letters on the coffee table begin to slip from their mooring. A moment of silence. And then he said, simply, "I thought so." And that was that. I had given him the certitude he had both been avoiding and awaiting. And then the moment was over, the test—if that was what it was—passed, and we proceeded to the table to open the packages. It was like Christmas all over again.

There would be other awkwardnesses, further attempts at privacy, further disclosures, each of which I would have to weigh against the need to tell the story of one of the giants of twentieth-century American poetry: the right to know measured and balanced against the need to respect an individual's right to privacy. It is always a difficult issue, this question of privacy and disclosure, for one person's attempt at discretion may be another person's sense of outrage that private matters have been violated, whether that person be a family member, a friend, a critic, a reviewer, or any one of ten thousand anonymous readers, each with their own say in the matter.

"Does he know the names of Williams's intimates or doesn't he?" one reviewer complained when my biography was finally published in the fall of 1981. Well, yes, I did have the names—or certainly enough of them, many of which I had refused to publish. An example. Interviewing a local druggist in Rutherford, a man who had known Williams for years, I learned something that endeared Williams to me more than ever. Williams and the druggist had been in a kind of charitable collusion for years. If someone came to Williams for medical help and Williams knew that individual could not pay for the visit or the treatment, he would write out a prescription, with a symbol at the top that told the druggist that Williams was not charging this person. Seeing that symbol, the druggist would also refuse to take any money. The system seems to have worked, and it surely must have helped save whatever shards of dignity the patients still possessed.

But over the years, the druggist had also become aware that Williams was having affairs with several of his female patients, women whom Williams had already portrayed in several of his plays, including *Many Loves* from the early 1940s and *A Dream of Love*, a decade later. It was as if, lacking the confessional or the therapist's counsel, Williams had had to portray his transgressions under the guise of drama.

Turn off the recorder, the druggist motioned to me now with his hand, not willing even to have the recorder pick up that he was asking me to turn off the machine. When I did, he began giving me names and addresses, at the same time insisting that what he was telling me would have to kept in strict confidence. I loved the man's sense of mystery, his sense of collusion, of an old secret finally shared. I would have to be careful, he added, since one woman in particular was now remarried.

I suppose something might have been gained by pursuing that lead. I might have compared her story with the portrait in *Many Loves* of the young woman ironing in her living room whom Williams had visited on his rounds forty years before. But at what cost to her and to her life now that she was in her seventies? And so I let the story go. Charity, I had long ago decided, covers a multitude of sins, and I needed balance in my biography. Sexual or alcoholic escapades have a way of running away with someone's life when you are retelling it for posterity, and portions of the good have especially to be retold, especially since they have a way of disappearing faster than the other stories. Relighting an old women's furnace after a house visit so that she would not be left alone in a cold house. Driving through an ice storm in the middle of the night to be there for a woman in labor. Sending a destitute writer fifty dollars for heating oil. Reporting a case of child abuse at a time when such an act was unheard of. Providing free medicine for the most destitute of one's patients. Refusing to charge more than fifty dollars for delivery, along with pre- and postnatal care because—as Williams put it—it was the woman who did all the work anyway. These things too needed to be said, and they certainly helped balance accounts. And since I was the one writing the biography, these facts were getting in there too.

Once, walking with him along the banks of the Hackensack River, Doc told me something I shall never forget. It was one of those quiet disclosures that nevertheless carry a profound impact. His father had written of this river many times in his poetry, fiction, and letters: the maternal landscape that had nurtured him, which he had seen die a little more with each passing year. How often, I wondered, had his father gone fishing with him along this very river? Never, Doc shot back. Not once. He had had to learn how to bait a line and cast and the rest of it from a neighbor. Doc was in his seventies then, his father already dead twenty years. And yet the memory still rankled. Why, I asked him? Why hadn't he taken him fishing? Too busy, he shrugged, catching himself. Too busy writing. Stealing every minute he could to write. That disclosure has served as a cautionary tale for me: the fear that some day it—or something equally devastating—might be repeated against me by one of my sons after I was gone.

Which reminds me of a story about the responsibilities that go with writing a biography of a contemporary. About ten years after my biography of Williams was published, at a time when I was already deep into my life of Berryman, I had a note from Doc Williams. He wanted me to set him straight about something. When he was a small boy, his father used to take him to visit various friends. The two of them would climb into the family's Ford flivver, and soon they'd be over in some neighboring town or crossing by ferry or tunnel into lower Manhattan. He'd never thought much about these visits. Or had he? For his letter suggested that he had harbored some sneaking suspicion all these years. Take, for instance, he said, this new book that had just come out about some woman named Evelyn Scott, a writer with something of a name in the 1920s, attractive, married, bohemian. An Englishman had discovered papers in a secondhand bookstore, and had followed up certain leads. I knew of course that there were letters from Williams to Scott that had wound up at the University of Texas. Now I wrote Texas, asking for copies of all those letters.

Then I began piecing together dates and events, and what I had taken as a friendship I now saw had been something more. Bingo. I wrote Doc back. Apparently his father had been more active even than I had thought. Evelyn Scott had been intimate with others as well, including Thomas Merton's father. And it had been in some ways a bizarre affair, because Williams could never commit to any other relationship than the one he had with Flossie. If he stole time, he also stole affection. But he wasn't leaving, of that he was sure.

Finally, Scott demanded that Williams say where they stood. Williams replied with stammering protestations. He was unwilling to profess his love for her, he said, or even praise new work of hers he thought inferior to her earlier work. He liked her, but he would not lie for her. He also hoped for both their sakes that she would burn his letters to her as he had burned hers to him. Sex, it seemed to suggest, was one thing, love another. He closed by appending a drawing of a horse eating oats and expelling the by-product from the other end.

That disclosure seems to have ended the affair. I explained to Doc what I thought the affair had meant to his father, what he had in a sense been willing to sign on to and where he had balked, and then I attempted to put the affair in perspective. In retrospect, it would have been better, I think, to have simply offered Doc the facts and let him draw his own conclusions. It's strange, now that I think of it, how I sometimes felt as if I had to defend his father as if I were some spin doctor, and this—strangely—to a man my father's age. Somehow, I realize now, I kept seeing Bill Jr. as the vulnerable younger man, and myself as his father's contemporary. Somehow, in the mash of time, Doc would always remain for me Williams's boy. Spending ten years with the memory of a man can do strange things.

And though I've addressed here mostly matters of privacy, that is, after all, only one of many problematic areas when it comes to writing lives. There are also class issues to consider, as well as racial, religious,

gender, and moral issues, all of which must be evaluated and reconfig-
ured in any attempt to get at the essence of subject X. One also learns—
often the hard way—that in each of these instances there are the biographer's own misprisions and blind spots, all of which tell us as much
about the biographer as they do about the subject of the biography.

For while it is necessary that the biographer evaluate and judge one's
subject, the way one judges will be used to judge us. We all know biographers who are out not so much for the truth, whose claims they
dismiss as Pilate once dismissed them. Far too often they are after the
offbeat, the different, the outrageous, the salacious, the dark secret,
the thing that will finally sink subject X. Such an approach does little
to serve the subject, the reader, or the biographer. True, there are no
unpoetic subjects, William Carlos Williams insisted. And so with biographies. But there is bad writing. The question is, finally, how well
the biographer puts together a story, which begins where it begins with
all writers: with the ability to craft a sentence, then another, and another, into a convincing narrative.

And why does one choose to spend time writing biography? What
makes the endeavor, after all, worth it? Certainly not the money,
though biography often pays better than poetry. For me I suppose
it's because biography has been a search for seriousness in what often
seems the randomness of life, providing at its best the same sense of
transformation poetry offers. I mean the struggle toward a more luminous self via language, the lifting up of the self in ways that life itself
seems often to balk at, whether the life seems outwardly uneventful or
even a failure—as to one degree or another we might say of Hopkins
or Dickinson or Stevens or Flannery O'Connor or Walker Percy or
William Carlos Williams. Or whether the life is filled with the uproar-
ious, terrifying stuff of which legends are made—as with Rimbaud,
Dylan Thomas, Hart Crane, Sexton, Plath, Lowell, or Berryman.

I began by mentioning Matthew Arnold's touchstones, and now I
want to end there, by quoting some lines that have haunted me for
years. As a practicing poet I find myself asking how X ever managed
to arrive at the lines he did. What, really, did it cost him? That is, I

think, where the focus of literary biography rests with me. Consider Williams—like Chekhov a busy doctor in the provinces—somehow managing to publish forty-six books in his lifetime. I think of him, after suffering several debilitating strokes, finally slowing down long enough to see the woman with whom he had shared his life, calling out to her at last, in an idiom that transformed American poetry, before death took him off. "It is difficult," he wrote Flossie,

> to get the news from poems
>   yet men die miserably every day
>   for lack
> of what is found there.
>   Hear me out
>   for I too am concerned
> and every man
>   who wants to die at peace in his bed
>   besides.

Or Hart Crane, at the end of a year of poetic silence in Mexico, shortly before he jumped from the stern of the S.S. *Orizaba* into the waters off Florida, remembering the bells of the cathedral at Guadalupe, at Taxco, as everywhere in Mexico, wondering after all if anything he'd written had the power to resonate as these bells could resonate, summoning the faithful to God each day:

> And so it was I entered the broken world
> To trace the visionary company of love, its voice
> An instant in the wind (I know not whither hurled)
> But not for long to hold each desperate choice.
>
> My word I poured. But was it cognate, scored
> Of that tribunal monarch of the air
> Whose thigh embronzes earth, strikes crystal Word
> In words pledged once to hope,—cleft to despair?

Or Robert Lowell, toward the end of his life, after the failure of his last marriage, after the whole effort to do it his way had been shot to hell, leaving behind three women and several children and step-children, all hurt by his whirlwind, bull-like, murderously innocent and lethargic presence. And so, the older poet, remembering the covenant he had broken with his youthful self, that boyish Catholic C.O., recalling at the end "The Queen of Heaven." He missed her, he wrote now:

> We were divorced. She never doubted
> the divided, stricken soul
> could call her Maria,
> and rob the devil with a word.

Or Hopkins, at the end, writing his agnostic, Jesuit-hating dearest friend, Robert Bridges, as he tried a final time to explain why he wrote so little now. In the last lines he ever wrote, as he lay dying with typhoid fever, he offered an explanation he must have known Bridges would only partly comprehend. "O then," he wrote,

> if in my lagging lines you miss
> The roll, the rise, the carol, the creation,
> My winter world, that scarcely breathes that bliss
> Now, yields you, with some sighs, our explanation.

Not *his* explanation, he quietly inserted, but *ours*. His and God's, the same who had lifted him up as he had to believe he had lifted up his own Son, to draw others after him in that mysterious, baffling kenotic emptying that remained always *terra incognita* for the self-sufficient, rational, befuddled Bridges. It is to understand moments such as these that I've given the better part of thirty years. Whether it has been worth the cost I no longer ask myself. This far into the venture, such considerations take a back seat to questions of the heart. One finds oneself there, the way one finds oneself married, or a seasoned teacher, or the parent of grown children who have already left home.

"One of the visible movements of the modern imagination," Wallace Stevens reminds us, "is the movement away from God." Which suggests its corollary—as the subtle master well knew—that one of the *invisible* movements of the modern imagination may therefore be *toward* that same God. And that is what I have attempted to track: the elusive flame within the pitchblende of this odd, arrogant, vital century now going out. And sometimes—if one is lucky enough and willing to dig deep enough and long enough—something authentic begins to glimmer in the dark.

1998

III. GOD AND THE IMAGINATION

Summoning the Dead

Politics and the Sublime in
Contemporary English Poetry

SEVERAL YEARS AGO I underwent self-hypnosis for purposes of quieting a troubled spirit. One of the exercises I undertook under the direction of a priest friend was to descend into what we may call for convenience's sake "gamma level," to meet whoever was there to meet me. The time and place seemed inauspicious enough: late winter, a turn-of-the-century, red-brick parochial schoolhouse in West Springfield. I can still hear the exposed pipes in the room clanging as I sat at my schoolroom desk along with a dozen others and began to descend into a terrifying, hopeful interior dark. Who, I wondered, would I meet at that depth, a depth not unlike that at which Jacques Cousteau says we begin to experience *délires des grandes profondeurs,* that state of euphoria where experienced divers begin to offer passing fish their baskets, helmets, and oxygen lines. Surely, I thought, the figure who would rise across my lines at those depths would be one of the figures I'd spent the past twenty years attending to for what they might teach me.

What a surprise, then, when the presence who began to swim into ken turned out to be Baudelaire. What had I to do with Baudelaire, or Baudelaire with me? Why, I couldn't even speak his language. But at that depth one apparently has no difficulties in communicating. What he said then I soon found myself dictating in a poem I call "Baudelaire at Gamma Level." It surprised me, the poem, because I recorded things there that I didn't even know I was capable of saying. Dry leaves skitter-ing across the cold pavement of a November afternoon in Paris, circa 1855, like the leaves at the oracle at Delphi that Justinian had closed to stop the possibility of such meetings from ever happening again. The following year I read the poem at the Bread Loaf Writers' Conference, after which the poet Bill Matthews came up to me and asked how I'd really come to write it. I told him then what I am telling you, though I had no idea how to get back there again. I understand better now what the critical embarrassment has been over Yeats's communing with the spirits and his wife's automatic writing. Whatever else it did, I think we are all agreed that communing with these otherworldly messengers gave his poetry a new urgency and seriousness.

John Berryman learned much from listening to Yeats, and tried his own underworld journey several times magnificently and comically, first in his long poem, *Homage to Mistress Bradstreet,* where he man-aged to summon the poet Anne Bradstreet across three centuries in order to petition her to serve him as both mistress and muse, with grotesquely mixed results. And again, hoping to resurrect his dead fa-ther, who had shot himself in a Florida dawn in the summer of 1926. The record of this loss and of the ensuing silence is there in *The Dream Songs* he has left us. In the cold underworld of his poem Berryman attempted to search out his own philosophers' circle, looking for the company of Theodore Roethke, Delmore Schwartz, and Randall Jar-rell. Now, with Jarrell silent, Berryman addressed him in a poem:

> In the chambers of the end we'll meet again
> I will say Randall, he'll say Pussycat
> and all will be as before
> whenas we sought, among the beloved faces,
> eminence and were dissatisfied with that
> and needed more. (DS 90)

But Berryman's dead almost never speak back to him. Rather, it is he, like Yeats, who speaks to the silent underworld. With a translator like Ezra Pound, on the other hand, things are different, for he often allows his dead to speak, translating their syllables into an appropriate American idiom. Consider for a moment how he begins his epic poem, the *Cantos*. It is a translation into a sort of vigorous American ersatz Anglo-Saxon of the Nekuia episode of the *Odyssey*, purported to be one of the oldest passages of that venerable yet eternally youthful poem. Like Pound, Odysseus has traveled to the underworld to learn something of what the future holds for him. He and his men pour libations of wine and honey and then offer up a sheep to the spirit of the dead Tiresias. Soon other dead begin appearing like so many hungry wolves around the perimeters of a cattleyard in midwinter:

> Souls out of Erebus, cadaverous dead, of brides,
> Of youths and of the old who had borne much.
> Souls stained with recent tears, girls tender,
> Men many, mauled with bronze lance heads,
> Battle spoil, bearing yet dreory arms,
> These many crowded about me.

But Odysseus is looking for one soul only, the Theban Tiresias, who at last presses forward to speak with him. What follows are Pound's words placed in the mouth of the prophet, words that will echo across the next half century during which Pound will work at his epic as the prophecy gathers its own tragic reverberations. "A second time?" Tiresias asks Odysseus,

> why? man of ill star.
> Facing the sunless dead and this joyless region?
> Stand from the fosse, leave me my bloody bever.

Odysseus obeys and the spirit drinks of the sacrificed blood. Only then does it tell him what is in store for him: "Odysseus / Shalt return through spiteful Neptune, over dark seas, / Lose all companions."

That is all. The ill-fated poet, having fed the dead with his own blood—for is not that the essential act of the translator?—learns that he shall return home, having outlived or estranged his companions. How could Pound have known that in 1916? True, he had lost his friend, the young sculptor, Gaudier-Brzeska, killed in the trenches at Neuville St. Vaast in June 1915. But he would also lose Yeats and Joyce and Ford Madox Ford by the time he returned—a broken man—to be incarcerated at St. Elizabeth's for his wartime broadcasts over Radio Rome, a man isolated for too long from the living.

This evocation of the dead is a serious business, something translators traffic in all the time, as they bring over into the vernacular the music of Homer and Sappho, of Virgil and Catullus and Horace and Propertius, of Dante and Villon and Baudelaire and Mallarmé, the Chinese of Li Po, the Russian of Pasternak. Here the poet stands as medium, letting the voices from across the dark rivers speak to us in more familiar accents. But there is another kind of translation, where the words are evoked out of thin air by the will of the poet.

The Romans were particularly adept at this sort of summons, but even among them Virgil stands out for his particular act of daring when he has the dead Hector address Aeneas, asleep even as his whole world is in flames around him. Troy has been betrayed; Greek soldiers are at that very moment running through the city streets, not unlike government security forces in El Salvador, or Russian troops in Afghanistan. Asleep, Aeneas begins to question the dead Hector, caked with blood and still bearing his disfiguring spear wounds, asking him to tell him from what region he has come. And then Hector's implied reproach. The dead have no time for such useless questions. Hector has come, not to answer but to advise. Troy, he tells Aeneas, is already lost, its king and queen with it. The future of whatever remains of that world rests now with him. Here, in Allen Mandelbaum's translation, is what Hector tells him:

> "Troy entrusts
> her holy things and household gods to you;
> take them away as comrades of your fortunes,
> seek out for them the great walls that at last,
> once you have crossed the sea, you will establish."
> So Hector speaks; then from the inner altars
> he carries out the garlands and great Vesta
> and, in his hands, the fire that never dies.

It's a powerful moment in our western tradition, one that can move us two millennia later. Remember that Virgil himself worked within a great tradition from which he gained his strength. Aeneas himself will be translated—and Virgil with him—as he travels west toward Rome, carrying with him the fire that will one day shine throughout the world.

And yet is it not Dante who is best remembered as the poet who summoned the dead, and who in turn summoned so many other poets to do the same, poets as diverse as Shelley, Baudelaire, Lowell, Berryman, and Seamus Heaney? Dante, we remember, it was who summoned Virgil to be his guide: a voice to steady his own voice and imbue it with some of the authority and greatness of the past. It is Virgil who is Dante's first master, his teacher, the one who corrects him, chastises, protects, and even cheers, until Virgil himself—the voice of human reason—falls away before the higher spiritual wisdom of Beatrice. Beatrice: that amalgam of Aristotelian and Christian wisdom— the feminine Hagia Sophia. Not even Virgil, that noble emblem of antiquity, will be able to comprehend her, so much greater is her knowledge, and so he must fade before her like hoarfrost before the rising sun.

Between 1967 and '68 Robert Lowell wrote an epic centered on the Viet Nam era (the poem he first called *Notebook* and, later, *History*). In that commentary—half Ezekiel, half Baudelaire—on our time, he translates the words of Buonconte da Montefeltro, the ghost whom Dante has address us in the fifth canto of the *Purgatorio*. In his midtwenties, before his forced exile from his beloved Florence, Dante had served with the Florentine forces against the Aretines at the battle of Campaldino. Only a year earlier Buonconte had led the Aretines to a brilliant victory against Siena. But in the encounter in which Dante took part, Florence proved victorious and Buonconte was himself killed, though his body was never recovered. Dante has already met Buonconte's father deep in hell, exactly where his creator (Dante) had placed him, damned because he had attempted to deceive God even as he asked God for forgiveness. But now, in one of the most beautiful passages in the whole of the *Purgatorio*, Dante sees that the son, though his former enemy, has been saved, one of those whom Hopkins called the "last-breath-penitents."

What violence or chance dragged you from the field at Campaldino, Dante asks Buonconte, so that we never found out what happened to your body? Amidst so many of those who died violent deaths—Cato, Cleopatra, Cicero, Caligula, Roland, Anne Boleyn—Lowell has focused on this figure for complex reasons of his own, giving us his foreshortened but no less powerful rendition of the dead man's own testament of those last hours:

> Where the Archiano
> at the base of the Casentino loses its name
> and becomes the Arno, I stopped running,
> the war lost, and wounded in the throat—
> flying on foot and splashing the field with blood.
> There I lost sight and speech, and died saying *Maria* . . .
> I'll tell you the truth, tell it to the living,
> an angel and devil fought with claws for my soul:
> *You angel, why do you rob me for his last word?*
> The rain fell, then the hail, my body froze,
> until the raging Archiano snatched me,
> and loosened my arms I'd folded like the cross.

I think I understand why Buonconte appealed to Lowell, for in a world become increasingly nihilistic for Lowell, there is in the figure of Buonconte some hope held out, something to suggest that our stories have significance, that—from the vantage of eternity—we ought not judge others, or ourselves. True, Buonconte had been Dante's enemy in wartime. But Dante will not pass judgment, since none of us can be present at the end. It is an important moment, this evocation of the younger Buonconte, in the unfolding of the *Commedia*, and Dante has struck upon the strategy of having the dead tell us what really happened.

The passage strikes us so forcefully because we know the dead no longer have anything to hide. As such, the dead can act as a corrective, retelling their stories as they happened, capable of the reporting we mortals almost never seem to be able to come by. Too much is at stake, too much is always at stake, to ever get the truth, as Williams reminds us, from the newspapers. Yes, the poet needs to tell the truth. But poets too are flawed, likewise wary of the consequences of telling the truth about themselves, about others, about their world.

Which is why the dead are so important to us. They give us the perspective we need in order to come closer to the truth. They can lift us, these presences with their unblinking eyes, be a conscience to us, remind us that, while we will soon enough make the great translation to the other side, our words remain to judge us. Virgil and Dante know this. Lowell too understood that, with three marriages in ruins, his friends dead, having been in and out of mental institutions far too often, and suffering at the last from a faulty heart, he had little left to lose. Given all that, he was willing to settle in his poems for a portrait of his troubled times before the lens of the strict observing eye was shut for good.

In the last weeks of his short, tortured life, Shelley also found himself summoning the dead. In the poem he left unfinished at the time of his drowning, "The Triumph of Life," sensing he had little more to lose, Shelley turned to Dante's *Commedia* to come to some tentative summation of life's meaning. T. S. Eliot, whose whole attitude and poetic tenor seem so different from his Romantic predecessor, has spoken of his admiration for the new seriousness he found in Shelley's last poem. And it *is* an extraordinary fragment, though it may be even darker than Eliot acknowledged. Life, the poem seems to say, first traps then kills us. The strongest among the living are but prisoners chained to Life's triumphal chariots, forced to pass in procession before the witnessing poet. At the end, the light we are told to follow turns out to be only the light that drew the fish Shelley saw in the waters off Lerici, light from the lamps of night fishermen, waiting to break their backs before they tossed them into baskets.

And though it is Rousseau, as one of the founders of Romanticism, who speaks to Shelley, the figure owes as much to Wordsworth who, by 1822, the year of Shelley's death, had sold out to the status quo. The light of the revolution had failed by then, Shelley knew. Even the great Napoléon—that Promethean light-bearer of the new order—was by that time dead. Nature was never a strong contender for Shelley, and even Eros had apparently failed him. That left the example of history. And if history teaches anything, Shelley tells us at the end, it is that life itself is the final ghastly illusion. The ghost of Rousseau, having witnessed the end of mortal beauty, wishes for nothing more now than to return to the atomizing oblivion from which it had sprung:

> In the eyes where once hope shone
> Desire like a lioness bereft
>
> Of its last cub, glared ere it died; each one
> Of that great crowd sent forth incessantly
> These shadows, numerous as the dead leaves blown
>
> In Autumn evening from a poplar tree.
> . . . .
>
> Mask after mask fell from the countenance
> And form of all, and long before the day
>
> Was old, the joy which waked like Heaven's glance
> The sleepers in the oblivious valley,
> And some grew weary of the ghastly dance
>
> And fell, as I have fallen by the way side,
> Those soonest from whose forms most shadows past
> And least of strength & beauty did abide.

Shelley was the poet of our adolescence, Eliot insisted, a figure endowed with first-rate poetic gifts, but whose mind remained essentially that of an irresponsible young man. This was so much the case for him, in fact, that he could only return to Shelley for matters of literary reference. Or so he wrote in the early 1930s. But ten years later, in his summative poem "Little Gidding," Eliot returned a final time to Shelley via Dante. For it was against the pressure of what Shelley had achieved in "The Triumph of Life," a poem he acknowledged to be "one of the supreme tributes to Dante in English," that he would reach new heights in his own poetry.

In the second movement of "Little Gidding" Eliot summons his own "familiar, compound ghost," a ghost whose body lies now—in 1942—on a distant shore. On at least one occasion Eliot acknowledged that the presence summoned from the refining fires of Purgatory—met in the pre-dawn hours on a London street immediately after German bombers had passed over and the all-clear had been sounded—was in fact his own master: William Butler Yeats. Twenty years before, in *The Waste Land*, he had summoned the figure of the Provençal poet, Arnaut Daniel, who, after telling his story, had turned back into the fire to get on with his own necessary refinement and expiation. Had not Yeats in advanced age, feeling his dying body tied to him like a can to a dog's tail, himself evoked the holy sages in the holy flames, unwinding into their new, antithetical life? And now Yeats's eminent disciple, Eliot, summons Yeats much as Shelley had summoned Rousseau. Once again, it is Dante who is the mediating text, the figure most available to Eliot as he reaches in his own poetry to address the living dead.

In 1940 Eliot had delivered the first annual lecture in honor of Yeats. There he had praised Yeats, while reserving judgment on what he took to be the poet's foolishness in assuming the stance of the wicked old man in his last years. But now, having gone before in death and having understood at last who the holy sages really were, Yeats returns to warn Eliot of what the future holds for him. What is there to lose now, here in the unreal city of London, as avenging angels in the form of German Stuka bombers drop incendiaries on the city? And in fact, the fires ringing London now look very much like the fires of hell itself. Even Yeats's voice, as Eliot hears it from beyond the pale, has changed from the voice of the wild old man to the voice of the stern prophetic father:

> But, as the passage now presents no hindrance
> To the spirit unappeased and peregrine
> Between two worlds become much like the other,

So I find words I never thought to speak
In streets I never thought I should revisit
When I left my body on a distant shore.

How wonderful and ironic this passage, where two worlds—those of
the living and the dead—for a moment present no hindrance to Eliot
as he undertakes to recreate the master's voice. True, Yeats would never
have thought to speak these words himself, except that now—in this
act of translation—he has been filtered through the intermediary fire
of Dante across to Eliot, who now invents a father to instruct the son.
Had not Yeats once written, in a moment of intense self-scrutiny, of

Things said or done long years ago,
Or things I did not do or say
But thought that I might say or do,
Weigh me down, and not a day
But something is recalled,
My conscience or my vanity appalled. ("An Acre of Grass")

Now this becomes, in Eliot's translation, Yeats's final Pascalian insight into the nature and significance of the pain incurred in looking
back to reenact

all that you have done, and been; the shame
Of motives late revealed, and the awareness
Of things ill done and done to others' harm
Which once you took for exercise of virtue.
Then fools' approval stings, and honour stains.
From wrong to wrong the exasperated spirit
Proceeds, unless restored by that refining fire
Where you must move in measure, like a dancer.

By the time Eliot came to write "Little Gidding," he had moved beyond
factional politics to a reconciliation of differences through something
like a unitive vision. Surely, he felt, the dead had long ago given up on
civil strife. Now, in death, he hoped, all would be well and all manner
of things be well.

Seamus Heaney too has invoked Dante's spirit in "Station Island," calling up the dead. These include not only the exiled James Joyce, who tells Heaney that he has paid his dues to Ireland and that it is time now to move on, but other, humbler presences as well: the young girl who was for years a dream fantasy; a friend who died early of heart disease; and yet another victim of the sectarian troubles in Northern Ireland. Station Island is an island on Lough Derg in Northern Ireland, Heaney explains, "where pilgrims—following the legend of St. Patrick—perform each summer the spiritual exercises which involve fasting and praying for three days." As such it is a near-perfect analogue for Dante's Mount Purgatory, the fasting and bodily exhaustion invoking a dream state not far removed from the concussion-like effects of aerial bombardment Eliot had evoked in "Little Gidding," both places not unlike Dante's waking dreamlike state as he moved through the fires of hell and purgation.

Reading "Station Island," you know you are in the presence of significant poetry. There is, for instance, a powerful description of the gangland-style execution of a storeowner somewhere in Northern Ireland. As Heaney comes to the edge of the waters at Lough Derg and kneels down, he senses someone behind him. And there is his dead friend, his forehead ripped open by a bullet. "Easy now," the dead man tells him, "it's only me. You've seen men as raw / after a football match." And then he too begins to recount his last moments. Here are Heaney's words, in that universally acknowledged plain-style Dante has given us, where each simile acts unobtrusively, shedding light and providing us with the sense that we are experiencing what the speaker experiences. The shopkeeper hears a knock at his door in the pre-dawn hours and knows that something is terribly wrong. He goes to the window, looks down, and sees a Land Rover and two men in the street below. They call up to him to open the shop and his wife, terrified, begins to cry:

> The knocking shook me, the way they kept it up,
> and her whingeing and half-screeching made it worse.
> All the time they were shouting "Shop!

Shop!" so I pulled on my shoes and a sportscoat
and went back to the window and called out,
"What do you want? Could you quieten the racket

or I'll not come down at all." There's a child here not well.
"Open up and see what you have got—pills
or a powder or something in a bottle,"

one of them said. He stepped back off the footpath
so I could see his face in the street lamp
and when the other moved I knew them both.

But bad and all as the knocking was, the quiet
hit me worse. She was quiet herself now,
lying dead still, whispering to watch out.

At the bedroom door I switched on the light.
"It's odd they didn't look for a chemist.
Who are they anyway at this time of the night?"

she asked me, with the eyes standing in her head.
"I know them to see," I said, but something
made me reach and squeeze her hand across the bed

before I went downstairs into the aisle
of the shop. I stood there, going weak
in the legs. I remember the stale smell

of cooked meat or something coming through
as I went to open up. From then on
you know as much about it as I do.

Heaney's affection for the dead man is clear. "Big-limbed, decent, open-faced," the man is unexceptional, apolitical, except that he has been chosen to be the sacrificial victim, this "rangy mid-fielder in blue jersey / and starched pants, the one stylist on the team / the perfect, clean, unthinkable victim?" Why did they do it? Because, the dead man answers for Heaney, there being no longer anything to fear from reprisals, they were "shites thinking they were the be-all and the end-all," smalltime gods. But it is enough, this explanation, and the complex feelings Heaney experiences in writing of such tragedies from the relative safety of the south of Ireland, or America, or the poem, breaks forth now as he addresses the dead man for the last time.

It is too much, this visit from an old friend, yet another victim like those he earlier addressed in *North* and *Field Work*. Heaney the penitent at Station Island asks now to be forgiven for having stood too long, too safely on the sidelines. "Forgive the way I have lived indifferent— / forgive my timid circumspect involvement," he hears himself say. And then the answer from the man who cannot help but stand as mute witness to a violence he himself did not understand:

> "Forgive
> my eye," he said, "all that's above my head."
> And then a stun of pain seemed to go through him
>
> and he trembled like a heatwave and faded.

If Seamus Heaney's predecessor for the poem that summons the dead is Dante, Derek Walcott's is—to go back to the beginning of this essay—the Shelley of "The Triumph of Life." In "The Hôtel Normandie Pool," Walcott, sitting by a hotel pool somewhere in the Caribbean—alone on New Year's Day 1980, is surprised to discover that he has just been visited by the Roman poet, Ovid. Virgil and Dante, Rousseau and Shelley, Yeats and Eliot, Heaney and Joyce. And now, two exiles facing each other in this New World Roman outpost: Ovid and Derek Walcott.

Walcott tells us that he is undergoing the bitter exile of divorce, and feels even further exiled by the political situation back home in Trinidad. New Year's: the meridian line between a new dawning and a poignant ending. The weather itself, like the political situation in the Third World, is as uncertain as Walcott's mood: gusty showers followed by violent sunshine reflecting off the troubled waters of the outdoor pool. He remembers couples from the night before dancing until the stroke of midnight, when the band had suddenly lurched into the strains of "Auld Lang Syne" and a battalion of drunk married men had resworn their marriage vows. Now he imagines his wife "sleeping with one arm around each daughter / in the true shape of love, beyond divorce." In his fiftieth year he finds himself praying contritely to the water—his sign—to change him into someone he can bear.

A sense of self-loathing weighs so heavily on him now that he struggles to escape his own reflection and—even more—his own voice. In a brilliant pun, he ends the first part of his poem by evoking the image of the "disfiguring exile of divorce." And with that, the mirror self Walcott has projected appears to him. A white tourist in sandals and terry-cloth robe and foam-blown hair joins Walcott. A figure of "Roman graveness" he "mummy-oils" himself and then nods in Walcott's direction. Walcott thinks he hears a Latin phrase, "some mineral glint" forming from his British schooldays: *"Quis te misit, Magister?"* he asks. *Who sent you, master?* Master. There you have it: the history of colonization rearing its glossy head. But this is his literary master, the one from whom he has learned. This is none other than Ovid, the poet Augustus Caesar exiled to Tomis on the Black Sea in *his* fiftieth year, an outpost as far from the beehive of Rome—at least psychologically—as this Third World island is from either New York or London. And now the poem itself begins to take on a new grandeur in the presence of the old master, magnifying "the lines / of our small pool to that Ovidian / thunder of surf between the Baltic pines."

But first Walcott draws the necessary parallels between the master and himself. You were once just another "drop in a surf of faces— / a fleck of spittle from the she-wolf's tooth," Walcott realizes, addressing the ghostly eminence. But now the light "splashes a palm's shadow at [Ovid's] foot," the sign of Ovid's final victory over time's annihilation. Things have not changed all that much since your time, Walcott reminds Ovid as much as himself, even if—in another sense—all things *have* changed. Look, for instance, at these beautiful emerald waters, he laments now, these lonely outposts of the new empire, "stained with sewage" the way all empires eventually stain everything with their "corruption, censorship, and arrogance."

And still the old divisions persist, where house slaves sigh for the "just and level" voice of the old British Commonwealth, while the "field slaves scream revenge." One empire crumbles, only to be replaced by another. The rhetoric of one group blares from the marketplace in a frantic effort to displace the old. Nothing changes finally but the faces. Walcott knows both sides: the English tradition of his white grandfather, the black traditions of his parents. Like Shelley's prisoners dragged in triumph by the chariot of Life, Walcott feels the effects of power from both sides:

> My own face
> held negro Neros, chalk Caligulas;
> my own reflection slid along the glass
> of faces foaming past triumphal cars.

And then Ovid answers. *I too missed my language in my exile,* he tells Walcott. *I too missed my child; I too did not know my rightful place among the barbarous strangers of Augustus Caesar's outflung empire. What saved me finally was the writing:*

> On a tablet smooth as the pool's skin,
> I made reflections that, in many ways,
> were even stronger than their origin. . . .

> since desire is stronger than its disease,
> my pen's beak parted till we chirped one song
> in the unequal shade of equal trees.

The final government for the exile, Ovid reminds Walcott, must remain the government of the word. It is enough to keep the attention riveted to the page before you, he exhorts all poets. For in the end all poets are *by nature* exiles:

> There, hammering out lines
> in that green forge to fit me for the horse,
> I bent on a solitude so tyrannous
> Against the once seductive surf of crowds
> that no wife softens it, or Caesar's envy.

There is one thing further Walcott needs to hear. He is a poet who has had to negotiate carefully between two worlds: the first-world cultures of old Britannia and her daughter, America, on the one hand, and his own indigenous island heritage on the other, those raw, energized black and Indian cultures of the Caribbean. "And where are those detractors now," Ovid consoles the outcast, where are all those who once said

> that in and out of the imperial shade
> I scuttled, showing to a frowning sun
> the fickle dyes of the chameleon?
> Romans—he smiled—will mock your slavish rhyme,
> the slaves your love of Roman structures, when,
> from *Metamorphoses* to *Tristia*,
> art obeys its own order. Now it's time.

The meeting is over. Ovid disappears into the pool to return to the final exile of the underworld. Only one question remains: why has Ovid appeared here, of all places,

> A small suburban tropical hotel,
> its pool pitched to a Mediterranean blue,
> its palms rusting in their concrete oasis?

And why has Ovid addressed Walcott in this godforsaken imperial waystation? Because, as Walcott knows, to make Ovid's image is to flatter the summoner himself. And this is true, not in the self-deprecating sense—as Walcott understands—but in the sense in which Walcott, like those poets who have gone before, knows he has been taken seriously in being visited by the old masters. Now he too must assume his role as witness.

In the twilight world between lyric and translation, in the region between dramatic monologue and drama itself, the strong poet has the power to call on powerful forces within the unconscious. This summoning of the dead, this calling on the *masters*, this reliance on *authority*, is one way in which we can momentarily escape the weight of our own voices and, by learning to listen to the presences thronging on the distant shore, raise our own voices to a new level of seriousness. We would do well to rethink our own pact with the dead, to think of those who have preceded us, not merely as the dead, but as by far the greater part of our living memories.

For these presences are in fact what Stevens meant by the noble horsemen in ourselves who ride the strong-backed wingèd steed: forces waiting for a sympathetic, patient ear. In listening to them we—both poet and reader alike—should not be surprised to find our own voices paradoxically rising beyond the minor slopes of Parnassus. We have it in us, after all, in spite of the despairing aphasic flood of words swirling about us every day, to reach once more into the shadows gathered deep within, where advisors greater than any fiction wait only to be blooded.

1984

The Intensest Rendezvous

On the Poems of John of the Cross

୧୧

AFTER REGISTERING summer-session students for his course in Western masterpieces at the University of Minnesota one June day in 1966, John Berryman went home and wrote a poem about the heavy cost of being a poet. "I say the subject was given of old," he wrote in what would become Dream Song 125, "prescribed the technical treatment, tests really tests / were set by the masters & graded."

And what were the tests the old bards set themselves? These:

> Bards freezing, naked, up to the neck in water,
> wholly in dark, time limited, different from
> initiations now . . .

Thus, apparently, in Ireland a millennium ago, unlike what young poets at Iowa or Bread Loaf or Berkeley or Massachusetts must undergo, where, dressed in their uniform "turtleneck sweaters [and] loafers," "clothed & dry & light," and with "unlimited time, till *Poetry* takes some," poets write according to their lights. Art now, Berryman added with another sardonic touch, was, in the minds of its youthful practitioners, "if anything 'fun.'"

Consider Berryman himself, like many of us who struggle with the word, "paralyzed with fear" that, even after a lifetime of grueling work—much of it given over to a maddeningly long stint at apprenticeship—he would still not be counted worthy to stand among the poets. For it was the poet, he believed, like the saint, who "springs for" the rest of us, footing the bill for a culture once the party was over and the culture itself had either disappeared or changed forever.

Consider too St. John of the Cross, squeezed into a cell—a cupboard, really—in the priory of the Carmelites in Toledo, Spain, in the winter and spring and beastly summer of 1578. So cramped were his quarters, in fact, that John could never quite stand up. There he languished, to be taken out each day and led to the refectory, flogged by each of the friars in turn in what was called the "circular discipline," the saint's bare back exposed to the leather whips until his neck and shoulders were permanently scarred.

Dysentery, lice, lack of warmth in winter, lack of fresh air in summer, lack of adequate nourishment, lack of companionship, of understanding, of light. His own Carmelite brethren, out of fear, out of zeal perhaps for maintaining the power that comes with holding to the status quo, no doubt meant business. They would break this thirty-six-year-old rebel and poet and mystic *(nel mezzo del cammin di nostra vita)* as others had tried to break that other unrecalcitrant, Teresa of Ávila.

After a time, they forgot about him. Eventually the beatings became boring, repetitious, unfruitful, and decreased from one a day to one a week. A new jailer took compassion on him and gave him paper and pen so that he could write down the lines haunting his ear. One thinks of the black G.I. assembling a small makeshift desk for Ezra Pound, stuck in a "gorilla cage" at an Army detention center outside Pisa in the summer of 1945. Pound, a proud man broken by his own recklessness, the intense camp lights pouring down on him like rain, his only companion a cricket, as he wrote his *Pisan Cantos.* "Pull down thy vanity," he warned himself, in a rare moment of self-understanding, "I say, pull down." Or Miguel de Cervantes in prison, writing whole sections of the life of his ascetic, half-cracked, idealistic knight who has given the language that misunderstood epithet, "quixotic." Or Emily Dickinson, writing lyrics into the pregnant silence from her cell room in Amherst, poems that still burn with an incandescent flame a century after they were penned. "Penned." Does all great writing derive from intense solitude? One thinks of the moving confessional poems of William Carlos Williams's old age, when he too, no less than his friend Pound, no less than his fabled unicorn, was penned, in his case to his room in Rutherford, free at last from a lifetime of duties and other preoccupations to write out at the end his love for his wife and family.

And then there's John, simple Juan de Yepes, John of the Cross, hearing, as Willis Barnstone, one of John's translators, tells us in his introduction, in the dark isolation of his cell:

> Muérome de amores,
> Carillo, ¿qué haré?
> —¡Que te mueras, alahé!

There's a scene from *The Godfather* that captures something of what is going on in this *villancico*, this popular Spanish street song. Fat Clemenza, one of the Corleone capos, is cooking spaghetti for some of the mob holed up during a gang feud. As he stirs the sauce, he chides young Michael Corleone, who is in love. "I'm so much in love," Clemenza mimics, "my heart's so much breaking for you I'ma gonna die." And so with the mocking response on the part of the beloved in the *villancico*, "You're gonna die? Well, go ahead and die!"

The realism of the popular lyric form must have tickled John as well. But he also heard something more, for soon he was taking the hackneyed Petrarchan-style lyrics—already turned on their head once— and turning them again, this time into the sublime lyrics of the "Cántico espiritual." Yes, of course, he says, the answer would be to go ahead and die—involving of course the European conceit of sexual intercourse as a dying to oneself. But John means a dying into life, dying as the necessary prelude to becoming one with the Beloved, the one who has waited patiently out in the darkness for the beloved. One comes to such knowledge, John says, by way of unknowing, the brilliant scientific language of Thomas Aquinas—as even Aquinas himself came to understand—failing to deliver a sufficient knowledge of the Truth of the heart. "Y todos cuantos vagan," John has it,

> de ti me van mil gracias refiriendo
> y todos más me llagan,
> y déxame muriendo
> un no sé qué que quedan balbuciendo.

Which might be rendered:

> Everything about me
> sends word of your myriad graces.
> And yet everything hurts,
> everything leaves me dying,
> stammering on about I don't know what's what.

"Words strain," Eliot has it in "Burnt Norton,"

> Crack and sometimes break . . .
>   slip, slide, perish
> Decay with imprecision, will not stay in place,
> Will not stay still.

"Qué . . . que . . . que," John stutters, reaching after the ineffable and trashing the poor language as if it were the fault of the poor phonemes and other charged particles to deliver what they cannot.

T. S. Eliot and Robert Lowell—those two American puritans—both incorporated the figure of John's dark night of the soul as well as John's ascent up the mountain into their poems, though Eliot, I think, understood John's meaning more deeply as he aspired toward it. So, in "East Coker," he freely adapts the maxims John gave us as aids for making the ascent up Mount Carmel. Here's Eliot:

> In order to arrive at what you do not know
> You must go by a way which is the way of ignorance.
> In order to possess what you do not possess
> You must go by the way of dispossession.

And here's John of the Cross, in a translation by E. Allison Peers, a copy of which Eliot owned and marked:

> In order to arrive at that which thou knowest not,
> Thou must go by a way that thou knowest not.
> In order to arrive at that which thou possessest not,
> Thou must go by a way that thou possessest not.

Was it not John who gave us the image of the blazing night in which occurs—to echo Wallace Stevens—"the intensest rendezvous"? Out of nothing, out of the terrible deprivations forced upon the prisoner, out of darkness, out of absence, out of hunger, while the house sleeps, the soul somehow finds itself wading through a lily-filled, cypress-scented garden, into the arms of her Beloved. I remember reading John's "Noche oscura" for the first time ten years ago. I had been discussing the pitfalls of the erotic with my confessor, when suddenly he reached for his bookshelf and took down a copy of "Noche oscura" and asked me to read it. I will never forget the force of the poem, nor how it took me by surprise and made me rethink the meaning of "the dark night." Up until then I had read the words to mean something like what Gerard Manley Hopkins experienced at forty, when he underwent an experience of spiritual deprivation that left him, he feared, nearly mad, but also gave rise to some of the most powerful religious poetry in the language. "I wake and feel the fell of dark, not day," he tells us:

> What hoürs, O what black hours we have spent
> This night! what sights you, heart, saw; ways you went!
> And more must, in yet longer light's delay.

And then, to underscore that none of this is mere literary rodomontade, he tells us, "With witness I speak this." In another sonnet, he ends with the strain of these words: "That night, that year / Of now done darkness I wretch lay wrestling with (my God!) my God."

Beyond the aspirin powders and cold compresses there is for Hopkins the sudden realization here that the real nature of the inner struggle has been nothing less than his soul's wrestling with his Master, who has—apparently—taken Hopkins at his word and lifted him alongside Himself to taste the desolation of the cross and the cry of the Psalmist:

"My God, my God, why have you abandoned me?!" What happened, then, between the summer of 1885 and the summer of '89, when Hopkins lay dying in a room in Dublin, his body wasted by typhoid, that made him whisper, "I am so happy. I am so happy. I am so happy"? What discipline, what sacrifices, what spiritual intimacies had been given him, that the dying Jesuit—not yet forty-five years old—could speak of being happy in such a dark time? *O dichosa ventura!* John has it. Lucky break!

But John's dark night is at another level. It is an emptying and a freeing of oneself from a too-great attachment to the things of this world. Years after he wrote "Noche oscura," John would give us ninety pages of commentary to "explain" his forty-line poem. Ninety pages in the Kavanaugh/Rodriguez translation of the *Dark Night* treatise, just to explicate the first ten lines of the poem! Not even Eliot could duplicate that feat in the ironic notes he appended to *The Waste Land.* John's theological gloss on the dark night, together with his commentary, *The Ascent of Mount Carmel* (on the same poem), eventually earned him the title of Doctor of the Church. But even the commentary, useful as it is, cannot supplant the incandescence and passion of the poem itself, which belong to another order of experience.

"Noche oscura" is made up of eight identical stanzas, rhyming *ababb,* each stanza consisting of lines of seven, eleven, seven, seven, and eleven syllables. It's an Italian form—the lira—transposed to Spanish by two Castilian poets active during the first half of the sixteenth century, and anthologized by one Sebastian de Córdoba in 1575. But it was John of the Cross who with his Midas touch turned the lyrics to gold:

> En una noche oscura,
> con ansias, en amores inflamada,
> ¡oh dichosa ventura!,
> salí sin ser notada,
> estando ya mi casa sosegada.

How simple and yet how difficult to render the music of this ecstatic poem into English. In his fine poetic sequence "Station Island,"

Seamus Heaney sets himself the task of translating John's "Cantar de la alma que se huelga de conoscer a Dios por fe," which he says he did as a penance. "Read poems as prayers," the priest had suggested, and Heaney proceeds to give us perhaps the best Englishing of John's poem we have, another of those composed by the saint in his dark cell and committed to memory, as another poet, Anna Akhmatova, would later commit to memory the hundreds of lines she composed in a Russian gulag under the Stalinist regime, the lines written down only afterward, when pen and paper became available. How haunting the simple form of John's poem: a couplet and a single refrain repeated twelve times, the poem packed with the theology of the transubstantiation— all of which Heaney manages to bring over from the Spanish. Here is the opening of John's poem:

> Qué bien sé yo la fonte que mana y corre,
>   aunque es de noche!

> Aquella eterna fonte está escondida,
> ¡qué bien sé yo do tiene su manida,
>   aunque es de noche!

> Su origen no lo sé, pues no le tiene,
> más sé que todo origen de ella viene,
>   aunque es de noche.

And here is Heaney's reading of the poem, its theology carried over intact:

> How well I know that fountain, filling, running,
>   although it is the night.

> That eternal fountain, hidden away,
> I know its haven and its secrecy
>   although it is the night.

> But not its source because it does not have one,
> which is all sources' source and origin
>   although it is the night.

221 The Intensest Rendezvous

By way of tribute on the four hundredth anniversary of the death, or better, perhaps, death into life of John of the Cross, I offer my own translation of "Noche oscura." Anyone, I think, who has ever fantasized a tryst with an ideal lover will catch something of John's sensual passion in these lines. For the rest—the mystical wounding, the losing of the self in the other without annihilating the self—things about which John's friend, Santa Teresa de Ávila, also speaks—one will have time enough to consider:

> One dark night,
> burning with love's long hungers,
> —oh happy happy chance!—
> the whole house asleep at last,
> I slipped away unnoticed.
>
> In darkness, in safety,
> disguised, down a secret ladder
> —oh happy happy chance!—
> hidden by darkness,
> the whole house asleep at last.
>
> On that happy happy night,
> in secret, when no one saw me
> and I saw nothing,
> with no other light for guide
> than the one that blazed away inside me. . . .
>
> And yet it guided me
> more surely than the sun at noon
> to where He waited for me
> —he whom I knew so well—
> to where no one could disturb us.
>
> Oh guiding night.
> Night sweeter than dawn.
> Oh night that mingled
> lover and beloved,
> when she was changed forever by her lover. . . .

On my blossoming breast,
which I had saved for him alone,
  he lay there sleeping
    all the while I caressed him
as scented cedars, swaying, fanned the air.

  Down from the tower walls breezes floated
all the while I lay there playing with his hair.
  Oh so tenderly his hand
  bent back my neck,
numbing all of my senses.

  I lay there forgetting who I was,
my face flush against my lover's,
    until everything stopped turning,
    and self faded from itself, faded too my cares,
until among the lilies even they were soon forgotten.

In a lifetime's searching among the words, most poets rarely ever touch the threshold of such knowing as John writes of here. If one is ever to begin to approach that knowledge, it will help, as Heaney's confessor reminds him, to read poems as prayers. And prayers as poems.

1991

The Ineffability of What Counts

❧

HE SITS ACROSS from me in his too-huge chair, my friend, the poet Philip Levine, and asks the modern question. Twelve stories above Greenwich Village, gray raindrops plastered against gray windowpanes. It is raining and it is going to rain. Poetry and religion, he thinks out loud to himself, the slightest hint of a smile crossing his face. And will you speak of Dylan Thomas, of "A Refusal to Mourn the Death, by Fire, of a Child in London"? I do not think so, I tell him, though now I know I will. I can feel again, as he begins to recite the poem by heart, that this time I may well be in over my head:

> Never until the mankind making
> Bird beast and flower
> Fathering and all humbling darkness
> Tells with silence the last light breaking
> And the still hour
> Is come of the sea tumbling in harness
> And I must enter again the round
> Zion of the water bead
> And the synagogue of the ear of corn
> Shall I pray the shadow of a sound
> Or sow my salt seed
> In the least valley of sackcloth to mourn
> The majesty and burning of the child's death.

With poetry of that order, and recited by a poet of Levine's uncommon abilities, I find myself awed into silence. I am willing to assent to the beauty of those lines. The majesty and sublimity of the language, cutting as they do across the Jewish, Christian, and Eastern traditions, the poem's Welsh cadences and diction close to Hopkins, even as its message of the eternal return of life-forms into other life-forms echoes the theologies of Whitman and Hardy.

Is not "A Refusal" religious poetry? Yes, though it is not what I am looking for, this celebration of the final extinction of the self. What I am after, I see better now, is discovering the imaginative possibilities of the spirituality with which I grew up. I mean my Roman Catholicism, which in my own experience has as often been maligned as praised.

Several years ago, in Augusta, Georgia, where I was giving a poetry reading, I walked through a desacralized Catholic Church. The fine old brick edifice had been turned over to the city years before to become a hall with offices and gift shops. I remember the young woman assigned to me as a guide pointing to the altar and asking what it was. The stained-glass windows were still in place, as well as a few of the Stations of the Cross by grace of an adamantine cement. There was an empty choir loft above us, though in the main part of the former church the pews were gone, along with the candle that had signaled the presence of the Spirit. In spite of the pamphlets describing the architecture and the church's history, being there was rather like being at a wake. Like Thomas's poem, with its bits of old familiar language and religious imagery, it had become a museum of forms.

Is the Catholic imagination as historical as that church was? Does it have a place in the panoply of voices in the marketplace today? "If the Catholic writer hopes to reveal mysteries," that other Georgian edifice, Flannery O'Connor, wrote almost forty years ago, "he will have to do it by describing truthfully *what he sees from where he is.*" She was speaking specifically of Catholic novelists, since she knew that Catholic poets, in fact poets in general, had by that point lost their audience.

Given Western culture's preoccupation with the secular and its sentimental clamoring after the new, there's only a slim chance that a sacramental perspective will even be recognized. It's no use lamenting this state of affairs, for here in our country that is the given. So you learn to play the game as best you can, which may mean, as it meant for Joyce, with a combination of cunning and exile. It is what serious writers do anyway, the gamble being that one may learn to hide too well. Camouflage, self-irony, ambivalence: all are effective. But if there's no key out of the maze provided for the writer, readers may find themselves locked inside the language, unsure how to unscramble the signs for themselves. Like Eliot's speaker, locked inside Ugolino's tower, without a key until the soul starves to death.

Every serious writer operates with the belief that what he or she has to say is important. Whether one is a symbolist or a realist, it's all part of the burden and the glory of language that it should communicate the self and the self's preoccupations. All rhetorical strategies being suspect these days, and authority and ideology alike being under fire, readers still seem willing to listen to personal witness. Lenin once said that if you are planning a revolution, be sure you wear a suit. So with myself. Except that when I look back now, I wonder at the enormity of the edifice I proposed for myself. It's as if I'd undertaken to build a cathedral I could never finish in my lifetime, and now that I can see the effulgence of autumn's auroras across the night skies, I am more than a little afraid. Already the leaves are gone and the first snowflakes tumble through the afternoon air, as I go on setting cement footings for my edifice of one.

I remember the surprise I felt reading Hopkins for the first time back in Dr. Paul Cortissoz's class at Manhattan College in the spring of 1962. Hopkins: a Catholic poet, hardly contemporary, to be sure, but writing in a language my ear and heart thrilled before. I remember coming home from the A&P nightshift to read "The Wreck of the Deutschland" and the sonnets of desolation late into the night. For those poems alone, I was willing to go on for a master's and a doctorate in English, the music of those poems playing in my ears then, as it still delights.

Two years later, at Colgate, finishing up my master's, one of my teachers, learning I was one of those rarities at Colgate, a practicing Catholic, recommended Robert Lowell's "Colloquy in Black Rock" and

"The Quaker Graveyard in Nantucket." In among the tortured language of desolation, of seawrack and oil spill from sperm whale and
torpedoed ship, there was Lowell's evocation in another key of the consolations of Our Lady of Walsingham, not unlike Eliot's ghostly Anglican community at Little Gidding, destroyed by Roundheads during
England's fratricidal Civil War. It was the calm Lowell had provided at
the eye of the storm:

> Our Lady, too small for her canopy,
> Sits near the altar. There's no comeliness
> At all or charm in that expressionless
> Face with its heavy eyelids. As before,
> This face, for centuries a memory,
> *Non est species, neque decor,*
> Expressionless, expresses God: it goes
> Past castled Sion. She knows what God knows,
> Not Cavalry's Cross nor crib at Bethlehem
> Now, and the world shall come to Walsingham.

Later I came to Berryman. That was after Williams and my search
for an American poetic. I was particularly struck by Berryman's loss
of faith with the death of his father. It took him forty years and the tortured syntax and dreamscapes of his early poems and his self-lacerating
Dream Songs before Berryman turned back to his God in the "Eleven
Addresses to the Lord." For all their double-edged irony and strain,
they are among the best religious poems of our time, written by a
man deeply wounded by drink, lust, and self-hatred. Reading them,
Lowell heard the authenticity of a search that he himself had all but
abandoned.

Finally, a word about T. S. Eliot: invisible, paring his fingernails, bid-
ing his time. He is someone so large on the poetic horizon that poets have had to avoid confronting his shadow in any way they could.
Eliot, after all, as Pound was fond of saying, could play the possum
to perfection. How often he seems to hide behind the lectern, to keep

a rigorous distance, a tight smile, when in fact his poems reveal just how vulnerable he is. It may well be that Eliot took modernism's measure perfectly, being the consummate modernist himself, and found its subversive strategies wanting, even as he embraced its music. My own poetry owes much to Eliot, from an early poem like "The Lesson," with its lines

> Some lessons you just can't
> forget. So with my own son here in this
> ritual reenactment, this nailing to the wall,
> for dark motives one calls "exercise"
> of virtue, righteous anger, discipline . . .

to "Crossing Cocytus," to the even larger canvas of "The Eastern Point Meditations," conceived at Gloucester in my forty-fifth year, as I sat facing the pounding waves of the North Atlantic and picked through the fragments of a life. Here is Eliot in "The Dry Salvages":

> The sea is the land's edge also, the granite
> Into which it reaches, the beaches where it tosses
> Its hints of earlier and other creation:
> The starfish, the hermit crab, the whale's backbone;
> The pools where it offers to our curiosity
> The more delicate algae and the sea anemone.
> It tosses up our losses, the torn seine,
> The shattered lobsterpot, the broken oar
> And the gear of foreign dead men. The sea has many voices,
> Many gods and many voices. . . .

And here is a passage from "Eastern Point Meditations":

> The wind was nearly screaming when I found my way
> out of the garden. Waves were crashing now against the worn,
> resisting rock. At the sea's edge in a light so strong
> you could have cupped your hands & caught it I sat
> like an Arapaho, wrapped up in my blankets, and stared out
> at the terrifying magnitude of waters. Three gulls swept

across my line of vision left to right, playing
the prevailing eastern wind with outstretched wings
as they searched the sea for food.

Bricoleurs that they are, poets make poems with whatever is at hand. Many have been ransacking Catholic edifices for centuries for durable stone and stained glass. Consider Yeats's "The Magi," for instance, whose wise men are fated to repeat their visit to the bestial floor at Calvary as Christianity draws to its predetermined close. Or Williams's rewriting of the Nativity in "Burning the Christmas Greens," where the poet sits facing the all-consuming fire in his grate, breathless for a new Nativity, a new political and aesthetic order to be born. Or Bishop, in "Over 2,000 Illustrations and a Complete Concordance," searching the old Christmas stories to warm herself—in the absence of her dead mother—with memories of her beloved landscapes of Nova Scotia.

Or Stevens, discoursing in blank verse on the abstract idea of the Good Man who, he insisted, had no shape. Though of course the Good Man did have a shape, as the poem itself, haunting in its unbearable loss, shows us through its crazed glass:

> At last the good life came, good sleep, bright fruit,
> And Lazarus betrayed him to the rest,
>
> Who killed him, sticking feathers in his flesh
> To mock him. They placed with him in his grave
>
> Sour wine to warn him, an empty book to read;
> And over it they set a jagged sign,
>
> Epitaphium to his death, which read,
> The Good Man Has No Shape, as if they knew.

"Our religion has materialized itself in the fact," Matthew Arnold wrote as long ago as 1880, "and now the fact is failing it." By then science and technology had moved into that space. What better refuge, therefore, for the religious sensibility, he argued, than poetry, which after all did not depend on hard, scientific fact, whatever that was. Twenty years later George Santayana, that nostalgic Catholic agnostic who spent the last dozen years of his life cared for by an order of Irish nuns in his cell in the shadow of the Roman Forum ("There is no God, and Mary is His Mother," Lowell would quote him as saying), would extend the claims for the self-sufficiency of the religious impulse in poetry. After all, poetry at its best, Santayana would insist, was "identical with religion grasped in its inmost truth," or would be if only religion would stop trying to act as if it really dealt with matters of fact. Exit the Exodus and Mt. Sinai, exit the Incarnation, exit the sweat and frightful din of the Passion, the whole intersection of the timeless with time in the perceived lives of countless millions. Exit the whole shebang.

But here is Hopkins, in his private retreat notes written six months before his death. Would it have mattered to his life or that of his contemporaries, he wondered, if Caesar had not conquered Gaul and Britain, or if he had not been assassinated when he was, or if Pompey had won out over Augustus, or if Augustus had lived another twenty years? Probably not. On the other hand, he saw, his own life—like the lives of untold millions of others—had been "in their whole direction, not only inwardly but most visibly and outwardly, shaped by Christ's." "Without that," he argued, "even outwardly the world would be so different that we cannot even guess it." In fact, his whole life had been literally "determined by the Incarnation down to most of the details of the day." This being the case, so much so that the work of the Incarnation would continue whether he willed it or no, why shouldn't he "make the cause that determines my life, both as a whole and in much detail, determine it in greater detail still and to the greater efficiency of what I in any case should do, and to my greater happiness in doing it?"

So, it seems, for myself. In my time, as a teacher of the great modernist poetic texts, I have tasted a potpourri of gnosticisms, including a number of rewritings of the Christian tradition like those one finds in Yeats, Lawrence, Stevens, Pound, and Williams. I marvel at what our poets have wrought. Still, there is something in me that only the religious call and response seems able to satisfy. Religious self-scrutiny, for instance, has yielded something authentic for me. "Then Sings My Soul," for instance, written on a retreat years ago, as I watched a dear friend suffering from terminal cancer. Or "The Eastern Point Meditations," begun in November 1984, after a week of prayer and self-examination at a Jesuit retreat house in Gloucester, Massachusetts.

We address this issue of poetry and religion either by direction or indirection. A translation of John of the Cross's "Noche oscura" or another, based on the eighty-eighth Psalm, which I heard read by a Franciscan in the ruined cistern beneath the compound of the high priest Caiaphas, above which now stands the church of St. Peter Gallicantu— Peter of the Cockcrow. The eighty-eighth: perhaps the very words Jesus uttered in his desolation, as he waited for dawn and the trial he would face before the Roman authorities. And Scripture tells us he uttered the opening of the twenty-second Psalm as he hung from the cross that afternoon. "Hanging by his wrists," my poem "The Cistern" closes,

> *Eli,*
> he would cry out, *Eli,* and again
> they would misread him, thinking
> he was calling on Elijah.
> As each of us will be: alone,
> friends scattered to the winds.
> Except for one out in the courtyard
> growing cold, poised now to deny him.
> *Darkness,* the psalmist ended.
> *The one companion left me.*

And then there's the route of indirection, as it was for Eliot and Flannery O'Connor. The trouble is that we live in a time when anything one says, from the banal to the sublime, is in danger of degenerating into a kind of white music. "Nothing speaks to him anymore," Nietzsche wrote, describing the plight of the last philosopher, "nothing at all but his own speech; and, deprived of any authority from a divinely ordered universe, it is only about his speech that his speech can speak with a measure of philosophical assurance." Not even the language of religious utterance can escape this general interiorizing of language. Walker Percy was right to speak of the exhaustion and depletion of the logocentric. If even the idiom of the Gospels is in danger of becoming counterfeit coin, echoed as it is in our ads, how shall we return luster to it?

But is that not where the artist comes in: as the reinventer, the remaker, of the language? Yes, as that spoiled priest Emerson might say, but only with certain qualifiers. For the poet who would attempt to create or recreate a viable religious language for his time it is necessary to remember that it is the *language* and *not* the underlying reality that needs to be reconstituted. It is words—if St. John's verbal pun on the verbal can be made to work again for us—that need to be realigned again with the Word. And how will this be done? Walker Percy speaks of watching the PBS series on Joseph Campbell and mythmaking, and seeing all religious myth ground down in the Cuisinart of Campbell's far-reaching imagination. But even as he watched Campbell, Percy added, he also made sure to say a decade of the rosary in order to touch a reality beyond theory.

When I look back at what I have written, I see that it was often in darkness that a paradoxical light was given off. As in the poem about my brother reading the Christmas story and bearing witness to the Mystery in the very act of warning his listeners about angels with eleven-foot wingspans hovering over Bethlehem:

> Fer chrissake think about it: here it is
> the middle of the night & these poor bastards
> freezin' their cullyones off when wham! they catch
> these mothers hoverin' over 'em like fuckin'
> Huey gunships, goin' *whucka whucka whucka.*
> Think about it: a buncha roaches like you & me
> feeding in the kitchen in the middle of the night
> when, whunck! goes the landlord's eyeballin' flashlight
> & us there grooling just begging to have ourselves
> be stompt & squished when this wingspan croons:
> *Do not be afraid.* You gonna stick around for that?
> *Whucka whucka whucka* & some fuckin' floodlight
> saying: Go thou *now* & catch the stable action

in yonder Bethlehem. Who, me? You're lookin'
at one first-class case of heart attack is what.

It is a way of speaking, of witnessing that may in its indirection speak for a time that is willing to accept angels, if not God.

For the poet for whom such things are important there is the groaning of the soul as it waits for the descent of the Holy Spirit to renew the face of the earth. If things are ever going to rise and converge, Flannery O'Connor reminds us, it will first mean taking a long look at where we are. There is, after all, no resurrection without a death. The death of loss, the death of what might have been. It is from that vantage that we begin.

"From the beginning till now," St. Paul wrote, "the entire creation, as we know, has been groaning in one great act of giving birth. And not only creation, but all of us who possess the first fruits of the Spirit. We too groan inwardly as we wait for our bodies to be set free." We were not there yet, he knew, and we would have to learn to bide our time. In the meantime, we had the Spirit to assist us. And then he added this further consolation: "For when we cannot choose words in order to pray properly, the Spirit himself expresses our plea in a way that could never be put into words, and God—who knows everything in our hearts—knows perfectly well what he means." Language, then, and—because language is metaphorical—the world it yearns for. That seems a fitting enough place with which to end. Or begin.

1993

Toward a Sacramental Language

Walker Percy calls us language animals, designating our ability to speak and write the Delta factor. If the beginning of history is Alpha and the end point Omega, he explains, the Delta factor lies somewhere in between. We become human just there, when we break "into the daylight of language." But whether this jump into language should be considered "good fortune or bad fortune, whether by pure chance, the spark jumping the gap because the gap was narrow enough, or by the touch of God," he adds, it is not for him to say.

On the other hand, you don't throw around a phrase like "by the touch of God" without catching someone's attention, Robert Coles notes in his study of Percy. If Percy the trained scientist thought it was not for him to say whether the human race came about by chance or by the touch of God, still, it was Percy the semiotician and novelist and spiritual seeker who wrote that sentence. And that means that Percy had to live "in such a way, long enough, with enough dedication and curiosity and maybe doubt, and maybe melancholy, for such a line of thought to be quite definitely and persistently *his*—a reflection of his way of spending his days, committing his energies."

True, the very terms for articulating this so-called "touch of God" in our literature seem ambiguous, imprecise, and misunderstood. Yet it is a dimension of language that seems necessary for any fuller sense of the mystery and multidimensionality of human experience. In our time the language of theological discourse among the general populace appears suspect and emptied of much of its former significance. But then, so does language. The language philosophers and behaviorists seem to have marched through the landscape of language like Sherman on his way to the sea, in the process smashing the symbolic edifices we once sheltered in.

What, in its wake, has been lost? First off, it is a fundamental contradiction for someone writing in the Muslim, Jewish, or Christian tradition to act as if there were no community to talk to, as if one could accept the idea of the totally alienated existential self. It helps, then, to know there are others listening as hard as ourselves, likewise trying to shape a language that will take into account a world we did not make and that sees the necessity of making room for the sacred.

No doubt the sacred takes many forms, each shaped both by one's sense of the sacred as well as by one's sense of the possibilities of the language to fetch forth the sacred. But it is also true, as Flannery O'Connor said, that a great deal of experience remains unknown to us. It is also true that each of us writes out of a particular human personality, and that "any attempt to circumvent it, whether this be an effort to rise above belief or above background, is going to result in a reduced approach to reality." To ignore the possibility of the sacred, then, results not in an enlarged but a *reduced* reality.

Like other writers in the Christian tradition, I share with O'Connor and Richard Wilbur (and Dante, and Cervantes, and Hopkins, and Berryman) a language that pays homage to the splendid grittiness of the physical as well as to the splendor and consolation of the spiritual. In a word, a sacramental language. If the Incarnation has indeed occurred, as I believe it has, then the evidence of that central act in human history—when the Creator took on our limitations with our bones and flesh—should have consequences that are reverberating down to our own moment. Evidence of God's immanent presence ought to be capable of breaking in on us each day, the way air and light and sound do, if we only know what to look and listen for.

Richard Wilbur is already on record as opting for a poetry that favors "a spirituality that is not abstracted, not dissociated and world-renouncing." Which is to say a language and a way of seeing filled with the things of this world. Like Herbert and Hopkins before him, he sees, in spite of our fallen condition, a world brimming with possibility and renewal. "The world's fullness is not made but found," Wilbur writes in a wedding toast for his son and daughter-in-law, a toast that recalls the liberal wine Christ had brimming from the water jugs at Cana: "Life hungers to abound / And pour its plenty out for such as you."

What then is our part? As the planet's language-bearing, self-conscious creatures, it is given us—as St. Ignatius says—to praise the Creator of all that we see and hear and touch. And yet and yet. The thing we would do we do not, St. Paul laments, and the thing we would not do we do. Such is our contradictory nature and the difficulties that flow from the fact of the fall. And so our literature, as Newman reminds us, is of necessity a fallen literature, since we are fallen creatures. But this is not the same as saying—as many of our mainstream poets and novelists would say—that the ultimate reality is the Void, the nostalgia of a late light falling in an empty room from which all the guests have departed.

Given our proclivities, we all find ourselves fascinated at moments with the idea of nothingness, drawn by our dark doubles, as Walker Percy was fascinated by the idea of a self-contained system of semiotics calling down an empty corridor. Or as Flannery O'Connor reminds us of our too-human greed and stupidity. Or as Richard Wilbur reminds us of the world-negating mind of Poe, a mind lost in a wilderness of self-reflecting mirrors. We all have our devils, and we had better do our best to recognize them lest they devour us.

In "Poetry and Happiness," Wilbur praises Robinson Jeffers's ability to name the things of this world in his poems, its cliffs and seas and hurt hawks. "Except for the consequences," Jeffers wrote once, "I'd sooner kill a man than a hawk." Place this misanthropic view against Dante's view in *The Divine Comedy*, Wilbur suggests, and "how peripheral and cranky Jeffers seems! Dante's poetry is the work of one man, who even at this distance remains intensely individual in temper and in style; and yet the world of his great poem was, for his first readers, quite simply *the* world. This was possible because he was a poet of genius who wrote from the heart of a full and living culture. He lived and wrote, in Stevens's phrase, 'at the center of a diamond.'"

To write *at the center of a diamond*. Asked once in an interview what poem he would most like to have written, Wilbur surprised his questioner by naming *The Divine Comedy*. Well, who wouldn't, I suppose? And yet, he might have answered with *The Odyssey* or *Paradise Lost* or *The Prelude* or—more modestly, perhaps—Keats's "To Autumn" or Hopkins's "The Windhover" or Frost's "Birches." But the reason *why* Wilbur chose Dante tells us something important about Wilbur's sense of the American literary landscape, and that brings us likewise to a consideration of Poe. It seems fitting that Wilbur should have come to a knowledge of Poe—the progenitor perhaps not only of an American Gnostic tradition but of a native variety of deconstructionism—while Wilbur hunkered in a foxhole, pinned down by the Germans at Monte Casino in the winter of 1944, even as the great and austere Benedictine abbey founded by St. Gregory was systematically reduced to rubble by Allied bombers intent on driving the Germans out. "A good part of my work could, I suppose," Wilbur has noted with classic understatement, "be understood as a public quarrel with the aesthetics of Edgar Allan Poe."

The reasons for this are not hard to find, I think, for Poe is Wilbur's dark double, a force to be contended with, sized up, measured, appreciated, saluted . . . and avoided. In Poe he finds a blasted spirituality that is self-delighting, "abstracted, . . . dissociated, . . . world-renouncing," all things Wilbur finds endemic to one strain of American poetry, one which his own poems so eloquently do battle with. Our century, Wilbur acknowledges, having himself known most of them firsthand, has surely had its share of "poets of great ability." And yet, when one examines the lives of these figures, what one finds is "alcoholism, aberration, emotional breakdowns, the drying up of talent, and suicide." Wilbur also notes the signs of destructive behavior in the poetry not only of the so-called Confessionals, but of the New York School, and in many of the so-called Language poets. The "key to all this unhappiness," Wilbur believes, lies in what he has called "the obligatory eccentricity" of the modern poet's world, an eccentricity stemming from America's lack of "a sufficient cultural heart from which to write." In the absence of anything like a shared culture, the writer has tried instead to create a voice unmistakably his or her own. And since—as Flannery O'Connor has said—where one's audience is hard of hearing, one has to learn to shout, a great deal of the American writer's emphasis for the past two hundred years has been on out-romanticizing our predecessors.

And while I've enjoyed the surprising shifts in style of the post-Romantic poets, I've also looked for constants, including the underlying theologies of these writers. I remember Robert Creeley counter-pointing William Carlos Williams's broad Catholic sympathies against his own Puritan proclivities, revealing what lay behind Williams's epic sweep in a poem like *Paterson* and pointing to his own minimalist instinct to block out a poem on a single sheet of paper. Most writers in our time have been reluctant to say where they stand on the issue of religion, as if to do so would somehow too easily type them.

Still, in reading a poet like Williams, I've found that it's not the lack of belief that rendered the poet largely silent on the score of religion, but rather the absence of a language adequate to manifesting the realities of the spiritual. And so the image of light and the power of symbols like common light and the myth of Kora—the Virgin—were often as close as Williams dared approach the subject, though they were at least a beginning.

"Perhaps God is a slob," Berryman has his alter ego, Henry, blurt out in Dream Song 238. And yet, in the end—in a kind of Augustinian loop—he turned to God in his sickness to write some of the most inspired and distinctive religious poetry of the last hundred years. It took another poet (and lapsed Catholic) to understand what Berryman had effected in *Love & Fame*: a poetry so right, and yet so oblique and sly at the same time, Robert Lowell noted, that even Corbière would have applauded. In the first of his "Eleven Addresses to the Lord," having in his own skin passed through a hell as vivid as anything in Dante's, Berryman at last turned to the God who had followed him for four decades down the back alleys of his desolation:

> Master of beauty, craftsman of the snowflake, inimitable contriver,
> endower of Earth so gorgeous & different from the boring Moon,
> thank you for such as it is my gift. . . .
> You have come to my rescue again & again
> in my impassable, sometimes despairing years.
> You have allowed my brilliant friends to destroy themselves
> and I am still here, severely damaged but functioning.

I still remember the cold, rainy afternoon at Colgate when I first read "The Quaker Graveyard in Nantucket" in the library stacks, relieved and overjoyed that a religious poetry of that magnitude was still possible in our time. What thunder in those lines, lines that held Milton and Melville in their web. Lines that embraced both Lowell's Puritan forebears as well as his newfound Catholicism:

> Waves wallow in their wash, go out and out,
> Leave only the death rattle of the crabs,
> The beach increasing, its enormous snout
> Sucking the ocean's side.
> This is the end of running on the waves;
> We are poured out like water. Who will dance
> The mast-lashed master of Leviathans
> Up from this field of Quakers in their unstoned graves?

Why did he turn away from being a "fiery Catholic C.O." to embrace instead the bleak nihilism of Baudelaire, Rimbaud, and Flaubert and the historical Gibbon, Macaulay, and Suetonius? Yet he too, at the end, could call on the Blessed Mother as to an old friend suddenly glimpsed in a crowd in some faraway country. In the ironically titled "Home," the poet finds himself in an isolation as empty as those in Edward Hopper's late canvases. The scene is a mental hospital—this one in England—as the poet slowly swims out of yet another of his manic episodes:

The immovable chairs have swallowed up the patients,
and speak with the eloquence of emptiness.
By each the same morning paper lies unread:
January 10, 1976.
I cannot sit or stand two minutes,
yet walk imagining a dialogue
between the devil and myself,
not knowing which is which or worse,
saying,
as one would instinctively say Hail Mary,
I wish I could die. . . .
The Queen of Heaven, I miss her,
we were divorced. She never doubted
the divided, stricken soul
could call Maria,
and rob the devil with a word.

As with Eliot and Wilbur, it is Dante Lowell remembers now, the *Commedia* the one book he had with him when he was strapped to a stretcher and rushed to the mental hospital. For Dante seems one of us, holding within his art what few modern writers have been able to sustain: a vision that encompasses the entire spectrum of human emotion, from desolation to transfiguration. It is Dante's sense of the world, a world shared by his enemies as well as by his friends, that allowed him to shape his epic. Are desolation, hope, and a sense of having won through so alien to the late twentieth century that we cannot grasp the heart of Dante's world? I hardly think so, and many poets—including figures as diverse as Yeats and Pound and Stevens—have constructed their worlds around the triadic structure of Dante's *Comedy.* How else, for example, explain Eliot's ascent from *The Waste Land* to "Ash Wednesday" and on to the *Four Quartets*? How else explain the shift from the desolation of

> A rat crept softly through the vegetation
> Dragging its slimy belly on the bank
> While I was fishing in the dull canal

> On a winter evening round behind the gashouse
> Musing upon the king my brother's wreck
> And on the king my father's death before him

to these lines from "Ash Wednesday," caressed with so much yearning—

> Suffer us not to mock ourselves with falsehood
> Teach us to care and not to care
> Teach us to sit still . . .

to these lines from the final, achieved movement of the *Four Quartets*, lines that brush up against the mystical, as if we were seeing what was always there, but for the first time:

> At the source of the longest river
> The voice of the hidden waterfall
> And the children in the apple-tree
> Not known, because not looked for
> But heard, half-heard, in the stillness
> Between two waves of the sea.
> Quick now, here, now, always.

When we write, we write for others, knowing that we will be heard only insofar as the values that underwrite our poems are held in common with our readers, even if what is found is found only in isolate flecks. What most characterizes American culture—Wilbur again—is "a disjunction and incoherence aggravated by an intolerable rate of change." Or, as William Carlos Williams says, because we are a people who cannot see the beauty around us, we are therefore "destined / to hunger until we eat filth / while the imagination strains / after deer / going by fields of goldenrod." As much as Williams would have liked the poet to be our guide, he realized that the poet in America is peripheral, leaving "No one / to witness / and adjust, no one to drive the car."

"Our center of political power, Washington, is a literary and intellectual vacuum," Wilbur noted during the heyday of Johnson's experiment with the Great Society, even as a war of attrition ground on halfway around he world. Moreover, the church in America was by then "broken into hundreds of sorry and provincial sects; colleges of Christian foundation hold classes as usual on Good Friday; our cities bristle like quartz clusters with faceless new buildings of aluminum and glass, bare of symbolic ornament because they have nothing to say; our painters and sculptors despair of achieving any human significance, and descend into the world of fashion to market their Coke bottles and optical toys; in the name of the public interest, highways are rammed through old townships and wildlife sanctuaries; all other public expenditure is begrudged, while the bulk of the people withdraw from community into an affluent privacy." Yes, there was money (then) for the arts and for education, and for "the growth of regional theaters and symphony orchestras." But these did not in themselves constitute a viable culture, for where art did not "arise from and nourish a vital sense of community," it was "little more than an incitement to schizophrenia." For Wilbur, the eighteenth century had tolled the death knell for anything like a moral consensus, and no poet in this country has ever been able to speak as confidently to an audience as Pope could speak to his.

It may help, as Wilbur and Walker Percy and Robert Coles and others have done, to analyze our historical and cultural predicament, but it is also important to realize that we will have to find a way of addressing our moment in a language that will at least get us a hearing. And that will mean learning to play a music our culture can understand and appreciate. Greg Wolff speaks of a scene in the film *The Mission* where a Jesuit father establishes a connection with the indigenous peoples of the Brazilian forests—the same who had sent his fellow Jesuits over the steep rapids nailed to wooden crosses—not by preaching *at them* but by playing his flute *for them*. It is a haunting melody the priest pipes for his audience, and soon men and women and children are leaving their hiding places to listen to this strange and wonderful music.

Think of this scene as a parable of the artist's entry into a world that does not yet understand what is meant by a sacramental vision of the world. And yet, because music is universal, the skillful writing of a fiction—a poem, a novel—will at least give the religious writer entry into that world. It will be a difficult balance, this maintaining our citizenship not only in the world of physical and historical fact—which we scant at our own peril—but in a spirit world capable of refreshing us.

"My guide and I came on that hidden tunnel," Dante writes at the end of his journey through hell,

> to make our way back into the shining world;
> and with no time for rest, we climbed—
> he first, then I—until I saw, through
>
> a round aperture, those things of beauty
> Heaven holds. It was from there at last
> that we emerged, to see again the stars.

It is this ability *to see again the stars* from our own front porches or apartment windows that underlines so much of Richard Wilbur's work and explains the import of a poem like "Love Calls Us to the Things of This World," where the poet finds his angels embodied in the morning laundry hanging from the back of a tenement. Awakened to the sound of cranky pulleys, the soul sees—as on the first day of Creation—bedsheets, blouses, and smocks filling with angels in the morning breezes. A moment of grace freely offered, a vision of the invisible inhabiting the visible. And then, just as quickly, the self-reflective, skeptical, questioning consciousness kicks in, and the shaken soul remembers that it is just another work day, until finally the transfigured moment is taken from us.

And yet, even as it is forced to confront another day, the soul is reluctant to leave behind what it has been privileged to witness. And just as Peter cried out for tents for his Lord and his two distinguished visitors, Moses and Elijah, so now the soul cries out that fresh laundry might somehow be enough:

> Oh, let there be nothing on earth but laundry,
> Nothing but rosy hands in the rising stream
> And clear dances done in the sight of heaven.

It is the nature of such unattended moments in and out of time to be glimpsed before the work of living insists on going on, and the soul must once again descend from its privileged vantage "in bitter love / To accept the waking body." And so the poet yawns and rises into a world where clean clothes—like the Logos donning the world of a subsistence workman in a hilltown in Galilee—cover the backs of thieves, lovers "go fresh and sweet to be undone," and even the "heaviest nuns" must negotiate (as we all must) the world of angels and the world of the fall, keeping our precarious balance "in a pure floating / Of dark habits."

Here's Flannery O'Connor again, this time in an essay she wrote about peacocks for *Holiday Magazine*. It's called "The King of the Birds," a model for the sort of writing I'm speaking of. An essay on the raising of peafowl, it's also a parable of how the divine reveals itself, and how the artist in turn reveals a glimpse of the divine to her readers. "Many people," O'Connor writes,

> are congenitally unable to appreciate the sight of a peacock. Once or twice I have been asked what the peacock is "good for"—a question which gets no answer from me because it deserves none. The telephone company sent a lineman out one day to repair our telephone. After the job was finished, the man, a large fellow with a suspicious expression half hidden by a yellow helmet, continued to idle about, trying to coax a cock that had been watching him to strut. He wished to add this experience to a large number of others he had apparently had. "Come on now, bud," he said, "get the show on the road, upsy-daisy, come on now, snap it up, snap it up."
>
> The peacock, of course, paid no attention to this.
>
> "What ails him?" the man asked.
>
> "Nothing ails him," I said. "He'll put it up terreckly. All you have to do is wait."

It's the being willing to wait on the vision that's so hard, isn't it? Especially when, we tell ourselves, there's so much that has to get done. And so with the peacock, who—like the divine—has its own mysterious timetable. O'Connor's lineman is willing to give the peacock a quarter of an hour to perform before he climbs back in his truck and drives off. And then, suddenly, unexpectedly, the peacock shakes himself and his tail rises around him. O'Connor shouts after the man to witness the transfiguring planets dancing on the outstretched canvas of the bird:

> "He's doing it!" I screamed. "Hey, wait! He's doing it!"
>
> The man swerved the truck back around again just as the cock turned and faced him with the spread tail. The display was perfect. The bird turned slightly to the right and the little planets above him hung in bronze, then he turned slightly to the left and they were hung in green. I went up to the truck to see how the man was affected by the sight.
>
> He was staring at the peacock with rigid concentration, as if he were trying to read fine print at a distance. In a second the cock lowered his tail and stalked off.
>
> "Well, what did you think of that?" I asked.
>
> "Never saw such long ugly legs," the man said. "I bet that rascal could outrun a bus."

How comic and human this parable is, and yet how brilliantly it speaks a theology and an epistemology of grace. Often, when we least expect it, the mystery displays its transforming beauty, sensibly marking our souls before hiding again behind a cloud. And what are we to make of it all? In O'Connor's anecdote one sees dancing planets where another sees only "long ugly legs." She knew in her short lifetime how her work might be misread or only dimly understood by even well-intentioned readers, and so it was. But that was not her concern. She wrote until sickness broke her, the work unfinished but so brilliant and curative that it could not be ignored. And she wrote of what she knew—rural Georgia and its Christ-haunted denizens—and thus opened a door onto that reality and—at the same time—an otherworldly dimension. In this she followed a literary strategy used by Christ himself, who gave us a world of parables as a way into the world of the spirit. The workaday world and the Spirit, each necessary, each informing and gracing the other. Mustard seeds, birds' nests, swept rooms, buried treasure, lit lamps, lilies, lost pennies. What similes, what metaphors, what words, after all, does one use to find the Kingdom of Heaven if not the things of this world?

1995

God and the Imagination

HOW SEDUCTIVE the promptings of the Gnostic imagination for the artist: the old temptation to think one sees the world as God sees it. It's tempting to think of such a radical displacement of the divine as a peculiarly American heresy, Emerson being its archangel and high priest, but we have no monopoly on such palace revolutions, as Mallarmé, Rilke, and Joyce remind us.

Still, we Americans do have our own version of this desire to be at the still point of the turning world. Here is Wallace Stevens, a poet who bumped his head often enough against the glass barrier of the mystery, as eager as any to punch through to certitude, to read tomorrow's Wall Street numbers today, though at least he had the humility to mock his penchant to hold the world up like some circus seal twirling a ball on its nose:

> He held the world upon his nose
> And this-a-way he gave a fling.
>
> His robes and symbols, ai-yi-yi—
> And that-a-way he twirled the thing.

But as he reached the end of a lifetime's preoccupation with the insistences of the symbolist imagination, Stevens reapproached the mystery of existence by attempting to empty himself of his own centrality. Not *meaning*, then, since definitions always remained elusive and problematic, but merely *being* in the midst of something larger than himself:

Here, now, we forget each other and ourselves.
We feel the obscurity of an order, a whole,
A knowledge, that which arranged the rendezvous,

Within its vital boundary, in the mind.
We say God and the imagination are one . . .
How high that highest candle lights the dark.

Out of this same light, out of the central mind,
We make a dwelling in the evening air,
In which being there together is enough.

The lines constitute Stevens's self-humbling before the Sublime. And yet even here the linguistic counters remain slippery, for what Stevens's words imply is that it is still the human mind that imagines and must therefore bring God into play. Having shifted back and forth all his life between the poles of the imagination and reality, Stevens offers a final axiom. It is one that begins as all modernist axioms do, ironically, in this instance with a subtle qualifier and an ambiguous we: "*We* say God and the imagination are one."

It is a position Stevens seems to have been long in arriving at. "Let us say," he seems to suggest, "that God and the imagination *are* in fact one." In the very act of affirming the two to be one, a light is lit, an order established, a single candle set blazing against the encroaching evening of our lives. It is the light, let us say, of Genesis, the same light therefore that emanates from the mind of God. But it is also the light of the human imagination, an imaginative space, sustained by the Creator himself, who (even if God is only imagined) gives this light its ground and authority. Having arrived at this position, construct though it may be, it is enough to find oneself in the company of one's Beloved, even if the Beloved is finally no more than a reflection of oneself.

And so you have it. Stevens has managed to create out of nothing a palpable imaginative space, an interiority without material dimensions, replete with its own achieved and accomplished music. And in truth, in a world of Heisenbergian uncertainties and shifting star masses, it may be enough simply for the dizzying, ever-shifting merry-go-round of the Faustian mind simply to slow down and let itself come to rest, if even for the moment.

Notice too that Stevens's article of faith might satisfy the veriest skeptic, since his mode of proceeding still gives precedence to the human imagination. There is, after all, a conditional here to this divinely infused space, one that resides in the very same linguistic counters that initiate the argument: "*We say* the imagination and God are one." And so the clairvoyant eye, the central mind of the artist, which leads us on to assume—like Walt Whitman, Stevens's precursor—what the central mind assumes, in a willing suspension of disbelief. *We say*, Stevens tells us, but it is an argument built as much on old myopias and on metaphysical exhaustion as it is on desire.

Consider too Rilke's massive imaginative displacements. Here, in Stephen Mitchell's translation, is the opening movement of Rilke's magnificent *Duino Elegies*, in which the poet summons the necessary angel of the imagination. Since Rilke's angel has the dazzling power and beauty to confront the very imagination that created it, we are in a universe not unlike the one Milton creates in *Paradise Lost*. Here is Rilke confronting the angel of the self:

> Who, if I cried out, would hear me among the angels'
> hierarchies? and even if one of them pressed me
> suddenly against his heart: I would be consumed
> in that overwhelming existence. For beauty is nothing
> but the beginning of terror, which we still are able to endure,
> and we are so awed because it serenely disdains
> to annihilate us. Every angel is terrifying.

But if Rilke's imagination quails before the Sublime, does it then turn back to a world it can understand, a world of people, birds, trees, stones, and landscapes—the world of creation—to sustain it? Rilke, inveterate Romantic that he was, would seem to say no. For, having obliterated time and human contact as both messy and problematic, Rilke understands—as that other word magician, Mallarmé, before him—that there is for the imperious, all-consuming, and (alas) self-lacerating imagination no place on earth to call home.

"Every angel is terrifying," Rilke writes,

> And yet, alas,
> I invoke you, almost deadly birds of the soul,
> knowing about you. Where are the days of Tobias,
> when one of you, veiling his radiance, stood at the front door,
> slightly disguised for the journey, no longer appalling. . . .
> But if the archangel now, perilous, from behind the stars
> took even one step toward us: our own heart, beating
> higher and higher, would beat us to death. Who *are* you?

Just who *is* this new angel of the imagination, summoned from the tombs at Karnak and the Koran as much as from the Bible? Whatever else it is, it is most certainly a powerful composite, rising from the pool of Narcissus, heady in its power, seductive in its beauty, beyond the limits of human history. If you listen to it, you will hear it calling you, as it called to Rilke, urging you to give yourself over to an imaginative freedom that ends with the self gazing into the abyss of a language cut loose from the Logos and with reference now only to its own sound.

It seems axiomatic among many of the major Western writers of the past two centuries that everything should be grist for the imagination. All systems—political, philosophical, and theological—are like so many ruined estates and roofless churches, empty of their former authority, there now only for the plundering. Even the Scriptures—especially the Scriptures—are there to be rewritten so that the old Hebrew and Christian "myths," exhausted now, might be broken up and reconstituted in the hope of engaging a drowsy Emperor, bored with the "given" and in endless search of the new. In the hands of a Rilke, a Yeats, a Joyce, a Pound, the single-minded devotion to art means, as one critic has said of Rilke, nothing less than "cannibalizing every basis for human relations," including religion itself, in order that we might nourish the primary faculty of the aesthetic. Art over all.

It should be no surprise to us in the West at this moment in our history to find that the weight of literary and critical tradition is on the side of the Gnostics, with their championing of self-referentiality and the kind of language play we find among those who call themselves— among other things—deconstructionists of the text. If there are special cases of orthodoxy of one shade or another in figures like Hopkins, Eliot, Marianne Moore, Walker Percy, Merton, and Flannery O'Connor, there are against these figures and in varying degrees the looming presences of Rimbaud, Baudelaire, Mallarmé, Joyce, Conrad, James, Faulkner, Hemingway, Woolf, Richard Wright, Pound, Williams, and Hart Crane.

Was it not Keats who spoke so memorably of the artist's giving over the incessant search for certitude that dogs us all? Better, he thought, to rest in uncertainties, to give over any attempt to follow what he called the egotistical sublime he'd found in such world orderers as Milton and Wordsworth. What Keats was after was an emptying of the self so that all other selves—"The Sun, the Moon, the Sea and Men and Women who are creatures of impulse . . . and have about them an unchangeable attribute"—might fill that void.

Keats's aesthetic displaces both theology and philosophy in favor of the imagination, and has for its main attraction the simplifying of the moral dilemma we are all faced with by ignoring the dilemma altogether. But is riding the crest of a perpetual incertitude finally workable? Hopkins, though his own poetics were shaped by Keats, thought not, insisting that, if Keats had lived long enough, he would have arrived at a more balanced position that included both the philosophical and the moral domain.

"We have borrowed, traded upon, made small change of the reserves of transcendent authority," the critic George Steiner noted a decade ago in a strategic response to the nay-saying critical climate of our time. "Very few of us have made any return deposit. At its key points of discourse and inference, hermeneutics [the science of meanings and interpretation] and esthetics in our secular, agnostic civilization are a more or less conscious, a more or less embarrassed act of larceny."

It has been my luck, if you will, to have been fed by a religious and literary tradition that has at times seemed robust and at other times faded and irrelevant. I mean here my sense of an analogical reality in the tradition I know best because I was born into it: Catholic Christianity, American style. To feed this felt presence (and pressure) in my own life, I have had to learn how to come back to the Scriptures as to a wellhead, and—since I share this world with others—to participate in some kind of communal liturgy. It is also true that the I who is writing this has wished his enemies harm and acted both the bully and the fool. Considering the price millions of others have paid to witness, mine has been a light-enough yoke.

Writing to the community at Corinth, Paul spoke of a great mystery. He and they, he told them, were growing "brighter and brighter as we are turned into the image that we reflect." He meant the image of the glorified Christ as something actually moving through the community, and turning them year by year into more incandescent flames. The Jesuit paleontologist and mystic Teilhard de Chardin had much the same idea when he spoke of all things rising through time toward the end point of the Spirit.

It is a great mystery Paul and de Chardin share, though they both knew progress in living the spiritual life comes slowly and painfully. I don't mean that there aren't moments in each of our lives filled with a sort of electric clarity and enthusiasm. Transformative moments, even, when we would be happy to set up a tent and let the traveling circus go by. But always, and because it is the necessary counterbalance of our human lives, we learn to trek back down the mountain to take up our quotidian work once more.

Flannery O'Connor seems to have been much taken with the ideas of the Jesuit paleontologist. But if she was fascinated by the concept that we were actually evolving toward a more spiritual nature, and that everything—humanity *and* nature—was indeed rising toward the Omega point of God, she also understood that things were taking their sweet time getting there. Many speak of ours as a post-Christian moment, as if the century had managed to leave Christianity behind. Which is too bad for me, having spent most of my life trying to better understand—like Hopkins and O'Connor before me—the meaning of the Incarnation: God's saturating the world with His own divinity. If, that is, the Good News is really good news and God really did enter into human history in human form, if indeed he emptied himself of his Godhead to enter this speck of a planet—one among some fifty billion galaxies in an ever-expanding universe that makes Galileo's discoveries look like some preschooler attempting his first shaky alpha.

But if the Word of God did come among us, as the Jesuit scholar and critic William Lynch has noted, Christ has turned "the whole order of the old imagination" on its head. Not by negating the old, but—as St. Paul understood—by raising things to a new order, "identical in structure with, but higher in energy than, every form or possibility of the old." It's a divine energy that must inhabit everything, from trees and thistles to insects and human beings, and—by extension—our human constructs as well. Moreover, this infusion of the Word should affect our own words as well, those fictive forms our dreams take.

But is a new order of the spirit really available for the religious imagination this late in history? And if so, what would be its characteristics? How does one know, for instance, when one is in the presence of an enhanced metaphor, much less an enhanced nature? If every artist, by dint of his or her calling, is—as Andrew Greeley maintains—a sacrament maker, "someone who sees the hints of grace in the world and in human life and illumines them for the rest of us," where is the evidence for that in the world around us? And if all true artists participate in the sacramental nature of things, then what of the religious artist who takes that insight and tries to enhance all human transactions, not by erasing nature or remaking it in one's image, but by seeing the incredible lightness of this real presence in everything?

Consider Hopkins, for whom the real presence of God in the things of this world was the main reason for his own conversion. Hopkins saw beauty everywhere: in the shadow play of sunlight breaking through trees, in the night stars, in bluebells, even in the complex pattern of ice spray on the slate urinals he was sent as a Jesuit novice to clean. Conversely, he was deeply distressed by the refusal of humankind to offer adequate thanks to the Creator of all that beauty in return. Having thought long and hard on the fallen, wounded world into which he was being sent, he found himself returning again and again to what it meant to live in such a world. Like St. Paul, he was aware that all life seems to reach out after light, a phenomenon he observed in the outstretched limbs of trees groping heavenward. Both heard nature's groaning after solace and consolation, a groaning one hears—by extension—in the Psalms, in the plainchant of Benedictines and Cistercians at their office, as well as in the existential loneliness of gospel, blues, and country music.

How many of us, like Hopkins, have not at some point tasted the world in its incredible beauty—in sweet violets, mountain range, blackbird, sunset—feeling that all of it is somehow "charged with the grandeur of God"? The stars, flaring out in the night heavens like "fire-folk sitting in the air . . . / bright boroughs, circle citadels." Dappled things, "skies of couple-colour as a brinded cow," "Fresh-firecoal chestnut-falls," "finches' wings," "silk-sack clouds." Despite murder, greed, and slander, have we not often experienced goodness in people who by their very being create a "cordial air" that seems to nest over everything, the way a "mothering wing" nests over its "bevy of eggs"? The air on those first mild nights of spring descending over "the new morsels" of leaf and bud? A sacred space, as Hopkins has it, "where all were good / To me, God knows, deserving no such thing." As I tasted it recently, at the Benedictine abbey at Weltemburg at a bend on the Danube. There, where a Roman garrison once guarded the river passes against German barbarians, and where a Benedictine father made a group of tired strangers welcome with his smile alone, and took us in, and fed us, making all luminous, quieting our querulous spirits by his very presence.

But Hopkins knew that things are too often otherwise. There is something perverse in the way we turn away from such peace, preferring our own restlessness. Why is it that the eye beholds what might be, only to turn away from that to a dimmer thing? How often the landscape itself seems to appeal to us to treat it more kindly, that we might stop fouling rivers, air, and soil by dumping waste—everything from the raw sewage pumped into the Hudson to radioactive effluents into the North Sea, the Siberian tundra, the coral reefs of once-splendid Caribbean islands. Looking at a landscape unchanged from the bronze age down to his own day, when strip mining ridged deep brows into the ancient hills, Hopkins could weep for the earth:

> And what is Earth's eye, tongue, or heart else, where
> Else, but in dear and dogged man? Ah, the heir
> To his own selfbent so bound, so tied to his turn,
>
> To thriftless reave both our rich round world bare
> And none reck of world after, this bids wear
> Earth brows of such care, care and dear concern.

Who else but humans—who did much of the damage in the first place—can speak for the earth, an earth that after all *means* giving praise back to the Author of all beauty? Consider humankind, so turned in on itself, so dogged, so willing to eat up as much of the world as it can, depleting its oils and ores and rain forests, its lakes and rivers and oceans, thinking neither of its own children nor of their children's children, and surely not the world after this one, in both of which accountings will surely be made. The earth: etched now with deep furrows, its face disfigured, turning its eyes on the raging, inchoate figure bent on destroying it. How little it takes, really, to destroy the inherent symmetry and beauty of things. A gouge across an oak-top table, poor restoration work with shoddy materials, graffiti on the face of a public building, the limbs of Binsey poplars that had danced for generations along a river suddenly lopped and bundled like so many amputated arms: beauty long in the making gone in a single afternoon.

Trees. Consider a passage from Flannery O'Connor's story "A Good Man Is Hard to Find." A family of six travels from Georgia down to Florida on vacation, though by day's end all will have died at the hands of a psychopath named the Misfit. The central figure in this story is the grandmother, someone not unlike most of us at moments: narrow-minded, selfish, self-absorbed. As the family drives toward their destination with fate, the grandmother tries pointing out to the children what she takes to be "interesting details of the scenery: Stone Mountain; the blue granite that in some places came up on both sides of the highway; the brilliant red clay banks slightly streaked with purple; and the various crops that made rows of green lace-work on the ground. The trees were full of silver-white sunlight and the meanest of them sparkled. The children were reading comic magazines and their mother had gone back to sleep. . . . They passed a large cotton field with five or six graves fenced in the middle of it, like a small island." "The meanest of them sparkled." O'Connor here is talking about trees, trees "full of silver-white sunlight," but she means the family as well, means the Misfit, means us. Each of us, after all, is capable of being "full of silver-white sunlight," and—given the chance—capable too, like Dante's souls ascending spark-like into the night sky, of giving off light.

Just before the Misfit kills her, the grandmother looks up into his twisted features and sees there a wounded child who for one brief moment realizes that he has turned from the Light. He looks as if he would cry. "Why you're one of my babies," the grandmother tells him, reaching out to the man who has ordered her family's executions and who now wears her dead son's sport shirt. "You're one of my own children." Then, as she reaches out to comfort him, he slams three shots into her chest. Self-damned, he is still the story's most astute theologian, and it is he who remarks as he stands over the grandmother's body that she "would of been a good woman if it had been somebody there to shoot her every minute of her life."

Here's O'Connor again, in another short story called "The Enduring Chill." A young man has left New York City to return home to rural Georgia to die. As he steps off the train he sees his mother, and behind her the vast dawn sky. The sky is "chill gray," with a "startling white-gold sun, like some strange potentate from the east, . . . rising beyond the black woods which surrounded Timbersboro. It cast a strange light over the single block of one-story brick and wooden shacks. [He] felt that he was about to witness a majestic transformation, that the flat of roofs might at any moment turn into the mounting turrets of some exotic temple for a god he didn't know. The illusion lasted only a moment before his attention was drawn back to his mother."

The imagery here prefigures the water stain on the ceiling of the young man's bedroom, a stain that has been there as long as he can remember. At the end of the story, the stain assumes the form of "a fierce bird with spread wings" with an icicle in its beak. O'Connor's cold young intellectual is possessed of that peculiar gruel-thin liberal sensibility O'Connor so distrusted, a sensibility made up of half ignorance and half overweening pride. Of course he is too good for rural Georgia and for the uneducated mother who has raised him. But after he has been cut down to size by a no-nonsense, crusty, old, hard-of-hearing Jesuit who has never even heard of James Joyce—much less being able to discourse on the subtleties of *Ulysses*—in short, after the young man has been shorn of his illusions, he is at last ready to see himself as he is: lonely, wounded, and afraid of dying.

Of course, to be stripped of one's illusions is not necessarily to come to a fresh sense of reality. That revelation will have to come as a grace if it is to come at all. But at least the young man is ready to see that God has been waiting patiently to enter. "The old life in him was exhausted," O'Connor writes. "He awaited the coming of the new. It was then that he felt the beginning of a chill, a chill so peculiar, so light, that it was like a warm ripple across a deeper sea of cold. His breath came short. The fierce bird which through the years of his childhood and the days of his illness had been poised over his head, waiting mysteriously, appeared all at once to be in motion. . . . He saw that for the rest of his days, frail, racked, but enduring, he would live in the face of a purifying terror. A feeble cry, a last impossible protest escaped him. But the Holy Ghost, emblazoned in ice instead of fire, continued, implacable, to descend."

No matter that O'Connor's descent of the Spirit should be different from Hopkins's image of the Spirit descending dove-like "over the bent / World" and brooding "with warm breast and with ah! bright wings." Different too from Eliot's dark dove descending in "Little Gidding" over war-ravaged London in the shape of a German Stuka dive-bomber breaking the air

> With flame of incandescent terror
> Of which the tongues declare
> The one discharge from sin and error.
> The only hope, or else despair
>   Lies in the choice of pyre or pyre—
>   To be redeemed from fire by fire.

Whether figured as brooding dove or tongue of fire or implacable Paraclete, the Spirit takes whatever shape it needs to meet us where we are.

There are other forms the sacramental imagination can use. Consider the fictive structures of Reynolds Price, Walker Percy, Andre Dubus, Doris Betts, Kathleen Norris, Patricia Hampl, or Ron Hansen. Hansen, who comes closest perhaps of the fiction writers I have mentioned to the crossover between poetry and fiction, is particularly instructive in this regard. In *Mariette in Ecstasy*, he presents a young nun living in a convent in upstate New York at the turn of the century who finds herself with the stigmata. As her doubting physician father and her religious community of sisters attempt to deal with the disturbing phenomenon of Christ's lovescape imprinted in the young woman's hands, Hansen's prose, sinewy and delicate by turns, begins to reveal another reality: a sacramental existence unfolding everywhere around us, though we may be too self-bent and preoccupied to give it a local habitation and a name.

Here is a passage from the novel, Whitmanesque in its breadth, in which the quotidian is suddenly alchemized by the simple act of the convent bells summoning the community—and us—to a moment of prayer in the midst of our daily rounds. *Laborare est orare*, the ancient communal maxim goes. *To work is to pray*:

> White sunlight and a wide green hayfield that languidly undulates under the wind. Eight sisters in gray habits surge through high timothy grass

that suddenly folds against the ringing blades of their scythes. Mother Céline stoops and shocks the hay with twine and sun-pinked hands.

Four novices stand taciturnly at a great scullery table plucking tan feathers from twenty wild quail shot by a Catholic men's club just yesterday. Horseflies are alighting and tasting the skins, or tracing signatures in the hot air. . . .

[A nun] is still huffing breathlessly in the campanile as she grins up at the pigeons shuffling along the rafters and frantically jerking their heads toward her. She gets a handful of sweet-corn kernels from her gray habit's pocket and scatters them on the flooring, and the pigeons heavily flap down and trundle around her sandals.

I could name others who share in this sense of a world larger than ourselves, a field in which something like a sacramental imagination is clearly at play. One thinks of the poetry of Whitman, Williams, and Stevens, of Bill Heyen and Charles Wright and Philip Levine—a poetry filled with the things of this world, each proclaiming the splendid luminosity of things. Or one thinks of Dubus, Merton, O'Connor, and Wilbur, where something more, a sense of the abiding presence of God in the things of this world, is made manifest. There are moments when we are graced with a creative insight into the mysterious, awe-filled world we did not create. And isn't it a matter, after all, of raising the quotidian to the level of spirit, of correcting an imbalance by learning to see the Spirit as it lifts everything into the light of that graced imagination of which Paul, taking his clue from an itinerant preacher who walked the Galilean hill country two thousand years ago, spoke so compellingly?

1996

"The Unshapeable Shock Night"
Pain, Suffering, and the Redemptive Imagination

ॐ

IN "90 NORTH" the poet Randall Jarrell imagines himself as a boy on a dream expedition to the North Pole. Having somehow arrived, and finding all his companions dead, he wonders what it is he's learned. "I reached my North," he ends,

> and it had meaning.
> Here at the actual pole of my existence,
> Where all that I have done is meaningless,
> Where I die or live by accident alone—
>
> Where, living or dying, I am still alone;
> Here where North, the night, the berg of death
> Crowd me out of the ignorant darkness,
> I see at last that all the knowledge
>
> I wrung from the darkness—that the darkness flung me—
> Is worthless as ignorance: nothing comes from nothing,
> The darkness from the darkness. Pain comes from the darkness
> And we call it wisdom. It is pain.

Jarrell was thirty when he wrote those lines. He had another twenty years to work and write, but he never moved—essentially—from the philosophical position he outlined in "90 North." By the time he was fifty he had suffered at least one breakdown. By fifty-one he was dead, struck down by a car he'd apparently thrown himself against. The circumstances strongly suggest suicide. A poet, a respected university professor: brilliant, nervous, high-strung, capable of eviscerating his enemies—of which he had many—with words that he used with rapier precision—walking out alone at night into oncoming traffic, the darkness swirling about him, then seeing the headlights up ahead and making his decision. If there is light at the end of the tunnel, his friend Robert Lowell would write of Jarrell's death, it is the light of an oncoming train. There's an admirable stoicism in the way Jarrell tropes the essential meaninglessness of life. But the actual suffering he underwent one imagines to be another thing altogether: without form, inchoate, a kind of elemental scream. And Jarrell is but one instance. The literature of despair would fill libraries, even though it is there—ostensibly—as a sweetener, a palliative, a temporary antidote to get us through the pain. Otherwise why bother reading it?

But the Christian imagination, informed by its deep Jewish roots, opens the possibility of another response to pain, another way of understanding human suffering. In this scenario suffering is not merely something to be endured because it cannot be avoided. Instead, it becomes the vehicle by which we encounter ourselves more fully. It means a humbling, a radical reassessment, a turning once again back to the metaphorical road from which we strayed. It means turning back to God. One feels awkward, even foolish, speaking like this, for there is always the fear that one may not be able to cope with such suffering oneself, that one is a sort of armchair player in all this. It is one thing to imagine suffering, another thing altogether to undergo the ordeal by fire. After all, helplessness, pain, and suffering can too often overwhelm and even annihilate us.

Gerard Manley Hopkins, S.J., completing his studies in theology in North Wales in the winter of 1875, read the accounts of a sea disaster—the wreck of *The Deutschland*—a steamer bound for the New World with five Franciscan nuns among its passengers, all of whom would perish in the mouth of the Thames in an accident that would claim more than fifty lives. Reading of the terrifying events with the guilt feelings of the survivor, Hopkins tried also to "read the unshapeable shock night" and so discover "the who and the why" of it all. In our literature, examples of redemptive suffering are scarce, and one has to look deeper to read the ambiguous signs of its presence. For the presence of redemptive suffering—even to the imagination—is as ambiguous as the cross itself: a contradictory sign, rejected by the wise of this world, but a sign too to be grasped at as a rare-dear gift. It all depends, finally, on how one reads that sign.

Consider the lives of two Catholic poets, Hopkins, who died in 1889, and John Berryman, who ended his life in 1972. No one can say Berryman was a stranger to suffering. For much of his life—in spite of leading a brilliant career as a scholar and as a poet—he was tormented. He lost his father through suicide or—worse—with the complicity of his mother. For twenty-five years he carried on a dialogue with God, alternately insulting and crying out to Him, denying Him in one breath, damning himself in the next. He could make you laugh with his incongruities, one moment shocking you, the next breaking your heart. Subtle though he was, he had to admit he was not as subtle as his divine Adversary. He tried adopting the theologian Origen's concept of the *apocatastasis*, the idea that at the end of time an all-merciful God would shut down hell and even Satan would finally bend the knee in adoration. Thus, after a few eons in purgatory, even he—Berryman— would eventually be able to slide through the cracks into heaven. Suffering would be long, a just payment for his sins, betrayals, malefactions. But it would not go on forever. One day, please God, it would all come to an end, and he too would be covered in the General Amnesty.

Berryman had always asked the big questions about pain, suffering, evil, redemption. But it was only at the end—in his mid-fifties—a confirmed alcoholic from whom nearly every shred of dignity had been stripped—after having caused no end of pain to his family, his friends, and himself, that he reached bottom. Having nearly killed himself with alcohol, he was admitted to St. Mary's Hospital in Minneapolis for treatment. In the past, he had been able to sign himself out pretty much at will. But this time he was told that—if he left—he would not be welcomed back. It is difficult to gauge, often, what the secret anchors are that hold us steady on the bobbing seas, but for Berryman it seems to have been his reputation as a teacher. And when that last anchor was in danger of being cut, he began visibly to go to pieces. "It seems to be DARK all the time," he wrote in stripped, minimal, exhausted quatrains:

> I have difficulty walking.
> I can remember what to say to my seminar
> But I don't know that I want to.
>
> I said in a Song once: I am unusually tired.
> I repeat that & increase it.
> I'm vomiting.
> I broke down today in the slow movement of K.365.
>
> I certainly don't think I'll last much longer.

It was in this setting that a miracle of grace—as he saw it—occurred. Berryman's counselor, an Episcopalian priest assigned to the hospital, saved Berryman his dignity by refusing to let him leave and then offering to take over his classes until he was sufficiently recovered. It was that gesture—totally unexpected under the circumstances—that Berryman took as the redemptive sign he had thirsted after for so much of his life: God's own rescue come through the mediation of a fellow human being. It was a gesture large enough, significant enough, that Berryman began a series of addresses to the Lord.

Astonished and incredulous that anyone, let alone God, should attend upon his miserable self-inflicted sufferings, he began the addresses in a state of heightened awareness and qualified exultation. It was as if he had just discovered that his tongue could sing praise of this magnitude. "Master of beauty, craftsman of the snowflake," he began, one artist praising Another:

> inimitable contriver,
> endower of Earth so gorgeous & different from the boring Moon,
> thank you for such as it is my gift.
>
> I have made up a morning prayer to you
> Containing with precision everything that most matters.
> 'According to Thy will' the thing begins.
> It took me off & on two days. It does not aim at eloquence. . . .

Whatever your end may be, accept my amazement.
May I stand until death forever at attention
For any your least instruction or enlightenment.
I even feel sure you will assist me again, Master of insight & beauty.

It is tricky, this attempt to read suffering in the context of redemption. Often one's way is lit only by irregular flashes. The idea, of course, is to learn to give over one's own will completely, to become—as Christ warned—like little children again, completely dependent on God. What followed that surrender was for Berryman a release, as of a great burden lifted. The difficulty was in the letting go, of falling back into God's hands. It is at one and the same time the easiest and the hardest thing to do, this reading of God's hand in the midst of the fire. Robert Lowell knew what sort of prayer Berryman had managed to offer: a modern prayer, replete with humor, doubt, indecision, petulance, false bravado, childish wheedling, and fear. Because he had been there himself, he knew that Berryman had managed to bring his whole complex, bifurcated humanity to bear on his suffering.

Four years earlier, in Dublin with his wife and daughter at Christmas, his drinking out of control, Berryman had called on the memory of the Jesuit poet, Gerard Manley Hopkins, who had died unknown in the same city seventy-five years before. The one sane milkman, he had called him then, the one poet who had somehow managed to hit the Milky Way, "while the Holy Ghost / rooted for" him. Just so, just so: a poet who had somehow won through, in spite of dying at forty-four, with nothing of his poetic stature known to the world. How could this be, Berryman wondered, that a man whose name was nearly obliterated should have such a lasting impact on so many twentieth-century writers? "Oil all my turbulence," Berryman wrote now in quiet astonishment,

> as at Thy dictation
> I sweat out my wayward works.
> Father Hopkins said the only true literary critic is Christ.
> Let me lie down exhausted, content with that.

Christ as literary critic? Berryman was echoing here a letter Hopkins had written ninety years before, a letter to his friend, the Anglican clergyman Richard Watson Dixon. To the question as to why he—Hopkins—had suffered himself to live on in obscurity—he who had written such extraordinary poetry—Hopkins wrote back that, if they both valued what he had written, much more so did Christ. What happened to his poems, he insisted, was up to God. If God chose to avail himself of what he'd written, all well and good. If God chose to see that the poems remained unpublished, unknown, then—hard as it might be personally—better that way. Someday he would see the work as God saw it, and that would be enough for him. "This is my principle," he ended, "and this in the main has been my practice: leading the sort of life I do here"—he was in the midst of the year-long retreat known as the Tertianship when he wrote this letter—"it seems easy, but when one mixes with the world and meets on every side its secret solicitations, to live by faith is harder, is very hard." Nevertheless, he meant with God's help to follow that course.

No wonder Berryman was so taken by Hopkins's example. And then, of course, there were the poems Hopkins had left behind: those immortal diamonds, by turns gentle and terrible in their beauty. Then, in the first flush of having written his "Eleven Addresses," Berryman made a miscalculation. In his darkest moments, Hopkins had spoken of the desolation he was undergoing as a kind of crucifixion. Now Berryman, elated at finding God again, told an interviewer that he too hoped now to be "nearly crucified." Months later, reading the galleys of his interview, Berryman would scribble the word, "Delusion," next to that statement. By then he'd already begun to understand what he'd actually asked for. Suffering, the kind of suffering he's asked for, was of course beyond him because he would still be in control, raising or lowering the temperature as he saw fit. *He* would direct the soldiers, the placement of the nails, the placement of the spear, forgetting that Jesus himself, praying among the olive trees of Gethsemane, had begged his Father to let the cup pass him by. But by then Christ was already being pressed into the pure oil of sacrifice. But first they would really have to kill him before he could rise from the dead. It was—we see—a necessary step in God's redemptive plan, but in the short run it would be just that: a gruesome, brutal crucifixion.

Consider the example of Christ, Hopkins once wrote Dixon, having learned that Dixon had suffered a defeat in being bypassed for a public position in poetry. "His career was cut short and, whereas he would have wished to succeed by success—for it is insane to lay yourself out for failure, prudence is the first of the cardinal virtues, and he was the most prudent of men—nevertheless he was doomed to succeed by failure; his plans were baffled, his hopes dashed, and his work was done by being broken off undone. However much he understood all this he found it an intolerable grief to submit to it. He left the example: it is very strengthening, *but except in that sense it is not consoling.*"

That was Hopkins's model, and he suffered isolation, obscurity, failure, and finally a too-early death, trying always to understand the baffling bans against him as in some way God's greater plan for him. No wonder the example of Alphonsus Rodriguez, his brother Jesuit, canonized in 1888, less than a year before his own death, so appealed to him. To have suffered loss of fame, loss of friendship, loss of country, loss of prestige, loss of advancement, loss of understanding even by his fellow Jesuits: all this was not perhaps the same as suffering from cancer, from loss of limb, whatever—but it stung all the same. It is a lot most of us will no doubt share if we live long enough. "Honour is flashed off exploit," he wrote, thinking of the life of the soldier—for after all he too was in every sense a soldier, slogging out his life as a teacher and a priest in the trenches, ready to march at a day's notice, to go where he was sent. But his life, like Rodriguez's, had been lived out mostly unnoticed:

> But be the war within, the brand we wield
> Unseen, the heroic breast not outward steeled,
> Earth hears no hurtle then from fiercest fray.
> Yet God (that hews mountain and continent,
> Earth, all, out; who, with trickling increment,

Veins violets and tall trees makes more and more)
Could crowd career with conquest while there went
Those years and years by of world without event
That in Majorca Alfonso watched the door.

How quietly Hopkins's sonnet ends, and yet how full of expectation, a quiet crescendo, victory won by acceptance, long-suffering, doing one's duty, however humble it might be. It is just this quiet giving over, this surrender, this willingness to accept suffering as part of God's larger plan by which the Potter might shape the clay, that Hopkins learned an important lesson. If he asked God to be lifted to a higher plane, it was not for glory, not for his art, but simply out of love for the one who had gone before. He wanted to imitate that life and make of his own life a lovescape like Christ's.

The crisis for Hopkins came in his forty-first year, in Dublin, a year after he had asked his Lord to be lifted up with him. The record of it is to be found in a series of sonnets he left behind among his personal possessions, having shown them to no one, not even to his closest friend, Robert Bridges. They are a record of one in the midst of suffering, a pain so intense Hopkins thought he might actually be going mad. We call it the dark night of the soul, but in the midst of it all Hopkins could feel only darkness so palpable it choked him: "I wake and feel the fell of dark, not day," he wrote, surrounded by a darkness that seemed to yawn without end, like the ocean itself:

What hoürs, O what black hoürs we have spent
This night! what sights you, heart, saw, ways you went!
And more must, in yet longer light's delay.

Ten years before that he had had to imagine the suffering of five German Franciscan nuns drowned during a raging winter storm. But now, in Dublin, what he was experiencing was his own drowning, a sense of loneliness that threatened to pull him under. You can feel that suffering in the starkness of the lines, without embellishment, hammer blows thudding one after the other:

> With witness I speak this. But where I say
> Hours I mean years, mean life. And my lament
> Is cries countless, cries like dead letters sent
> To dearest him that lives alas! away.
> I am gall, I am heartburn. God's most deep decree
> Bitter would have me taste: my taste was me;
> Bones built in me, flesh filled; blood brimmed the curse.

Left to his own resources, he realized here, there was nothing to fall back on, nothing but a self that, feeding on itself, must starve to death. By himself he could do nothing. If it is hell we are looking for, it is here:

> Selfyeast of spirit a dull dough sours. I see
> The lost are like this, and their scourge to be
> As I am mine, their sweating selves; but worse.

In another sonnet written soon after, Hopkins came to the realization that the force he had been wrestling with, that had played him—he thought—as a cat plays a mouse, did after all have a local habitation and a name. Having been knocked down, pawed over, conquered, he needed to know who this Other was. And who was it cheering at his overthrow? Himself or this Other? "O which one?" he asked, as it dawned on him that he had been wrestling not only with depression but with God Himself, his own cry echoing Christ's from the cross. Had "each one" won then, he asked now, exhausted with that year of "now done darkness I wretch lay wrestling with (my God!) my God"?

Fellow Jesuits in his community at St. Stephen's Green would remember Hopkins grading exams until the early hours of the morning, suffering through migraine headaches, unable to find the respite he so desperately sought. Other poems of his suggest an eventual lull, with Hopkins coming out the other side of the storm, asking himself to be more patient with himself. Patience, like the ivy covering an old ruin, all "Purple eyes and seas of liquid leaves" adorning the scarred walls of the self. "My own heart let me more have pity on," he wrote afterward, assessing the damage his suffering had wreaked on him:

                                                      let
Me live to my sad self hereafter kind,
Charitable; not live this tormented mind
With this tormented mind tormenting yet.

Time, finally, to "call off thoughts awhile / Elsewhere" and "leave comfort root-room." And so, apparently, he did, turning to his teaching and his studies. Other poems came, including several masterpieces. But three and a half years later, when he went through the physical crisis that would end in his death—typhoid brought on by the antiquated sewer system at the college—he struggled one final time to try and understand why his life seemed to be one huge failure. "Thou art indeed just, Lord, if I contend / With thee," he wrote on the Feast of St. Patrick's, 1889. He was, of course, echoing Jeremiah's complaint made twenty-five centuries before.

Why was it that the ways of sinners seemed to prosper, when everything he put his hand to in the service of God seemed to end in disappointment? All about him life was quickening again, "banks and breaks . . . leavèd how thick" and laced again "With fretty chervil." Even "the sots and thralls of lust" seemed in their spare hours to thrive more than he did, he who could fairly say he had spent his life upon God's cause. Where was the justice in all this? Where was the justice in never breeding even one work that woke? The irony of course in all this is—as we in hindsight know—that the words he was writing held the answer he was looking for, for his poems have now entered the highest canons of literature and seem destined to remain there.

It is perhaps impossible to prove this, except to point to the poems themselves and wonder who else if not God was watching over his servant. Hopkins's prayer asking to follow his master and to win through by defeat seems after all to have been answered. At the very end he told Bridges that, if Bridges wondered why he wrote so little now, the answer was that the inspiration seemed to be missing. And this he explained in a sonnet that, even as it laments the loss of inspiration, is itself inspired. The words rise and fall, like air escaping, paralleling the loss of the arch, original Breath that is a brilliant metaphor for the Holy Spirit. For this, Hopkins ended, was not just *his* explanation, but the Spirit's as well, the same Spirit with whom he had long ago set up house: "O then," he ended, recalling now in a kind of great return to the opening lines of Genesis,

> if in my lagging lines you miss
> The roll, the rise, the carol, the creation,
> My winter world, that scarcely breathes that bliss
> Now, yields you, with some sighs, our explanation.

The quiet acceptance of God's plan, insofar as Hopkins could discern that plan, has been for many a sort of talisman, a nearly perfect end. Not my will, one of the most self-willed of all poets could say at the end, but Thine be done. Even as he lay dying, barely able to move, he found the peace that had so long eluded him. Thank God, he told his parents, at least there would be no more student papers to read. His only concern now was how to comfort his grieving parents. And his own final words, recorded by the brother in attendance on him at the end, were reported to be, "I am so happy. I am so happy. I am so happy." Death by enteric typhoid does not usually end in so calm and resigned a fashion. But with Hopkins it did, and I must believe it had everything to do with the way he transformed his suffering into a redemptive act, gaining the strength he needed from that very gesture.

1999

Index

The Life of Poetry

POETS ON THEIR ART AND CRAFT

Carl Dennis
Poetry as Persuasion

Paul Mariani
God and the Imagination: On Poets, Poetry, and the Ineffable

Michael Ryan
A Difficult Grace: On Poets, Poetry, and Writing

Sherod Santos
A Poetry of Two Minds

Ellen Bryant Voigt
The Flexible Lyric